MW01595318

Conversations
with an
Atheist

Conversations
with an
Atheist

JANINA BALABAT

CREATION
HOUSE
A STRANG COMPANY

Conversations With an Atheist by Janina Balabat
Published by Creation House
A Strang Company
600 Rinehart Road
Lake Mary, Florida 32746
www.creationhouse.com

Scripture quotations are from the New King James Version of the Bible. Copyright © 1979, 1980, 1982 by Thomas Nelson, Inc., publishers. Used by permission.

Cover design by Marvin Eans

Library of Congress Control Number: 2007938623
International Standard Book Number: 978-1-59979-266-8

First Edition

08 09 10 11 — 9 8 7 6 5 4 3 2 1
Printed in the United States of America

CONTENTS

PART II: THE NEW TESTAMENT

DEDICATION

I dedicate this book to all whom the Lord has led to its pages; to all of you who have everything; to you who are rich, famous, and honored, but lack peace in your hearts; to you who do not know where you came from, why you are here, or where you are going; and to you who do not see any purpose to your life. My prayer is that everyone reading this book will find the Lord's purposes for their existence.

I also dedicate this book to those citizens who have few worldly possessions, or even nothing; to you who are not known and pushed aside; to you who are lonely and feel forgotten by everyone; to you who are in constant pain and feel as though you are needed by no one. My desire is that all citizens reading this book find the One who said, "Yet I will not forget you. See, I have inscribed you on the palms of My hands" (Isa. 49:15–16).

PREFACE

I WAS LISTENING TO A RUSSIAN CHRISTIAN RADIO BROADCAST one evening a long time ago. The broadcast conductor was an evangelist named Mark, and he was trying to convince Russian atheists of God's existence. Mark read a letter sent to the radio station by an atheist, in which he asked for simple, live, visible proof of God's existence; convincing proof that one can see and come close to.

When I heard this request, it was as though I was struck by lightning—I jumped from the sofa and was mentally transferred to the first page of the Scriptures. I began thinking about this simple, live proof constantly, but my work, home, garden, and husband left me with little extra time. Nonetheless, this request sent deep roots into my heart, and I often pondered this theme—all the while my thoughts remaining on the first pages of the Bible.

I am an accountant. All my life I have worked with figures. I used to prepare income taxes for Americans. This job gave me great satisfaction, and I felt very happy, especially when my clients had refunds. I loved what I was doing, and I devoted myself to it very much. I was always busy and spent a lot of time outside the home. I was very proud of my accomplishments after I came to the USA.

But God Almighty decided to take my career away from me and put in my hands a hard physical task. He caused me to stay home while He made a writer out of me. I am very thankful to Him for it because His ways and His thoughts are much better and higher than mine (Isa. 55:8—9). Our almighty God is good. He is an awesome God, full of surprises. You never know what He can make out of a person who loves Him, believes in Him, and trusts Him wholeheartedly. But, sometimes He acts in a strange, mysterious manner, and leads a person through long, hard journeys to their ultimate great success.

Time went by quickly and unnoticed. My husband, Paul, grew ill and needed my attention. I wasn't able to work outside the home any longer. Paul, often in good humor, said, "I cannot die so fast because I do not have anyone to leave my young, beautiful, and good wife to." I do not know how much truth existed in those words, but he repeated them often. His words became reality. My husband died over the course of eleven years of hard illness. During this period, he was on the operating table six times. He suffered a stroke twice, and in the last three to four years, he was attacked with various illnesses. When we returned to the doctor, we heard that which a person never wants to hear.

This period of life was not easy for me. I spent many sleepless nights and worked hard during the day. But I didn't live by circumstances. Circumstances in the life of man are often hard, and there remains no point in thinking and living by them. I lived—and still live—by the Word of God, with God's promises. The Word of God says that God will never give trials to man that he cannot handle (1 Cor. 10:13). This is true. These words are alive and active, and by these words I live.

In order to occupy myself in light of my husband's illness, I began a side project working on finding this simple, live, and tangible proof—the result of which became this book. This proof, which you can see, touch, and smile upon, will respond to you. I decided, by using the Word of God, to prove to the atheist from the radio show that almighty God is alive and active today in the twenty-first century.

I traveled through the pages of Scripture, from the first book to the last. God was with me. He opened His great revelations to me, and I started to write them down on paper. My husband, lying in bed, often said, "Janina, read me what you have written today." I slowly read, and Paul listened with great respect and attention. Upon my question, "Do you want to add, delete, or change anything?" he, after a long silence, would reply, "It is well written." Paul had great and wonderful ideas that I didn't have, but he had a difficult time realizing them. I was the opposite—decisive and quick to bring good ideas to life. I think this was a good combination.

Once, he said, "Janina, collect this material, sort and polish it, and then publish a book from it." When I heard this suggestion, I was so excited. I grabbed onto the idea like a child grabs a colorful toy, and I said, "Your desire will be fulfilled, and a book will be published."

Time passed and my husband's diseases progressed rapidly. He couldn't remain at home any longer. At one point while sitting next to him on the hospital bed, I saw how life was slowly but surely leaving him. I saw how his memory left and returned. When he opened his foggy eyes, he looked at me and asked, "The book, is it published?" I decisively answered that it wasn't yet, but I promised that it would be. Three months before the book was published, my husband left for eternity.

The book was published in Poland, in the Polish language, with the title *Sun Above the Valley—Good News.* Now I have translated it into English in a version that includes additional thoughts.

In the English version, I first strongly emphasize that God

Almighty exists and is active and alive today. I underline visible and tangible proof of God's actions. Nobody can deny His existence; not scientists or atheists, and neither the educated nor non-educated public, because our own eyes witness His presence. Secondly, I describe, step-by-step, God's plan of salvation for mankind, as outlined in the Bible.

I believe that by reading this book, more than one atheist will admit that God does exist. More than one scientist will learn of God's plan of salvation; more than one person will accept Jesus Christ as their personal Savior. And more than one soul will be saved, reconciled with God the Father, and will receive eternal life.

I believe that this book will be translated into many different languages and will be spread around the world, because every citizen of this planet must know this visible and tangible proof of God's existence and His plan for salvation of mankind. I also believe that this book will be published until Jesus Christ returns for His precious bride—the church.

This book draws heavily from the Bible. I think there are more words from the Scriptures than there are my own words. The Bible is the most powerful, active book on Earth. *Conversations With an Atheist* isn't mine. It is God's book. He gave me these thoughts, and I simply wrote them on paper. I was used only as a pencil in His hands. I am very thankful to God that He chose me as His vessel, as His tool to do this work. All glory and praise belong to Him, to God Almighty, Creator of the universe; to Jesus Christ, my personal Savior and Redeemer; and to the Holy Spirit, my Helper.

QUESTIONS TO
THE ATHEIST

THERE ARE MANY DIFFERENT KINDS OF QUESTIONS IN THIS world. Everyone has questions, young and old and everywhere in between. Educated people have questions, simple people have questions, and illiterate people have questions. Wealthy and poor people have questions; believers and unbelievers have questions.

In order to give answers to some questions, which can be considered complicated, you have to study the subject for a long time. In contrast, the other questions, the simple ones, are straightforward and might simply require observation and a little thought. I have found that the simple questions hold great meaning for life.

I also have a question, a simple one. I have framed my question to a figurative atheist in a hypothetical conversation for the purpose of demonstrating this debate between believers and nonbelievers. Mostly, my question is directed to anyone who doesn't believe that God exists; or that He created heaven and Earth, the sun and moon, and every living creature on this planet; or that

God created all of mankind, talks to His creation, watches after His creation, and that He loves His creation and wants fellowship with us. My question is for the one who doesn't believe God has created them for a special purpose.

Yes, my question is for you, dear atheist. And even if you answer this question, you can still remain an atheist for your entire life. You don't have to change any of your beliefs because you answer my question—you may even die an atheist. But if you can't answer this simple question of life, then you need to think deeply and propose a question to yourself:

> Why can't I answer this question? I know much about life. I have read many books. I've even written some myself. But to this simple question, I have no answer. Why? Why don't I know? Why can't I answer?

My question is very simple. We meet this question everywhere on a daily basis: on the street, at the store, at work, at school, on the bus, at parks, at church, and even at home. We even meet this question in small, old cottages, where only grandfather and grandmother remain. This question constantly is before our eyes.

This question is simple. You might even say that this question is childish. If so, then fine—if a question is childish to you, then I'll start from childhood. Children are born all over this planet. My question is: who maintains the balance between boys and girls? Who decrees that life on this planet continues? Parents cannot maintain this balance. If a father wants to have seven sons, the opposite may in fact happen. The ratio has been kept, as our own eyes witness this phenomenon.

Therefore, who maintains this balance? Those of us who have lived fifty or sixty years know what a short amount of time that is and how fast it passes. Now consider how this planet would be if during this time only boys or only girls were born all around the world. How would the world look? If this occurred, this planet would become empty. It would die. You would hear only the wailing and moaning of this emptying and dying planet. But we do not see such events. Today, our planet blooms and breathes with life and activities. People live, people work, people travel around the world, airplanes full of people fly around this globe, even people visit outer space. Therefore, who is He that doesn't want to witness a dying planet?

Other important questions now arise. Who began human reproduction, and for what purpose? Who started the multiplication of the creatures—birds, fish, animals, and reptiles? Each living thing, in its own time, carries out the necessary events in reproduction, and the planet continues to be filled with life. Who gives people, and likewise animals, such a strong desire to leave offspring?

Who created a manner for plant reproduction? Each tree, bush, flower, and blade of grass has a specific method for reproduction. Who began this and for what purpose? Who wants our planet to be filled with people, animals, and plants? Who wants there to be life? Who is He?

Who placed the desire for life into the nature of people? When a person gets ill, they immediately go to the doctor and say, "Help me. Save my life. I want to live." The question, who gives people the desire for life? remains unanswered.

Who also gives animals this desire? Try to catch a rabbit, a fox, or another living creature. They fight as much as possible, because they know that being caught may be the end of their life—and they want to live. People, and similarly animals, strive to remain alive. The majority of people treasure their life and fight for it if need be, because the desire to live is innate. And again, the question exists:

who placed the deep and large desire for life into living beings? Who is He that doesn't want this planet to be empty?

Who placed the desire for action into the soul of mankind? The desire to do something is evident in little children. They cannot sit still. They turn, looking for some activity. Kids want to create something. When they are on the shore of an ocean or a lake, our eyes witness how hard children can work. Some build castles out of sand, while others dig holes, and with great effort use buckets and try to fill the holes with water.

They're little kids, yet they have great plans and ideas. Sometimes they want to move the entire ocean. And when they grow up, they want to be pilots and fly high to see the world from a bird's-eye view. Some want to be chefs and prepare delicious meals; others want to be farmers and cultivate crops to feed the world. Still others want to be doctors and heal people, or postal workers to bring you news or bills for you to pay. Others want to be leaders and rulers of countries. Each person strives for something, for some activity in order to discover something, to gain knowledge, and maybe even invent something new.

The questions still exist:

- Who granted the desire and tendencies for action?
- Who is He?
- Where does He live?
- Where can we find the place He inhabits?
- Has anyone seen Him?
- Who can call Him by name?
- Where can you learn more about Him?

- Who knows the reasons why He wants life on this planet to continue?

Dear atheist, can you tell me why we are born? Why do we live, worry, work, and fight just to save our life and be able to live a little longer? Why do we strive to live if death inevitably will meet us at the end? The questions exist: What is the purpose to life? What benefit is there in treasuring your own life?

Dear atheist, don't you think that there must be some secret to life? Don't you think that there is some mystery? Do you not think that a Power ought to be at work that places the desire for life into the hearts of people? Don't you think that there is Someone who needs this planet to be full of life and has a purpose for not only mankind in its entirety, but for each individual?

Dear atheist, if you have never thought of this theme, if these questions have never interested you, you have a chance now to take a moment to ponder them. Decide on the answers to these simple questions.

ANSWERS FROM
THE ATHEIST

I CAN PICTURE THAT MY DEAR ATHEIST FRIEND STOPPED FOR a moment and listened attentively as I asked all of my questions. He grew slightly uncomfortable and his face turned red. He found himself in deep silence. He then began talking to himself, "I'm such a powerful person. I know so much of life, of nature, and not only of things on Earth, but of the nature of the other planets. I've read many educational books. Yet, I do not have answers to these life questions. Why can't I answer? Why don't I have any answers? Why don't I know? Why don't I know who set everything up so wonderfully? Why don't I know my Creator?"

Suddenly, his face lit up and he smiled. He even began to laugh. He loudly exclaimed, "This is the work of nature! It is she that controls the balance of human life. It is because of her that our mother Earth breathes life."

My dear atheist, your answer makes a valid point, but who is Nature? We will now discuss this matter further.

Nature must work very hard. Nature must not sleep or doze off, day or night, in order to maintain the balance of life on all continents. Nature must be omnipotent and omnipresent. Nature must hold the globe in the palm of her hand without removing her eyes from it, and she must continually fill it with life.

Nature must be very wise. She must, at the proper time, start reproduction for all life forms: for ants, camels, grasshoppers, eagles, frogs, elephants, fish, and serpents. She must start the multiplication of plants, apple trees, potatoes, lilies of the valley, forget-me-nots, and oak and pine trees. This is not a simple task. The animal kingdom, like humankind, must also fulfill their role and multiply. The planet fills with life and continues to exist. Isn't this a miracle? Yes, it's a marvelous miracle.

Nature is a good caretaker. She is very skilled not only at creating, but at providing the necessities that support growth and development. Before a child is born, Nature prepares fresh, warm, and nourishing milk in the mother. Once born, this child drinks the milk and begins growing and developing into an adult.

Nature is life, and Nature loves life. Nature doesn't want living things to be born only to immediately starve. Nature foresees everything. She has prepared everything in advance for life on this planet to continue and decorate the world.

Nature acts with love. She shows great love to her creation. Nature pours love into the hearts of parents so that they will love, cherish, and protect their children. If you try to take a child from its mother, the mother will do everything in her power to save her child.

Nature does not only pour love into human hearts, she does the same for the animal kingdom. Try to remove a baby bird from its mother—she will harm you. Once, while working outside next to my home, I came to a bush and bent over next to it to remove thorns. At once, I heard a piercing scream and felt sharp claws on my shoulder. A blue jay had attacked me. There was a nest in this bush and in this nest were little birds—the babies of this blue jay. Mothers have great love toward each of their children. Sometimes, mothers don't even worry about their own life when they have to protect their young ones.

Nature is also a great architect! She possesses power that the human brain cannot even begin to comprehend. We can examine a simple example of this. Dear atheist, just look in the mirror. See yourself and see how unique you are. There are more than six billion people on this planet, and each living soul is both unique and unrepeatable. Dear atheist, imagine what a great power must oversee this. Nature is wonderful. We are her witnesses.

Nature is beautiful, and she truly loves beauty. She created such great trees and flowers. There are many types of roses, all of which produce a great combination of scents. Then there are the narcissus, tulips, forget-me-nots, lilies of the valley, daisies, dahlias, cornflowers, and gladioluses. Flowers bring great joy. Houses, halls, and offices are decorated with flowers during special occasions. People of all ages observe flowers when they are in a park. They breathe in the aroma and they forget their problems and their hurt. Flowers bring great joy to all of mankind and nature created these flowers for our joy. She created them to bring us cheer and give us something beautiful to look upon.

Not only has nature created beauty for the eyes, but she has also remembered to fill our stomach. She has prepared tomatoes, cucumbers, onions, garlic, pumpkins, cantaloupes, apples, pears, potatoes, beets, white cabbage, and cauliflower. Nature knows that man likes sweetness, and she has therefore created the little bee, which works so hard all of its life to prepare sweet honey to satisfy a person's life, to enhance it and make it sweeter and happier.

How wise Nature is! She concerns herself with men. How much love she extends, and how much goodness she creates for men.

Nature needs to know a person's desire. She must know our feelings. She knows what we like and what we dislike. Nature knows the heart and soul of man. When she creates everything, she must surely recognize our feelings. She knows you, dear reader, and me. Isn't Nature wonderful?

Nature must have a good sense of humor. She has created the green frog with its large eyes. She has created the segmented ant, the humped camel, the long-necked giraffe, the striped zebra, the bushy-tailed squirrel, the poky porcupine, the deer with the antlers, the slow elephants, and the silly turtle. How much variety exists and how beautiful everything is. The work of Nature is a miracle.

Nature doesn't make mistakes. Time has passed, year after year, century after century, and the balance between the male and female ratio has been prolonged and kept. Abnormalities in ratios cannot be found over the course of history. Nature has never made a mistake. She holds the world in her hand, and fills it with life without mistakes. She is perfect and she loves to maintain order. It's hard to imagine a scenario where only boys were born on one continent, and girls on another. Disorder would prevail! But we have never heard of such an example because nature doesn't err; order is always maintained. Not only does Nature keep order on Earth, she does so in space as well. When we look into the sky, we cannot comprehend or measure the distance of its great expanse, nor can we count the number of stars and quantify the number of heavenly bodies. Further, these heavenly bodies do not remain stationary—they orbit continuously. Each star quickly circles on an orbit that was established by nature.

Under the direction of Nature, catastrophes do not happen and collisions do not occur out in space. History doesn't tell of stars that have fallen into Mars or that Mars hit the moon. Nature evidently has great authority. Isn't Nature wonderful? Yes, Nature does great miracles. Nature is in constant contact with her creation. She looks after its development. She takes care of, treasures, and loves her creation, and she has a specific and great purpose for the work of her hands.

Human wisdom cannot explain the actions of Nature, her strength, her concern, her control, and love for her creation. I believe that libraries could not fit all the books that can be written about Nature's wisdom and activities. Further, you cannot find authors to record all of her deeds.

Dear atheist, have you seen Nature? Can you explain where she can be found? Do you know the location of her existence? Can you describe her? Can you meet with her? Can you talk with her? Can you have fellowship with Nature? For example, if you were to want a child or lots of money or good health, would you be able to turn to Nature and ask her to do something, using any means, to grant you your heart's desire? Have you ever thought of Nature, of her actions, of her greatness, concern, goodness, of her love to you personally? Many questions can be directed to Nature, and it is impossible to sort through them all. But who is Nature?

Nature actually is the Creator—and our Creator is over nature. The Creator of heaven and Earth, the Creator of life—our Lord God—and all of nature is a fulfillment of the commands of the almighty Father God.

It is He who has created heaven and Earth, the sun and moon, and all living things, including the human race. It is He who gives life. It is He who wants this Earth to breathe with life. It is He who has a great and specific purpose for His creation.

It is He who unconditionally loves all mankind, including you and I, dear atheist. It is He who wants fellowship with His creation. It is He who wants fellowship with me personally, and with you, dear atheist.

My dear atheist is not smiling now. He has scratched his head a few times while immersed in deep thought. He has begun to lack peace and has grown unsettled. His heart has been filled with the desire to know more of the Creator of life. Questions have been born in his heart, such as, Where can I learn more about the Creator, of His love, of His goodness, of His actions, and of His will? Who can direct me to the proper Source? And what—who—is this Source? How can you have fellowship with Him? How can I feel His presence? Where and when can I personally meet with Him? And where can I hear His voice? Where? And by what means?

Dear atheist, all of your questions are good questions and they have been heard by the Lord. He was always listening, and He has heard your wonderings. The desire of your heart will be filled, and all of your questions will be answered.

PART I

The Old Testament

1

THE BIBLE

W
HAT IS THE Bible? This is my own understanding of the Bible and what I see in the words that are written on its pages. Dear reader, you can agree with my points or you may not; that is up to you. You have complete rights to your choices. But I think that it will not hurt anyone to know another's opinion, another point of view. Your knowledge may increase because of this. Therefore, be kind and read with great attention.

We know that every country on this globe has its own constitution. Rulers set laws and regulations for their citizens, and the constitution describes the obligations people have toward their country and to other people. What one can and cannot do is described in the constitution. The constitution is taught in schools to young children. Each citizen is required to know the laws and regulations of his or her country. Each citizen who fulfills the laws is an honored citizen. Those citizens who do not follow the law are punished, and their freedom is limited. This kind of citizen is known as a lawbreaker.

Almighty God, the Creator of heaven and Earth and all mankind, didn't leave His people, His Creation, without instruction as to how to live and act. He didn't leave us without any direction, without a constitution. The Creator of life created one constitution for all human citizens of this land. The godly constitution is called the Bible and it is the Word of God.

The Bible contains many books. It is known as the Word of God because God Himself talks to His creation through it. God established laws for people, and the only way we may learn of them is through His Word. The Bible is also known as the Holy Word because God, who spoke the word, is holy. Therefore, the laws in the Bible are also holy.

The Bible is translated into almost every language that is spoken on Earth. No other book is as available to the entire human race, because God, our Creator, prepared no other book to serve as our constitution.

In this world there are many good and intellectual books. People read them and agree with them, but with time, these books age and can only be found in a museum or in the remote corners of libraries. Even the most interesting books are read once or twice, and then are tossed onto a bookshelf and read no more.

The Bible, on the other hand, is read daily. Little kids read and study this book in Sunday school, and as they grow older, they keep on reading it. As people age, they continue reading the Bible, which at some point, might be read and re-read one hundred times over. What is interesting is that every time the Bible is read, different revelations are seen. Why is this? This is because God talks through the words of this book to His people, His creation. The Bible was and will be the most popular book on this planet.

The Holy Word is made of two parts, the Old and New Testaments, and it has a total of sixty-six books. Thirty-nine are in the Old Testament, and twenty-seven are in the New Testament. The Old Testament contains the life, laws, and the Lord's will up until the birth of Jesus Christ. The New Testament contains the life, laws, and will for the world following Christ's birth.

As we see, the Bible was written over the course of many years by many different authors. What I find amazing is that in spite of having so many different authors, the Bible does not contain any contradictions. Only pure harmony is found in it, and each book contained inside has one purpose. Why is this? This is because the author was the Holy Spirit.

The Bible itself is not religion. It isn't merely a ceremony that is found in any particular church. The Bible is the book of life, a living and working book.

> For the word of God is living and powerful, and sharper than any two-edged sword, piercing even to the division of soul and spirit, and of joints and marrow, and is a discerner of the thoughts and intents of the heart. And there is no creature hidden from His sight, but all things are naked and open to the eyes of Him to whom we must give account.
> —HEBREWS 4:12–13

No other book can change a person in such a way as the Bible can. Alcoholics can be made sober. Thieves, liars, and burglars can be transformed into charitable, honest people. No doctor or psychologist can change the heart of man, turn him from lies, hatred, envy, pride, evil thoughts, evil tendencies, or evil deeds as the Bible can. No other book can make a Christian out of an atheist. No other book can change a man from a persecutor of Christians into a good preacher, a lover of God, and a lover of His Word and commands. No other book can inspire a man to follow God.

Questions now arise: Why does the Bible have such power? Why and how can the Bible make something positive from something negative, something good from bad, and turn hatred into love? The

Bible can do such things because God speaks to us through His holy Book, and God is love.

No other book on this planet has as many followers and lovers as the Bible. Additionally, no other book has as many enemies and persecutors as the Bible. Many attempts have been made to eliminate the Bible from the face of the Earth. But no one has been able to accomplish this; no one has yet been successful because this Book is holy. It is a constitution, prepared by God for His creation.

The citizens who believe in God, love their Creator, and have fellowship with Him also love this Book. They treasure and honor it highly. They read it daily to learn God's will and laws. They try to obey the laws and carry out the will of God in their lives. They live with this Book. They want to hear the voice of their Maker daily. For these citizens, the words in this Book are bread for their soul. But the citizens who do not believe in God, or in the fact that He is near, have not tasted His goodness. Those who believe that He is real but too far away have also never tasted His goodness. They have never experienced His love in their life. They do not have fellowship with Him, and they do not like this Book. When the Bible is mentioned, fear is born in their hearts. Their heart lacks the desire to read the Word because they do not live in accordance with God's laws, and they know very well that the Bible will judge them. It will expose them. It will reveal their improper actions and it will judge their conscience, all of which will deprive them of peace. They know very well that the words in this Book are alive and active.

The Word of God is a mirror. When we look into a mirror, we see ourselves, how we appear to others. We see our physical body. We see our characteristics and our shortcomings. When we read the Holy Word, we also see ourselves. We see our spiritual state, our innermost person. The Bible shows us what level we are with God in regards to His laws, His will, and His rules. Reading the Word of

God will allow us to see our spiritual status. By reading this godly constitution, we can discover if we are within the circle of God's will for salvation, or if we are out of bounds. The only way we can know the truth—God's truth—is by reading the Bible, and only then can we listen to the voice of God and have fellowship with Him.

When we pray, we open our hearts up to God. We bring our needs to Him and give Him thanks, and though this is very good, in and of itself it is a one-way relationship. But when we pray, talk with God, and read His Word, our fellowship with Him is full. We are then able to hear His voice, learn His will, and what He wants from us. Through prayer we lay down our needs, but by reading the Word of God we learn what He needs. By reading God's Word, we learn His commands and of His goodness and love for His Creation. Complete communication occurs between God and people when we read the Bible and pray.

You can write and talk of the Bible for a long time. Dear atheist, while reading this, how do you see yourself? Do you see yourself as big or little, rich or poor, educated or uneducated, popular or unpopular, young or old? You have full rights to read the Bible, this godly constitution. You have complete rights to listen to the voice of God, your Creator, and you have full rights to have fellowship with Him. You were created in the likeness of God. You have full rights to talk with Him, to discuss various issues with Him, and to ask of Him and receive from Him.

We live in a new era. Dear atheist and highly respected reader, begin reading the Word of God from the New Testament. After you read it, and after great thought, read the Old Testament. Remember that God loves His creation, and you are His amazing creation—and a very important one at that.

2

THE GOSPEL

WE OFTEN HEAR THE WORD *GOSPEL*. WE HEAR PEOPLE, say, "Read the gospel." The Bible says that Jesus "went about all Galilee, teaching in their synagogues [and] preaching the gospel of the kingdom" (Matt. 4:23). The gospel says, "A young evangelist came from afar and he will preach the gospel—let's go listen to him." As a matter of fact, what is the gospel? What does this word mean? How can this word direct our life? What does it refer to? To whom does the gospel pertain? Does it pertain to anyone living in the twenty-first century, the century of technology, computers, and desires to explore other planets? Does it pertain to me and to you, dear reader? We'll find all the answers in God's Word, the Bible.

The Bible that is issued by the Catholic church possesses a dictionary, and the dictionary says that the gospel, which is a Greek word, means "good news" and "victory." In the New Testament, the good news refers to the salvation and victory that is accomplished through Jesus Christ. What a wonderful definition! The words *victory* and *salvation* are in this definition, and we must stop and contemplate these because there are many questions associated with them, especially with the word *salvation*.

What must we be saved from? What threatens us? Who needs salvation? The sick? The elderly? The young? Only those who are strong? Are the rich in need, but not the poor? Or vice-versa? Is it only the educated and those who hold high positions? Or is it the simple and the uneducated? What's the difference between the saved and those not saved? Why do we need salvation? Where can we find it? Who has it to give it away? Can we buy it with money or trade some other material thing for it? Can we earn it with physical labor? Or can we inherit it? How can we get salvation? Are there many ways or is there only one way?

All of these questions are normal and important. The answers can be found only on the pages of God's Holy Constitution.

One of my dear and very attentive readers asked why there are so many verses from the Bible in this book. Why are there so many words from the pages of God's Constitution? My answer is this: the authority of these words does not come from people, but from almighty God, the Creator of heaven and Earth and of the human race. All of these words came from Him and are written on the pages of the Holy Scriptures. It is He who established such a plan of salvation for the human race. These are His laws and commands, and each citizen should know them.

My dear atheist has read intently and desires to listen to a few words from the Bible. His heart greatly desires to know what words begin the Bible, what is written on the first page and in the first chapter. He wants to hear the voice of God, his Creator, and the Creator of each of us.

To my dear atheist, I will tell you that there is no problem with this desire. We have the Bible in our hands, and we will discuss it until your desire is met. May God richly bless you as you read through His holy truth. God loves you and has a special purpose for you, a specific task for you to perform while you are on this planet.

3

THE CREATION OF
THE UNIVERSE

W E WILL NOW READ GOD'S WORD, HIS CONSTITUTION, beginning with the first book, Genesis:

> In the beginning God created the heavens and the earth. The earth was without form, and void; and darkness was on the face of the deep. And the Spirit of God was hovering over the face of the waters. Then God said, "Let there be light"; and there was light. And God saw the light, that it was good; and God divided the light from the darkness. God called the light Day, and the darkness He called Night. So the evening and the morning were the first day.
>
> —GENESIS 1:1–5

Today, in the twenty-first century, our own eyes see heaven and Earth. Our own eyes see light and darkness, day and night. We see what was created in the beginning:

Then God said, "Let there be a firmament in the midst of the waters, and let it divide the waters from the waters." Thus God made the firmament, and divided the waters which *were* under the firmament from the waters which *were* above the firmament; and it was so. And God called the firmament Heaven. So the evening and the morning were the second day. Then God said, "Let the waters under the heavens be gathered together into one place, and let the dry *land* appear"; and it was so. And God called the dry *land* Earth, and the gathering together of the waters He called Seas. And God saw that *it was* good.

—GENESIS 1:6–10, emphasis added

Today our own eyes see dry land, continents, islands, and peninsulas. We see oceans, seas, rivers, and lakes, and we say that this is good. We use the dry land. We walk and drive on it; we eat what it produces. We also use the water found in the oceans, seas, rivers, and lakes. We sail to far lands and to different continents on it; we transport materials via the waterways. It is good to live on this earth that God, our Maker, created.

For the Lord is the great God, And the great King above all gods. In His hand are the deep places of the earth; The heights of the hills are His also. The sea is His, for He made it; And His hands formed the dry land.

—PSALM 95:3–5

We will continue with Genesis, the first chapter:

Then God said, "Let the earth bring forth grass, the herb that yields seed, and the fruit tree that yields fruit according to its kind, whose seed is in itself, on the earth"; and it was so. And the earth brought forth grass, the herb that yields seed

according to its kind, and the tree that yields fruit, whose seed
is in itself according to its kind. And God saw that it was good.
So the evening and the morning were the third day.

—GENESIS 1:11–13

What have we noticed about the earth as we read verses 11
through 13? We noticed that the earth listened to the voice of
the living God and did as the Lord God decreed. Also interesting
is that even now, in the twenty-first century, the earth listens to
its Creator and carries out His will. Our own eyes see, we all
are witnesses, to the fact that the earth allows plants to grow in
virtually every soil type. When the wind blows some dirt on the
roof of a home, and it rains and the sun heats it up, something
there starts to turn green. The earth listens to the voice of God
and fulfills His desire. To the eyes of man, Earth is spirit-less and
inanimate. But according to God, the earth is alive and obedient.
She listens to the voice of her Creator and carries out His will. The
earth allows growth on all the continents, be they in the south,
north, east, or west; be they dry or luscious. Isn't it wonderful that
our planet Earth is a believer and is obedient to God? Yes, I think
so. Our Earth is alive and is a believer. She believes in God and
believes God, and we all are witnesses to this. Our own eyes daily
see her lovely growth. And not only do our eyes see that this earth
is alive and is a deep believer, but our stomachs witness this also.
When black and white bread, cucumbers, garlic, red tomatoes, a
full bowl of raspberries, dark cherries, white mushrooms, yellow
cantaloupe, red beets, sweet carrots, cauliflower, and potatoes
are available to us, then our eyes see and our stomachs support
the fact that our Earth is truly alive. We have plenty of evidence
showing that she is a believer who listens to the voice of her Maker
and fulfills His will.

God commanded the grass and trees to produce seeds. And

all of the plants listened to God's will, and they continue to do so to this day. They act exactly how God told them to. Ponder this wonderful miracle. Tiny poppy seeds, though dry like a bone, will produce a plant when put in the ground, watered, and warmed by the sun. The resulting plant will grow and bloom and its beauty will bring much joy to our eyes and heart. The plant will then bear seeds and bring forth one hundred times as many seeds as it started from.

There is life in these little seeds. It is interesting to note that our eyes cannot see the life in these little seeds. Even the most precise laboratories on Earth cannot find or observe the life in them. They cannot describe its size, taste, color, or weight—even though there is life in each of God's seeds. God's Word and will live inside them. The little seeds are deep believers. They are alive. They listen to the voice of the living God and fulfill His commands. Each little seed created by God is alive, a believer, and is obedient to its Maker. And this is a fact; it isn't a story. We are all witnesses to this phenomenon. Seeds create plants, and when we find ourselves in a park, a forest, or a field, we enjoy seeing their beauty and breathing in their aroma.

God created this. He commanded the plants to grow, and because the land is obedient to her Maker, plants are produced. The earth, after hearing His voice, did all she was commanded to. Then God told the creation to create seeds. And this was also done with obedience, as we see with our own eyes. The earth does her work when it rains and when the sun shines. She grows plants, flowers, and trees. She fills this land with beauty and aroma. All of this is God's work; He created all of it. He is the One who wants the land to breathe with life and look beautiful.

Man cannot put life into a created seed; only God, the Creator of heaven and Earth, can give life. Atheism is dead; therefore its work is dead. God is alive and His acts are of life. Let's continue reading the rest of chapter 1:

> Then God said, "Let there be lights in the firmament of the heavens to divide the day from the night; and let them be for signs and seasons, and for days and years; and let them be for lights in the firmament of the heavens to give light on the earth"; and it was so. Then God made two great lights: the greater light to rule the day, and the lesser light to rule the night. He made the stars also. God set them in the firmament of the heavens to give light on the earth, and to rule over the day and over the night, and to divide the light from the darkness. And God saw that it was good. So the evening and the morning were the fourth day.
>
> —GENESIS 1:14–19

The things that God established in the beginning exist even today—there aren't any changes. We have night and day, spring, summer, fall, and winter. The large light governs the day, and it shines like it did in the beginning. It warms and lights up our world, and God saw that that was good. I think that we all can say that this is still good. The warmth of the sun makes us feel better, both physically and spiritually. Our sense of humor and our mood improve. The smaller light, the moon, governs night.

Moonlit nights are wonderful any time of the year and in all continents. A countless quantity of stars decorates the firmament, the heavens. The most educated people in the twenty-first century cannot describe where the beginning and the end of the universe are. No one can count the stars. But the Creator:

…counts the number of the stars; He calls them all by name. Great is our Lord, and mighty in power; His understanding is infinite.

—PSALM 147:4–5

God can only create beauty like this; no one else is capable. Let's continue reading Genesis:

Then God said, "Let the waters abound with an abundance of living creatures, and let birds fly above the earth across the face of the firmament of the heavens." So God created great sea creatures and every living thing that moves, with which the waters abounded, according to their kind, and every winged bird according to its kind. And God saw that it was good. And God blessed them, saying, "Be fruitful and multiply, and fill the waters in the seas, and let birds multiply on the earth." So the evening and the morning were the fifth day.

—GENESIS 1:20–23

We see from verse 20 that God spoke to the water. This means that the water is also a living substance, which can hear His voice. Further, the water has not changed since the time of its creation until now. It remains alive and an active listener of God's commands, even today.

I live in California, in the suburbs of San Francisco. There isn't much rain here in the summer. Over the course of six to eight months, a single drop might not fall from the sky. But because I want to have green plants and trees around the house, I water the plants on a regular basis. Once, while watering my garden, I left some water in my bucket. I returned a few days later to water my garden with the leftover water. To my amazement, I found many living creatures in the small quantity of water left in this bucket. When I touched this bucket slightly, they began to move as though they wanted to hide somewhere to escape. I looked at them for a long time, and I felt two conflicting feelings. One was joy, and the other was sadness. My heart began to beat faster, and I began talking with God, saying, "Creator, this water is alive."

This revelation brought me much happiness and ecstasy, because it reminded me that the Word of God is powerful and is working today. Later, I proposed a few questions to myself: "Do I hear the voice of my Creator in my daily life? Do I carry out His commands without protest, mistakes, violence, or grumbling?" I began to analyze my own life, my daily conduct, my actions. I returned to my Creator and prayed:

> Dear God,
>   Teach me to listen to Your voice at all times, during the day and at night, in times of happiness and during life's storms, in grief, in sickness, and in health. Give me strength to fulfill Your commands without error.
>   In Jesus' name, amen.

On the pages of God's Constitution, it is written that God commanded the seas to bring forth all kinds of living things. The water was obedient and did as instructed by God. Even to this day, the water hears the voice of God and carries out His command. It fills rivers, oceans, seas, and lakes with life. A nature film entitled *World Under Water* shows the variety of sea creatures. No one can count the number of different fish species that are out there. I love watching films of this sort, and I admit I cannot take my eyes from the beautiful, colorful, and unique animals that films like this show. Water is alive, and the animals found in it listen to their Creator and fulfill His commands.

The land, the plants, the stars, and water are alive. They deeply believe and are obedient to their Creator, even to this day.

And let birds fly above the earth across the face of the firmament of the heavens.

—GENESIS 1:20

Many educated people, even scientists, cannot prove which came
first: the chicken or the egg. But those who read God's Word can
say, with faith, that God created the beings first and provided them
with the means to multiply. He created a specific way for each type
of creature to reproduce:

> Then God said, "Let the earth bring forth the living creature
> according to its kind: cattle and creeping thing and beast of the
> earth, each according to its kind"; and it was so. And God made
> the beast of the earth according to its kind, cattle according to
> its kind, and everything that creeps on the earth according to
> its kind. And God saw that it was good.
>
> —GENESIS 1:24–25

The Lord God commanded the land to bring forth life, and the
earth, after hearing the voice of the living God, did as it was told.
Every creature, to this day, listens to the voice of its Creator—this is
why I find what David said in his psalm to be truly amazing.

> Let everything that has breath praise the Lord.
>
> —PSALM 150:6

In the first chapter of this book, I proposed a question: who is
responsible for filling the Earth with life? After reading the first
chapter of the first book of the Bible, we have found that it is our
Lord God, Creator of heaven and Earth, who wants this world to
have life. God created animals because He didn't want the planet to
be empty, dead. Our almighty God is very humorous. It is He who
created all living things, in all sizes and shapes. It is He who made

green frogs, humped camels, poky porcupines, the deer with antlers, elephants, kittens, puppies, chickens, horses, cows, whales, the ants, pigs, and sheep. This is His work and our minds cannot ever fully comprehend what and how He created everything.

God blessed His creation and told it to multiply and fill the earth. God's plan for our earth is truly great. Today, in the twenty-first century, we are all witnessing the fact that God's plan is being carried out. Our own eyes see His wonderful creations, including the flowers, trees, shrubs, and the countless types of big and small animals.

Our God has a great sense of humor. Educated people know many complex details about all the life forms that exist on Earth, as well as details about other planets. But many of them, in spite of the access to information, do not know who established the methods for each creature to multiply by. And because they cannot answer this simple question of life, these people face a great problem: the mystery of why plants and animals reproduce. They cannot understand it themselves, and therefore, they cannot explain it to others. In contrast, those who read the Word of God and believe God and in God, do not encounter such a mystery. For these, plant and animal reproduction is a fulfillment of God's command.

Not only did God create all living creatures, but He loves and cares for each and every one of them. He remembers each living thing, be it big, medium, or small. God is life and He would hate for His Creation to die of starvation—which is why He creates food for us. God remembers and cares about newborns—those weak, helpless creatures—and by various means, prepares food for them. Let's read what the Word of God says of this:

> He sends the springs into the valleys; They flow among the hills. They give drink to every beast of the field; The wild donkeys quench their thirst. By them the birds of the heavens

have their home; They sing among the branches. He waters the hills from His upper chambers; The earth is satisfied with the fruit of Your works. He causes the grass to grow for the cattle, And vegetation for the service of man, That he may bring forth food from the earth.... The young lions roar after their prey, And seek their food from God.

—Psalm 104:10–14, 21

Who covers the heavens with clouds, Who prepares rain for the earth, Who makes grass to grow on the mountains. He gives to the beast its food, And to the young ravens that cry.

—Psalm 147:8–9

Can you hunt the prey for the lion, Or satisfy the appetite of the young lions, When they crouch in their dens, Or lurk in their lairs to lie in wait? Who provides food for the raven, When its young ones cry to God, And wander about for lack of food?

—Job 38:39–41

Look at the birds of the air, for they neither sow nor reap nor gather into barns; yet your heavenly Father feeds them. Are you not of more value than they?

—Matthew 6:26

Dear reader, have you ever thought that all created things might be believers and that the bushy-tailed squirrels, sharks, high-flying eagles, crows, crocodiles, and all others have fellowship with God? That they listen to His command to multiply and fulfill it? Each created thing, in its time, carries out the command to multiply and fill this earth with life. This occurs precisely as God decreed it—we are all witnesses to it. Isn't this wonderful? Of course it's wonderful! God's creations are miracles. I think that we can agree with the words of David and say:

O LORD, how manifold are Your works! In wisdom You have made them all. The earth is full of Your possessions—This great and wide sea, In which are innumerable teeming things, Living things both small and great.

—PSALM 104:24–25

For these great creations, we can only say, praise God, the Creator of heaven and Earth!

Praise the LORD! Praise the Lord from the heavens; Praise Him in the heights! Praise Him, all His angels; Praise Him, all His hosts! Praise Him, sun and moon; Praise Him, all you stars of light! Praise Him, you heavens of heavens, And you waters above the heavens! Let them praise the name of the LORD, For He commanded and they were created. He also established them forever and ever; He made a decree which shall not pass away. Praise the LORD from the earth, You great sea creatures and all the depths; Fire and hail, snow and clouds; Stormy wind, fulfilling His word; Mountains and all hills; Fruitful trees and all cedars; Beasts and all cattle; Creeping things and flying fowl; Kings of the earth and all peoples; Princes and all judges of the earth; Both young men and maidens; Old men and children. Let them praise the name of the LORD, For His name alone is exalted; His glory is above the earth and heaven.

—PSALM 148:1–13

4

THE CREATION OF
THE FIRST MAN

MY DEAR ATHEIST LISTENED TO MY DESCRIPTION OF creation, of the plant and animal kingdoms, and with great interest wanted to know where the first man came from. We'll find the answer to this question in the pages of the Bible. Let's continue reading the first book, Genesis:

> Then God said, "Let Us make man in Our image, according to Our likeness; let them have dominion over the fish of the sea, over the birds of the air, and over the cattle, over all the Earth and over every creeping thing that creeps on the Earth." So God created man in His own image; in the image of God He created him; male and female He created them.
> —GENESIS 1:26–27

I do not think that these words are referring to the physical appearance of both God and man. The Word of God teaches that "God is Spirit" (John 4:24) and "No one has seen God at any time" (John 1:18). But we see people and we see each other. We may physically touch each other. So what does "in our image, in our likeness" mean? I think this is referring to the spiritual aspect of people. To have been created in the image of God means that one has the choice and the power to make decisions. We can decide to do God's will and to act according to it or against it. God didn't create us to be programmed workers who only do what we are instructed. God created us with the ability to think and take charge of our life. I think that "in our likeness," is referring to our actions. "In the likeness of God" means to be like the Creator in conduct and actions and to accept His laws into our daily life and to fulfill His commands. It means to listen to His voice, to have fellowship with Him, to submit yourself under His management, and to carry out His will. In other words, we have the choice to make God the Lord of our existence.

> Let them have dominion over the fish of the sea, over the birds of the air, and over the cattle, over all the earth and over every creeping thing that creeps on the earth.
> —GENESIS 1:26

Having read the remainder of verse 26, we see what great rights God gave us. God gave us authority. He put all that He created under our control. God gave us the entire planet and all that is on it—all the plant and animal life.

> The heaven, even the heavens, are the Lord's; But the earth He has given to the children of men.
> —PSALM 115:16

What a wondrous God—and He regards us highly! He treasures you, dear reader, and me also.

"Male and female He created them." These words hold the answer to the question, who keeps the balance between males and females? The answer is simple. The Creator, God, maintains the balance. It is He who created males and females, and to this day He keeps the balance. This isn't a fabrication; this isn't a fairytale. It is a fact. We all are witnesses to this fact in our own life. Wherever we turn our gaze, we, through our own eyes, see men and women. In history, we do not find that sometime, somewhere, on some continent, in some country, only boys were born over the course of ninety-nine years. This is not recorded anywhere. There is also no record showing that at one time the last boy died and the world became empty and dead. This isn't recorded on the pages of history because this has never happened. The fact that this balance is maintained is proof that only God, the Creator, handles the natural development of mankind. No one else can do this. Parents cannot maintain the balance. Only God can maintain this balance, and no one can contradict this fact. Let's continue with the first chapter:

> Then God blessed them, and God said to them, "Be fruitful and multiply; fill the earth and subdue it; have dominion over the fish of the sea, over the birds of the air, and over every living thing that moves on the earth."
>
> —Genesis 1:28

It is God who gave us the permission to multiply. It is Him who prevents this world from lacking people and becoming empty, dead. It is He who established the methods by which each living thing can reproduce. It is He who wants the planet to breathe with life. What a great assignment Lord God gave to us to fill the earth with human life. He also gave us the power and authority to have dominion over all plant and animal life. In other words, you can say that God made us kings over all the earth. God is great, as are His actions!

When I consider Your heavens, the work of Your fingers, The moon and the stars, which You have ordained, What is man that You are mindful of him, And the son of man that You visit him? For You have made him a little lower than the angels, And You have crowned him with glory and honor. You have made him to have dominion over the works of Your hands; You have put all things under his feet, All sheep and oxen—Even the beasts of the field, The birds of the air, And the fish of the sea That pass through the paths of the seas.

—Psalm 8:3–8

Our God is wonderful, and His works are great also. Let's continue reading chapter 1:

And God said, "See, I have given you every herb that yields seed which is on the face of all the earth, and every tree whose fruit yields seed; to you it shall be for food. Also, to every beast of the earth, to every bird of the air, and to everything that creeps on the earth, in which there is life, I have given every green herb for food"; and it was so.

—Genesis 1:29–30

Not only did God create animals and people, but He also prepared food for them and us alike. At first, the animals ate from the goodness of the earth just as man did. God prepared food because God is life and wants His Creation to live, multiply, decorate the earth, and give Him praise.

Then God saw everything that He had made, and indeed it was very good. So the evening and the morning were the sixth day. Thus the heavens and the Earth, and all the host of them, were finished. And on the seventh day God ended His work which He had done, and He rested on the seventh day from all His work which He had done. Then God blessed the seventh day and sanctified it, because in it He rested from all His work which God had created and made.

—GENESIS 1:31–2:3

The seventh verse of the second chapter tells how God made the first man:

And the LORD God formed man from the dust of the ground, and breathed into his nostrils the breath of life; and man became a living being.

—GENESIS 2:7

God breathed into man the breath of life. Therefore, in each man, there is the breath of God, a tiny portion of Him. Some people call the breath of God a soul, a spirit, and some say that the breath is conscience. All these terms are really of little consequence. What is important is that each person has this breath. In each person there is a portion of God. We often hear, "My conscience bothers me," or, "I can't do this because my conscience will condemn me; it prevents me from doing something bad." Our conscience is surely made of the breath of God.

Lord God made the first man and looked after his conduct, actions, and mood. And He noticed an interesting detail. Let's read more from chapter 2:

And the LORD God said, "It is not good that man should be alone; I will make him a helper comparable to him."

—GENESIS 2:18

We see that while watching the first man, God noticed that he wasn't satisfied; he wasn't happy, content. He was alone and without friends that were comparable to him. Therefore, God decided to create a helper for him. But first, God gave the first man a great assignment to complete. What was it? What was his task? Let's continue reading chapter 2 together:

> Out of the ground the LORD God formed every beast of the field and every bird of the air, and brought them to Adam to see what he would call them. And whatever Adam called each living creature, that was its name. So Adam gave names to all cattle, to the birds of the air, and to every beast of the field. But for Adam there was not found a helper comparable to him.
>
> —GENESIS 2:19–20

God assigned Adam a great task. As is evident, the first man was intelligent and had a good memory, a sharp mind, and was bright enough to complete this large and important assignment. God paraded His entire creation in front of the first man, and he named each type of creature. Adam named each creature successfully and therefore completed this task perfectly. Adam got to see all the living creatures that God created.

I can imagine this scene. Adam is standing, and in front of him walks a large creature he names *cow*. And then a little creature with a bushy tail walks by and he names that one a *squirrel*. A large, clumsy creature wanders slowly by and Adam names him *elephant*. A black, medium-sized creature, with its wings flapping, walks by and is given the name *crow*. Then a proud, long-necked creature parades by and Adam names it *giraffe*. The giraffe might have passed Adam without even glancing in his direction. Each species walked by Adam like this and was named. Without directing much attention to Adam, the animals then scattered, each in his own direction. Not a single animal spoke, smiled, or winked at Adam. Because of this, a helper was not found for the first man. All creatures went their separate ways, with their own kind, and Adam was left alone, possibly with a sad and heavy heart. This didn't go unnoticed by God, who was looking after Adam. God saw his lonesome state. Let's continue reading the second chapter to see what happened next:

> And the LORD God caused a deep sleep to fall on Adam, and he slept; and He took one of his ribs, and closed up the flesh in its place. Then the rib which the LORD God had taken from man He made into a woman, and He brought her to the man.
> —GENESIS 2:21–22

Surely we can imagine how the first man reacted when his eyes first beheld the young, beautiful woman. I think we all can envision this scene and the joy Adam must have felt, and also how loudly he exclaimed:

> This is now bone of my bones And flesh of my flesh; She shall be called Woman, Because she was taken out of Man.
> —GENESIS 2:23

God created the first woman with a rib from the first man. What I find interesting is that God didn't make the woman from any portion of the man's head. She is therefore not in position to govern him. Neither was she created from the man's leg. She is therefore not below him. But she was created from a rib, which is so close to the heart. She is therefore to be loved and treasured by him.

> Therefore a man shall leave his father and mother and be joined to his wife, and they shall become one flesh. And they were both naked, the man and his wife, and were not ashamed.
> —GENESIS 2:24–25

From these words we see that God Himself created the marital life. It is He who made the man and woman, blessed them, and gave them the command to multiply and fill this earth with human life. God named the man Adam, and Adam named his wife Eve because she was to become the mother of all mankind.

Now we will focus back to our time. When we look at the conduct of today's Adam, we can say that today's Adam acts just like the first one did. When today's Adam looks at his own Eve, his heart beats faster, his blood warms, and he proclaims, "She is mine; she belongs to me." And he clenches his fist and with a raised tone yells, "Just let anyone look at her or touch her! He will receive his reward—right on his nose." So many years have passed since the Creation, but this Adam hasn't changed.

Let's look deeper at the following words: "It is not good for man to be alone. Let's make him a helper." After God made Adam, and after observing him for a while, God saw that it wasn't good for man to be alone. To solve this, God created a woman, a wife for Adam. Now a question arises: does God see and look after the twenty-first century Adam? Of course He does. God looks and sees the Adam of today's time—there is no doubt about that. For example, in today's time, no Adam must fly to another planet to find himself a wife. Likewise, he doesn't need to go to other countries in search of a helper. Today, our own eyes see that God hasn't changed. He sees today's Adams just like He saw the first Adam. It is God who controls the development of mankind. It is He who maintains the balance between men and women, and this is a fact, which we all witness. No one—not the rich, the poor, the educated, the un-educated, the wise, or simple—can deny this fact. I think that today, when Adam looks at his helper, his Eve, he must loudly exclaim: "God saw the first man and that it wasn't good for him to be alone, therefore He prepared a helper for him. This same God saw me, saw that my heart was heavy when I was alone, and

He has prepared such a beauty for me. I am a blessed man! Praise be to God of heaven and Earth!" I think that everyone will agree with me that Eve, woman and wife, is always beautiful at all ages and very important for this planet because without her our Earth would be dead.

The wife is tangible and living proof that you can look at, touch, smile at, and receive reciprocal feelings from. When a loving husband wholeheartedly smiles at his wife, then his Eve will have a hard time acting differently because the feelings are sure to be mutual. Eve, the wife, is proof that God hasn't changed and that He is the same today, in the twenty-first century, as He was in the beginning when He created the first man. God looked after the first Adam, and He has looked after each Adam since then. Dear Adam, it doesn't matter where you were born, on what continent, in what country, whether in a large city, a village, or in the center of Siberia. Just remember that God sees you and knows your needs regarding your Eve.

What if over the course of seventy-nine years or over any number of consecutive years, only girls were born in Poland and boys in Africa? Eventually, these kids grew up and the boys visited the pretty, curly haired girls in Poland. Some boys, the wealthy ones, flew in planes, while others took trains or walked if they were extremely poor. When they came to Poland, they took all the girls for wives, and kept the little ones for the future, for their sons. But this is not the story of life. If this had occurred, it would have undoubtedly left Poland disorganized and rather empty.

Dear reader and most interested atheist, have you ever heard of this occurring? Have you read of such an event on the pages of history books? Of course you have never heard or read of such a phenomenon. It isn't recorded in history books because it never happened. Our great God, the Creator of heaven and Earth, is the

God of order. He is sovereign and maintains the balance between males and females, for the benefit of each Adam.

Dear atheist, you can be an atheist—you don't have to change your belief. You can even die an atheist, but only if you can answer the question, who maintained the balance between males and females in the entire world, starting with the beginning of time up through to today? When you find someone other than God the Creator, then by all means, remain an atheist. But if you don't find anyone else and you can't answer this question, then immediately turn to the living God; to the One who created you and remains your Maker; to the One who loves you, wants to save you, and awaits your return.

Right now, start to talk to Him. Ask Him whatever you want and He will answer you. "Call to Me, and I will answer you, and show you great and mighty things, which you do not know" (Jer. 33:3). Remember, He keeps His words.

Our God doesn't sleep. He holds the entire planet in the palm of His hand and daily fills it with life. The balance is maintained by God, the Creator of heaven, Earth, and mankind—it is the result of His work. Regardless of where Adam is born, on a small or a large continent, in a small or large country, in a large city or in a village, our good God sees him and provides for him.

Dear Adam, have you thought of how much love God gives you? Have you treasured His goodness? If you have never thought of this or have never been truly interested in this question, you have time to think of these things today and to remember that there is Someone who remembers you, loves you, and wants you to have joy and blessings throughout your life on this earth. He is Someone who doesn't want you to feel lonesome. Regardless of where you were born, what your material situation is, where you live, what your education level is, what your profession is, remember one thing: God loves you, looks after you, and will never forget you because you are His creation; you are the work of His hands. Just as God saw the first Adam, so He sees you today. Isn't our God wonderful? Yes, and not one compares to Him.

Let's return to Adam and Eve and see how their life continued:

> The Lord God planted a garden eastward in Eden, and there He put the man whom He had formed. And out of the ground the Lord God made every tree grow that is pleasant to the sight and good for food. The tree of life was also in the midst of the garden, and the tree of the knowledge of good and evil. Now a river went out of Eden to water the garden, and from there it parted and became four riverheads. The name of the first is Pishon; it is the one which skirts the whole land of Havilah, where there is gold. And the gold of that land is good. Bdellium and the onyx stone are there. The name of the second river is Gihon; it is the one which goes around the whole land of Cush. The name of the third river is Hiddekel; it is the one which goes toward the east of Assyria. The fourth river is the Euphrates. Then the Lord God took the man and put him in the garden of Eden to tend and keep it.
> —GENESIS 2:8–15

We can see from these verses that God made a great place for the first people to dwell in. This place had great trees that were beautiful to look at and also bore delicious fruit. But we must note that there were special trees in the Garden of Eden: the Tree of Life, in the center, and the Tree of the Knowledge of Good and Evil. God also gave great wealth to the couple, as there were gold and onyx stones in the garden. From the garden a river came out and was divided into four rivers, which indicates that this garden must have taken up a good portion of the land. Even though it was large, God told the first people to tend it. Tending a garden as big as this would require work, but God provided everything the people needed to be able to do so. I think that we all can agree that it was very nice of God to worry about man so. This was a period of blessing for the young couple. The Word of God doesn't tell us how long this period lasted, but this was a great time in their lives. From what God gave the first people, we can conclude that God loves His creation and creates the best for him.

We have read so much about what God has prepared, and now we come to a question: does God require something in return? We'll soon find the answer to this question on the pages of God's Constitution. In order to maintain a mutual relationship between God and man, God gave man one command:

> And the LORD God commanded the man, saying, "Of every tree of the garden you may freely eat; but of the tree of the knowledge of good and evil you shall not eat, for in the day that you eat of it you shall surely die."
>
> —GENESIS 2:16–17

Adam and Eve were specifically instructed not to eat from the tree of the knowledge of good and evil. It was the only command God gave them. God gave them everything: beauty, blessings, riches, authority, and power to rule over all of the Earth and over all creation. God made man the owner and king of this planet Earth. In return, God only required obedience—which is why He laid down the first rule. The first people received everything they needed for their life from God. They received so much, and in comparison, God required so little in return—just obedience. When we receive from God and are obedient to Him, we have fellowship with Him. And the fellowship that we have is the foundation for our connection and relationship with the Creator.

We will now return to the present to see if God has changed since Adam and Eve's time. There is much evidence showing that God hasn't changed. He still provides us with many things, including health, blessings, bread, and freedom. Nature still provides fruit and beautiful plants for us to enjoy. We receive everything from God the Father, our Creator. We receive so very much. And God requires so little of us—just obedience. And that is why He laid down His commandments for His creation, for us.

God observed the first man, Adam, so likewise He looks upon us today. God sees if we fulfill His will or if we disregard it; if we obey His laws or if we violate them.

The Word of God teaches us that God is also a Spirit; no one has ever seen God. But our own eyes have seen and continue to see the work of His hands. Wherever we turn, wherever we find ourselves, we see the actions and work of God. We see trees, shrubs, grass, and flowers that grow, multiply, and fulfill God's will. All these plants decorate the planet and fill it with their life. If we think deeper, we realize that it is only God who can multiply all of these plants. When we see the animals at the zoo, we notice that there are different types of animals, of various sizes and breeds. They have been reproducing since the beginning of time. And if we think deeper, we realize that they are fulfilling the command of God to "multiply and fill this Earth with life." At night, when we look up at the sky, we see numerous stars. This also is the work of God. The heavenly bodies are alive and believers of God. They fulfill His commands to circle without catastrophe, fill the space, and rule over either the day or night.

Many people can, in great detail, explain how the human organism functions. Yet, in spite of knowing many specifics about the human body, they cannot describe who established the method of reproduction or who commanded people to multiply. In contrast, those who believe in God and believe God, those who read the

Word of God, though they might be simple folks, have no trouble describing who maintains the balance between the sexes. They firmly believe that God, the Creator of heaven and Earth, created the first man, Adam. They believe that God saw that it wasn't good for Adam to be alone and therefore created a helper, Eve, for him. They believe that He blessed them and commanded them to multiply and fill the earth, a process that continues even today, as we witness. It is good to be a believer.

God is a Spirit—this is the truth. No one has ever seen God—this is true also. But we see the work of His hands everywhere we look. There isn't a place in the world where the work of God's hand is invisible.

5

THE GREATNESS AND MIGHT OF GOD THE CREATOR

WE HAVE READ ABOUT THE ACTIONS OF OUR LORD GOD to a good extent. We have heard, "God has created, God has formed, God has done, God has said, God has made, God has seen, and God is looking." Now my dear reader and highly respected atheist, would you like to know if this constitution, the Bible, says more about the qualities of God and His character, His features, and His actions? Does God say anything about Himself? Let's travel together though the pages of the Bible and find answers to these questions:

> Who has measured the waters in the hollow of His hand, Measured heaven with a span And calculated the dust of the earth in a measure? Weighed the mountains in scales And the hills in a balance? Who has directed the Spirit of the Lord, Or as His counselor has taught Him? With whom did He take counsel, and who instructed Him, And taught Him in the path

of justice? Who taught Him knowledge, And showed Him the way of understanding? Behold, the nations are as a drop in a bucket, And are counted as the small dust on the scales; Look, He lifts up the isles as a very little thing. And Lebanon is not sufficient to burn, Nor its beasts sufficient for a burnt offering. All nations before Him are as nothing, And they are counted by Him less than nothing and worthless.

—ISAIAH 40:12–17

God came from Teman, The Holy One from Mount Paran. Selah. His glory covered the heavens, And the earth was full of His praise. His brightness was like the light; He had rays flashing from His hand, And there His power was hidden....He stood and measured the earth; He looked and startled the nations. And the everlasting mountains were scattered, the perpetual hills bowed. His ways are everlasting.

—HABAKKUK 3:3–4, 6

But the LORD is the true God; He is the living God and the everlasting King. At His wrath the earth will tremble, And the nations will not be able to endure His indignation. Thus you shall say to them: "The gods that have not made the heavens and the earth shall perish from the earth and from under these heavens." He has made the earth by His power, He has established the world by His wisdom, And has stretched out the heavens at His discretion. When He utters His voice, There is a multitude of waters in the heavens: "And He causes the vapors to ascend from the ends of the earth. He makes lightning for the rain, He brings the wind out of His treasuries."

—JEREMIAH 10:10–13

And now we shall read what God says about Himself:

Thus says God the Lord, Who created the heavens and stretched them out, Who spread forth the Earth and that which comes from it, Who gives breath to the people on it, And spirit to those who walk on it.

—Isaiah 42:5

Thus says the Lord, your Redeemer, And He who formed you from the womb: "I am the Lord, who makes all things, Who stretches out the heavens all alone, Who spreads abroad the earth by Myself."

—Isaiah 44:24

For thus says the Lord, Who created the heavens, Who is God, Who formed the earth and made it, Who has established it, Who did not create it in vain, Who formed it to be inhabited: "I am the Lord, and there is no other."

—Isaiah 45:18

Indeed My hand has laid the foundation of the earth, And My right hand has stretched out the heavens; When I call to them, They stand up together.

—Isaiah 48:13

I, the Lord, search the heart, I test the mind, Even to give every man according to his ways, According to the fruit of his doings.

—Jeremiah 17:10

"Am I a God near at hand," says the Lord, "And not a God afar off? Can anyone hide himself in secret places, So I shall not see him?" says the Lord; "Do I not fill heaven and earth?" says the Lord.

—Jeremiah 23:23–24

Who has performed and done it, Calling the generations from the beginning? "I, the LORD, am the first; And with the last I am He."

—ISAIAH 41:4

Thus says the LORD: "Heaven is My throne, And earth is My footstool. Where is the house that you will build Me? And where is the place of My rest? For all those things My hand has made, And all those things exist," Says the LORD. "But on this one will I look: On him who is poor and of a contrite spirit, And who trembles at My word."

—ISAIAH 66:1–2

To whom then will you liken God? Or what likeness will you compare to Him? The workman molds an image, The goldsmith overspreads it with gold, And the silversmith casts silver chains. Whoever is too impoverished for such a contribution Chooses a tree that will not rot; He seeks for himself a skillful workman To prepare a carved image that will not totter. Have you not known? Have you not heard? Has it not been told you from the beginning? Have you not understood from the foundations of the earth? It is He who sits above the circle of the earth, And its inhabitants are like grasshoppers, Who stretches out the heavens like a curtain, And spreads them out like a tent to dwell in. He brings the princes to nothing; He makes the judges of the earth useless. Scarcely shall they be planted, Scarcely shall they be sown, Scarcely shall their stock take root in the earth, When He will also blow on them, And they will wither, And the whirlwind will take them away like stubble. "To whom then will you liken Me, Or to whom shall I be equal?" says the Holy One. Lift up your eyes on high, And see who has created these things, Who brings out their host by number; He calls them all by name,

By the greatness of His might And the strength of His power; Not one is missing. Why do you say, O Jacob, And speak, O Israel: "My way is hidden from the LORD, And my just claim is passed over by my God"? Have you not known? Have you not heard? The everlasting God, the LORD, The Creator of the ends of the earth, Neither faints nor is weary. His understanding is unsearchable. He gives power to the weak, And to those who have no might He increases strength. Even the youths shall faint and be weary, And the young men shall utterly fall, But those who wait on the LORD Shall renew their strength; They shall mount up with wings like eagles, They shall run and not be weary, They shall walk and not faint.

—ISAIAH 40:18–31

"You are My witnesses," says the LORD, "And My servant whom I have chosen, That you may know and believe Me, And understand that I am He. Before Me there was no God formed, Nor shall there be after Me. I, even I, am the LORD, And besides Me there is no savior. I have declared and saved, I have proclaimed, And there was no foreign god among you; Therefore you are My witnesses," Says the LORD, "that I am God. Indeed before the day was, I am He; And there is no one who can deliver out of My hand; I work, and who will reverse it?"

—ISAIAH 43:10–13

Thus says the LORD, the King of Israel, And his Redeemer, the LORD of hosts: "I am the First and I am the Last; Besides Me there is no God. And who can proclaim as I do? Then let him declare it and set it in order for Me, Since I appointed the ancient people. And the things that are coming and shall come, Let them show these to them. Do not fear, nor be afraid; Have

I not told you from that time, and declared it? You are My witnesses. Is there a God besides Me? Indeed there is no other Rock; I know not one."

—ISAIAH 44:6–8

I am the Lord, and there is no other; There is no God besides Me. I will gird you, though you have not known Me, That they may know from the rising of the sun to its setting That there is none besides Me. I am the LORD, and there is no other; I form the light and create darkness, I make peace and create calamity; I, the LORD, do all these things. Rain down, you heavens, from above, And let the skies pour down righteousness; Let the earth open, let them bring forth salvation, And let righteousness spring up together. I, the LORD, have created it. Woe to him who strives with his Maker! Let the potsherd strive with the potsherds of the earth! Shall the clay say to him who forms it, 'What are you making?' Or shall your handiwork say, 'He has no hands'? Woe to him who says to his father, 'What are you begetting?' Or to the woman, 'What have you brought forth?'" Thus says the LORD, The Holy One of Israel, and his Maker: "Ask Me of things to come concerning My sons; And concerning the work of My hands, you command Me. I have made the earth, And created man on it. I—My hands—stretched out the heavens, And all their host I have commanded."

—ISAIAH 45:5–12

Even to your old age, I am He, And even to gray hairs I will carry you! I have made, and I will bear; Even I will carry, and will deliver you. To whom will you liken Me, and make Me equal And compare Me, that we should be alike? They lavish gold out of the bag, And weigh silver on the scales; They hire a goldsmith, and he makes it a god; They prostrate themselves, yes, they worship. They bear it on the shoulder, they carry it And set it in its place, and it stands; From its place it shall not move. Though one cries out to it, yet it cannot answer Nor save him out of his trouble. Remember this, and show yourselves men; Recall to mind, O you transgressors. Remember the former things of old, For I am God, and there is no other; I am God, and there is none like Me, Declaring the end from the beginning, And from ancient times things that are not yet done, Saying, "My counsel shall stand, And I will do all My pleasure."

—Isaiah 46:4–10

Inasmuch as there is none like You, O Lord (You are great, and Your name is great in might), Who would not fear You, O King of the nations? For this is Your rightful due. For among all the wise men of the nations, And in all their kingdoms, There is none like You.

—Jeremiah 10:6–7

Many, O Lord my God, are Your wonderful works Which You have done; And Your thoughts toward us Cannot be recounted to You in order; If I would declare and speak of them, They are more than can be numbered.

—Psalm 40:5

Who is like You, O Lord, among the gods? Who is like You, glorious in holiness, Fearful in praises, doing wonders?

—Exodus 15:11

O Lord God, You have begun to show Your servant Your greatness and Your mighty hand, for what god is there in heaven or on earth who can do anything like Your works and Your mighty deeds?

—Deuteronomy 3:24

No one is holy like the LORD, For there is none besides You, Nor is there any rock like our God.

—1 SAMUEL 2:2

Therefore You are great, O Lord GOD. For there is none like You, nor is there any God besides You, according to all that we have heard with our ears.

—2 SAMUEL 7:22

Also Your righteousness, O God, is very high, You who have done great things; O God, who is like You?

—PSALM 71:19

Among the gods there is none like You, O Lord; Nor are there any works like Your works. All nations whom You have made Shall come and worship before You, O Lord, And shall glorify Your name. For You are great, and do wondrous things; You alone are God.

—PSALM 86:8–10

The Word of God teaches us that praise and glory belong only to God Himself. On the pages of the Holy Book we find a command: give praise and thanks to God. And this command does not only pertain to people—it pertains to all of nature. It pertains to deserts, cities, villages, oceans, and to every land and sea creature. Every breathing thing must praise God because He is the Creator. Everything He created is for His glory and praise, and all of it is alive and should listen to His will.

Sing to the LORD a new song, And His praise from the ends of the earth, You who go down to the sea, and all that is in it, You coastlands and you inhabitants of them! Let the wilderness and its cities lift up their voice, The villages that Kedar inhabits. Let the inhabitants of Sela sing, Let them shout from the top of the mountains. Let them give glory to the LORD, And declare His praise in the coastlands.

—ISAIAH 42:10–12

Sing, O heavens, for the LORD has done it! Shout, you lower parts of the earth; Break forth into singing, you mountains, O forest, and every tree in it! For the LORD has redeemed Jacob, And glorified Himself in Israel.

—ISAIAH 44:23

Sing, O heavens! Be joyful, O earth! And break out in singing, O mountains! For the LORD has comforted His people, And will have mercy on His afflicted.

—ISAIAH 49:13

God the Father has clearly stated that His praise will remain His. His praise will not go to other gods or to man's work.

I am the LORD, that is My name; And My glory I will not give to another, Nor My praise to carved images.

—ISAIAH 42:8

For My own sake, for My own sake, I will do it; For how should My name be profaned? And I will not give My glory to another.

—ISAIAH 48:11

This warning is for all of creation; it is for me and for you, too, dear reader, because His glory isn't for another. Glory and praise are only due to our holy God, Creator of heaven and Earth, because He is the one and only, and there is no comparison to Him.

As we read the Holy Word, we find that God has many names.

Let's read about the time when Moses first heard the voice of the living God:

> Now Moses was tending the flock of Jethro his father-in-law, the priest of Midian. And he led the flock to the back of the desert, and came to Horeb, the mountain of God. And the Angel of the LORD appeared to him in a flame of fire from the midst of a bush. So he looked, and behold, the bush was burning with fire, but the bush was not consumed. Then Moses said, "I will now turn aside and see this great sight, why the bush does not burn." So when the LORD saw that he turned aside to look, God called to him from the midst of the bush and said, "Moses, Moses!" And he said, "Here I am." Then He said, "Do not draw near this place. Take your sandals off your feet, for the place where you stand is holy ground." Moreover He said, "I am the God of your father—the God of Abraham, the God of Isaac, and the God of Jacob." And Moses hid his face, for he was afraid to look upon God. And the LORD said: "I have surely seen the oppression of My people who are in Egypt, and have heard their cry because of their taskmasters, for I know their sorrows. So I have come down to deliver them out of the hand of the Egyptians, and to bring them up from that land to a good and large land, to a land flowing with milk and honey, to the place of the Canaanites and the Hittites and the Amorites and the Perizzites and the Hivites and the Jebusites. Now therefore, behold, the cry of the children of Israel has come to Me, and I have also seen the oppression with which the Egyptians oppress them. Come now, therefore, and I will send you to Pharaoh that you may bring My people, the children of Israel, out of Egypt." But Moses said to God, "Who am I that I should go to Pharaoh, and that I should bring the children of Israel out of Egypt?" So He said, "I will certainly be with

you. And this shall be a sign to you that I have sent you: When you have brought the people out of Egypt, you shall serve God on this mountain." Then Moses said to God, "Indeed, when I come to the children of Israel and say to them, 'The God of your fathers has sent me to you,' and they say to me, 'What is His name?' what shall I say to them?" And God said to Moses, "I AM WHO I AM." And He said, "Thus you shall say to the children of Israel, 'I AM has sent me to you.'" Moreover God said to Moses, "Thus you shall say to the children of Israel: 'The LORD God of your fathers, the God of Abraham, the God of Isaac, and the God of Jacob, has sent me to you. This is My name forever, and this is My memorial to all generations.' Go and gather the elders of Israel together, and say to them, 'The LORD God of your fathers, the God of Abraham, of Isaac, and of Jacob, appeared to me, saying, "I have surely visited you and seen what is done to you in Egypt."'

—EXODUS 3:1–16

I am the LORD, that is My name; And My glory I will not give to another, Nor My praise to carved images.

—ISAIAH 42:8

But I am the LORD your God, Who divided the sea whose waves roared—The LORD of hosts is His name.

—ISAIAH 51:15

For thus says the High and Lofty One Who inhabits eternity, whose name is Holy: "I dwell in the high and holy place, With him who has a contrite and humble spirit, To revive the spirit of the humble, And to revive the heart of the contrite ones.

—ISAIAH 57:15

The Portion of Jacob is not like them, For He is the Maker of all things, And Israel is the tribe of His inheritance; The LORD of hosts is His name.

—JEREMIAH 10:16

Thus says the LORD, Who gives the sun for a light by day, The ordinances of the moon and the stars for a light by night, Who disturbs the sea, And its waves roar (The LORD of hosts is His name).

—JEREMIAH 31:35

In Exodus, God calls Himself I AM and Jehovah. He also calls Himself the God of Abraham, Isaac, and Jacob. In Isaiah He calls Himself God, Lord, the Lord of hosts, holy, everlasting, Creator of all things, and Maker.

The Word of God teaches us that God's wisdom is uncharted, unexplored. Let's read about this topic from Romans:

Oh, the depth of the riches both of the wisdom and knowledge of God! How unsearchable are His judgments and His ways past finding out! "For who has known the mind of the LORD? Or who has become His counselor?" "Or who has first given to Him And it shall be repaid to him?" For of Him and through Him and to Him are all things, to whom be glory forever. Amen.

—ROMANS 11:33–36

People cannot know, comprehend, or understand God's wisdom with their limited mind. People can see only a piece of God's handiwork.

He has made the earth by His power, He has established the world by His wisdom, And has stretched out the heavens at

His discretion. When He utters His voice, There is a multitude of waters in the heavens: "And He causes the vapors to ascend from the ends of the earth. He makes lightning for the rain, He brings the wind out of His treasuries."

—JEREMIAH 10:12–13

I think that each of us would like to have a little more wisdom. What the Bible says about wisdom is very interesting. I read these words with great delight, and each time I read them, I know more about the author of wisdom, the Creator of wisdom. My desire is for my dear readers to read the following words concerning wisdom:

But where can wisdom be found? And where is the place of understanding? Man does not know its value, Nor is it found in the land of the living. The deep says, 'It is not in me'; And the sea says, 'It is not with me.' It cannot be purchased for gold, Nor can silver be weighed for its price. It cannot be valued in the gold of Ophir, In precious onyx or sapphire. Neither gold nor crystal can equal it, Nor can it be exchanged for jewelry of fine gold. No mention shall be made of coral or quartz, For the price of wisdom is above rubies. The topaz of Ethiopia cannot equal it, Nor can it be valued in pure gold. "From where then does wisdom come? And where is the place of understanding? It is hidden from the eyes of all living, And concealed from the birds of the air. Destruction and Death say, 'We have heard a report about it with our ears.' God understands its way, And He knows its place. For He looks to the ends of the earth, And sees under the whole heavens, To establish a weight for the wind, And apportion the waters by measure. When He made a law for the rain, And a path for the thunderbolt, Then He saw wisdom and declared it; He prepared it, indeed, He searched it out. And to man He said, 'Behold, the fear of the Lord, that is wisdom, And to depart from evil is understanding.

—Job 28:12–28

Does not wisdom cry out, And understanding lift up her voice? She takes her stand on the top of the high hill, Beside the way, where the paths meet. She cries out by the gates, at the entry of the city, At the entrance of the doors: "To you, O men, I call, And my voice is to the sons of men. O you simple ones, understand prudence, And you fools, be of an understanding heart. Listen, for I will speak of excellent things, And from the opening of my lips will come right things; For my mouth will speak truth; Wickedness is an abomination to my lips. All the words of my mouth are with righteousness; Nothing crooked or perverse is in them. They are all plain to him who understands, And right to those who find knowledge. Receive my instruction, and not silver, And knowledge rather than choice gold; For wisdom is better than rubies, And all the things one may desire cannot be compared with her. "I, wisdom, dwell with prudence, And find out knowledge and discretion. The fear of the Lord is to hate evil; Pride and arrogance and the evil way And the perverse mouth I hate. Counsel is mine, and sound wisdom; I am understanding, I have strength. By me kings reign, And rulers decree justice. By me princes rule, and nobles, All the judges of the earth. I love those who love me, And those who seek me diligently will find me. Riches and honor are with me, Enduring riches and righteousness. My fruit is better than gold, yes, than fine gold, And my revenue than choice silver. I traverse the way of righteousness, In the midst of the paths of justice, That I may cause those who love me to inherit wealth, That I may fill their treasuries. "The Lord possessed me at the beginning of His way, Before His works of old. I have been established from everlasting, From the beginning, before there was ever an earth. When there were no depths I was brought forth, When there were no fountains abounding with water. Before the mountains were settled, Before the hills, I was brought forth; While as yet He had not made the earth or the fields, Or the primal dust of the world. When He prepared the heavens, I was there, When He drew a circle on the face of the deep, When He established the clouds above, When He strengthened the fountains of the deep, When He assigned to the sea its limit, So that the waters would not transgress His command, When He marked out the foundations of the earth, Then I was beside Him as a master craftsman; And I was daily His delight, Rejoicing always before Him, Rejoicing in His inhabited world, And my delight was with the sons of men. "Now therefore, listen to me, my children, For blessed are those who keep my ways. Hear instruction and be wise, And do not disdain it. Blessed is the man who listens to me, Watching daily at my gates, Waiting at the posts of my doors. For whoever finds me finds life, And obtains favor from the LORD; But he who sins against me wrongs his own soul; All those who hate me love death."

—PROVERBS 8:1–36

The fear of the LORD is the beginning of wisdom, And the knowledge of the Holy One is understanding.

—PROVERBS 9:10

The fear of the LORD is the beginning of wisdom; A good understanding have all those who do His commandments, His praise endures forever.

—PSALM 111:10

For "who has known the mind of the LORD that he may instruct Him?" But we have the mind of Christ.

—1 Corinthians 2:16

God is the God of all people because He created everything—the nations that exist on all the continents, islands, and peninsulas. And He calls everyone to Himself. He wants to have fellowship with His creation. God doesn't want His creation to aimlessly roam without knowing its Creator or the purpose for their lives. God wants to have fellowship with me, as well as with you, dear reader, because you and I are His creation—a fact that is written in God's Constitution.

Look to Me, and be saved, All you ends of the earth! For I am God, and there is no other. I have sworn by Myself; The word has gone out of My mouth in righteousness, And shall not return, That to Me every knee shall bow, Every tongue shall take an oath. He shall say, "Surely in the LORD I have righteousness and strength. To Him men shall come, And all shall be ashamed Who are incensed against Him. In the LORD all the descendants of Israel Shall be justified, and shall glory."

—Isaiah 45:22–25

Only God can forgive His creation their sins. He can forgive me of my lawlessness; and you of yours, dear reader; and also yours, my highly respected atheist. We only must do one thing: confess our transgressions. And do you know what will happen when we do so? God will throw our sins into the sea of forgetfulness and never again will He remember them. Isn't our God wonderful? Yes, He is wonderful. He is great, and His works are great. There is no other. How wonderful it is to know such a God and to have fellowship with Him.

I, even I, am He who blots out your transgressions for My own sake; And I will not remember your sins.

—Isaiah 43:25

I have blotted out, like a thick cloud, your transgressions, And like a cloud, your sins. Return to Me, for I have redeemed you.

—Isaiah 44:22

"But if a wicked man turns from all his sins which he has committed, keeps all My statutes, and does what is lawful and right, he shall surely live; he shall not die. "None of the transgressions which he has committed shall be remembered against him; because of the righteousness which he has done, he shall live. "Do I have any pleasure at all that the wicked should die?" says the Lord God, "and not that he should turn from his ways and live?... Again, when a wicked man turns away from the wickedness which he committed, and does what is lawful and right, he preserves himself alive. Because he considers and turns away from all the transgressions which he committed, he shall surely live; he shall not die.... Cast away from you all the transgressions which you have committed, and get yourselves a new heart and a new spirit. For why should you die, O house of Israel? "For I have no pleasure in the death of one who dies," says the Lord God. "Therefore turn and live!"

—Ezekiel 18:21–23, 27–28, 31–32

Who is a God like You, Pardoning iniquity And passing over the transgression of the remnant of His heritage? He does not retain His anger forever, Because He delights in mercy. He will again have compassion on us, And will subdue our iniquities. You will cast all our sins Into the depths of the sea.

—Micah 7:18–19

Each person in this world desires comfort and spiritual substance for daily life. But where can you find such a comforter, someone you can turn to in life's difficult times? God's Word has the answer to this question:

> I, even I, am He who comforts you. Who are you that you should be afraid Of a man who will die, And of the son of a man who will be made like grass?
>
> —Isaiah 51:12

> Thus says the Lord who made it, the Lord who formed it to establish it (the Lord is His name): "Call to Me, and I will answer you, and show you great and mighty things, which you do not know."
>
> —Jeremiah 33:2–3

> I, the Lord, search the heart, I test the mind, Even to give every man according to his ways, According to the fruit of his doings.
>
> —Jeremiah 17:10

God turned to His creation in ancient times, and He isn't any different now in the twenty-first century. Let's read the following words which God, the living God, Creator of heaven and earth, said. These words are true and active today, just as they were generations ago:

> Listen to Me, you who know righteousness, You people in whose heart is My law: Do not fear the reproach of men, Nor be afraid of their insults. For the moth will eat them up like a garment, And the worm will eat them like wool; But My righteousness will be forever, And My salvation from generation to generation.
>
> —Isaiah 51:7–8

Fear not, for I am with you; Be not dismayed, for I am your God. I will strengthen you, Yes, I will help you, I will uphold you with My righteous right hand.'

—ISAIAH 41:10

When you pass through the waters, I will be with you; And through the rivers, they shall not overflow you. When you walk through the fire, you shall not be burned, Nor shall the flame scorch you.

—ISAIAH 43:2

The LORD is good, A stronghold in the day of trouble; And He knows those who trust in Him.

—NAHUM 1:7

How good it is to be a Christian. Christian people may be happy to know the living God and have fellowship with Him. They receive God's abundant blessings daily.

Blessed is the man who trusts in the LORD, And whose hope is the LORD. For he shall be like a tree planted by the waters, Which spreads out its roots by the river, And will not fear when heat comes; But its leaf will be green, And will not be anxious in the year of drought, Nor will cease from yielding fruit.

—JEREMIAH 17:7–8

Blessed is the man Who walks not in the counsel of the ungodly, Nor stands in the path of sinners, Nor sits in the seat of the scornful; But his delight is in the law of the LORD, And in His law he meditates day and night. He shall be like a tree Planted by the rivers of water, That brings forth its fruit in its season, Whose leaf also shall not wither; And whatever he does shall prosper.

—PSALM 1:1–3

Lord, You have been our dwelling place in all generations. Before the mountains were brought forth, Or ever You had formed the earth and the world, Even from everlasting to everlasting, You are God.

—Psalm 90:1–2

Our great God, Maker of all, loves and remembers His creation. He loves and remembers you, dear reader and highly respected atheist, regardless of who you are. He turned to His creation in the past, and today He turns to me and to you with the following words:

Seek the Lord while He may be found, Call upon Him while He is near. Let the wicked forsake his way, And the unrighteous man his thoughts; Let him return to the Lord, And He will have mercy on him; And to our God, For He will abundantly pardon.

—Isaiah 55:6–7

Have you not known? Have you not heard? The everlasting God, the Lord, The Creator of the ends of the earth, Neither faints nor is weary. His understanding is unsearchable. He gives power to the weak, And to those who have no might He increases strength. Even the youths shall faint and be weary, And the young men shall utterly fall, But those who wait on the Lord Shall renew their strength; They shall mount up with wings like eagles, They shall run and not be weary, They shall walk and not faint.

—Isaiah 40:28–31

What a great promise there is in those words for each and every one of us. And this promise is alive and active today.

Three thousand years ago, King David, the psalmist, wrote a bit about the actions of God, His strength, power, greatness, and love.

I think that it will be good for both my reader and I to forget our problems, our tasks, and even our pain, and to go back to those ancient times to read a few of his psalms. We will gain strength from reading these psalms because the words and thoughts in them are alive and active, even in the twenty-first century. What happened three thousand years ago is also going on now. Our own eyes see that God hasn't changed toward His creation—to me and to you, dear reader. God remembers His creation and directs His love and mercy toward us.

When I read God's Word, I forget about myself. I forget my problems and even of what ails me physically. I may still hurt, though not as much, and sometimes my pain stops altogether. The Word of God has power and comfort. The Word of God calms pain. The Word of God provides support when everything seems to be hopeless. The Word of God lives where everything else seems to be dying because the Author of the words of the Bible is life— our Lord God *is* life! Let's read the psalms of David together:

> The heavens declare the glory of God; And the firmament shows His handiwork. Day unto day utters speech, And night unto night reveals knowledge. There is no speech nor language Where their voice is not heard. Their line has gone out through all the earth, And their words to the end of the world. In them He has set a tabernacle for the sun, Which is like a bridegroom coming out of his chamber, And rejoices like a strong man to run its race. Its rising is from one end of heaven, And its circuit to the other end; And there is nothing hidden from its heat. The law of the LORD is perfect, converting the soul; The testimony of the LORD is sure, making wise the simple; The statutes of the LORD are right, rejoicing the heart; The commandment of the LORD is pure, enlightening the eyes; The fear of the LORD is clean, enduring forever; The judgments of

the Lord are true and righteous altogether. More to be desired are they than gold, Yea, than much fine gold; Sweeter also than honey and the honeycomb. Moreover by them Your servant is warned, And in keeping them there is great reward.

—Psalm 19:1–11

Rejoice in the Lord, O you righteous! For praise from the upright is beautiful. Praise the Lord with the harp; Make melody to Him with an instrument of ten strings. Sing to Him a new song; Play skillfully with a shout of joy. For the word of the Lord is right, And all His work is done in truth. He loves righteousness and justice; The earth is full of the goodness of the Lord. By the word of the Lord the heavens were made, And all the host of them by the breath of His mouth. He gathers the waters of the sea together as a heap; He lays up the deep in storehouses. Let all the earth fear the Lord; Let all the inhabitants of the world stand in awe of Him. For He spoke, and it was done; He commanded, and it stood fast. The Lord brings the counsel of the nations to nothing; He makes the plans of the peoples of no effect. The counsel of the Lord stands forever, The plans of His heart to all generations. Blessed is the nation whose God is the Lord, The people He has chosen as His own inheritance. The Lord looks from heaven; He sees all the sons of men. From the place of His dwelling He looks On all the inhabitants of the earth; He fashions their hearts individually; He considers all their works.

—Psalm 33:1–15

When someone says to me, "Thank you for what you have done for me," even if it was a very small thing, my heart sometimes melts. When we come into the presence of God with thanksgiving, with joy, saying, "Thank You, Lord, You have done so much for me," I think His heart melts also.

> Oh come, let us sing to the LORD! Let us shout joyfully to the Rock of our salvation. Let us come before His presence with thanksgiving; Let us shout joyfully to Him with psalms. For the LORD is the great God, And the great King above all gods. In His hand are the deep places of the earth; The heights of the hills are His also. The sea is His, for He made it; And His hands formed the dry land. Oh come, let us worship and bow down; Let us kneel before the LORD our Maker. For He is our God, And we are the people of His pasture, And the sheep of His hand. Today, if you will hear His voice: Do not harden your hearts, as in the rebellion, As in the day of trial in the wilderness, When your fathers tested Me; They tried Me, though they saw My work.
>
> —PSALM 95:1–9

Lord God wants us to be active constantly (no vacation) sharing good news in all circumstances and always date to day until we depart from this Earth.

> Oh, sing to the LORD a new song! Sing to the LORD, all the earth. Sing to the LORD, bless His name; Proclaim the good news of His salvation from day to day. Declare His glory among the nations, His wonders among all peoples. For the LORD is great and greatly to be praised; He is to be feared above all gods. For all the gods of the peoples are idols, But the LORD made the heavens. Honor and majesty are before Him; Strength and beauty are in His sanctuary. Give to the LORD, O families of the peoples, Give to the LORD glory and strength. Give to the LORD the glory due His name; Bring an offering, and come into His courts. Oh, worship the LORD in

the beauty of holiness! Tremble before Him, all the earth. Say among the nations, "The LORD reigns; The world also is firmly established, It shall not be moved; He shall judge the peoples righteously." Let the heavens rejoice, and let the earth be glad; Let the sea roar, and all its fullness; Let the field be joyful, and all that is in it. Then all the trees of the woods will rejoice before the LORD. For He is coming, for He is coming to judge the earth. He shall judge the world with righteousness, And the peoples with His truth.

—PSALM 96:1–13

The Bible teaches us to remember what the Lord had done for us. Forget not each thing big or small that you receive from Him. I think God will be very pleased when we say, "Lord, I remember that day when You first spoke to me. Lord, I remember that verse through which You spoke to me long ago. Lord, I memorized by heart that verse through which You spoke to me recently." My personal testimony: Lord, I remember that you healed me in 1971. I want to tell You that organ in my body works perfectly now. I will always remember that You are my Healer, and You are alive and active today. Thank you so much. I love You, Lord!

Bless the LORD, O my soul; And all that is within me, bless His holy name! Bless the LORD, O my soul, And forget not all His benefits: Who forgives all your iniquities, Who heals all your diseases, Who redeems your life from destruction, Who crowns you with lovingkindness and tender mercies, Who satisfies your mouth with good things, So that your youth is renewed like the eagle's. The LORD executes righteousness And justice for all who are oppressed. He made known His ways to Moses, His acts to the children of Israel. The LORD is merciful and gracious, Slow to anger, and abounding in mercy. He will not always strive with us, Nor will He keep His anger forever. He has not dealt with us according to our sins, Nor punished us according to our iniquities. For as the heavens are high above the earth, So great is His mercy toward those who fear Him; As far as the east is from the west, So far has He removed our transgressions from us. As a father pities his children, So the Lord pities those who fear Him. For He knows our frame; He remembers that we are dust. As for man, his days are like grass; As a flower of the field, so he flourishes. For the wind passes over it, and it is gone, And its place remembers it no more. But the mercy of the Lord is from everlasting to everlasting On those who fear Him, And His righteousness to children's children, To such as keep His covenant, And to those who remember His commandments to do them. The Lord has established His throne in heaven, And His kingdom rules over all. Bless the Lord, you His angels, Who excel in strength, who do His word, Heeding the voice of His word. Bless the Lord, all you His hosts, You ministers of His, who do His pleasure. Bless the Lord, all His works, In all places of His dominion. Bless the Lord, O my soul!

—Psalm 103:1–22

God is life. He creates and prepares food for every living soul, for men, and every living thing. Glory to Him!

Bless the Lord, O my soul! O Lord my God, You are very great: You are clothed with honor and majesty, Who cover Yourself with light as with a garment, Who stretch out the heavens like a curtain. He lays the beams of His upper chambers in the waters, Who makes the clouds His chariot, Who walks on the wings of the wind, Who makes His angels spirits, His ministers a flame of fire. You who laid the foundations of the earth, So that it should not be moved forever, You covered it with the deep as with a garment; The waters stood above the mountains. At Your rebuke they fled; At the voice of Your thunder they hastened away. They went up over the mountains; They went down into the valleys, To the place which You founded for them. You have set a boundary that they may not pass over, That they may not return to cover the earth. He sends the springs into the valleys; They flow among the hills. They give drink to every beast of the field; The wild donkeys quench their thirst. By them the birds of the heavens have their home; They sing among the branches. He waters the hills from His upper chambers; The earth is satisfied with the fruit of Your works. He causes the grass to grow for the cattle, And vegetation for the service of man, That he may bring forth food from the earth, And wine that makes glad the heart of man, Oil to make his face shine, And bread which strengthens man's heart. The trees of the LORD are full of sap, The cedars of Lebanon which He planted, Where the birds make their nests; The stork has her home in the fir trees. The high hills are for the wild goats; The cliffs are a refuge for the rock badgers. He appointed the moon for seasons; The sun knows its going down. You make darkness, and it is night, In which all the beasts of the forest creep about. The young lions roar after their prey, And seek their food from God. When the sun rises, they gather together And lie down in their dens. Man goes out to his work And to his labor until the evening. O LORD, how manifold are Your works! In wisdom You have made them all. The earth is full of Your possessions—This great and wide sea, In which are innumerable teeming things, Living things both small and great. There the ships sail about; There is that Leviathan Which You have made to play there. These all wait for You, That You may give them their food in due season. What You give them they gather in; You open Your hand, they are filled with good. You hide Your face, they are troubled; You take away their breath, they die and return to their dust. You send forth Your Spirit, they are created; And You renew the face of the earth. May the glory of the LORD endure forever; May the LORD rejoice in His works. He looks on the earth, and it trembles; He touches the hills, and they smoke. I will sing to the LORD as long as I live; I will sing praise to my God while I have my being. May my meditation be sweet to Him; I will be glad in the LORD. May sinners be consumed from the earth, And the wicked be no more. Bless the LORD, O my soul! Praise the LORD!

—PSALM 104:1–35

What a great privilege Almighty God, Creator of the universe, gave to those who believe in Him and believe Him. He gave them the right to call upon His name. Our planet is very small in comparison to the universe and there is no comparison for man. God wants to have fellowship with man; He wants to hear his voice. Dear reader, the Lord God wants to hear your voice also. Call upon Him today.

Oh, give thanks to the LORD! Call upon His name; Make known His deeds among the peoples! Sing to Him, sing psalms to Him; Talk of all His wondrous works! Glory in His holy name; Let the hearts of those rejoice who seek the LORD! Seek the LORD and His strength; Seek His face evermore! Remember His marvelous works which He has done, His wonders, and the judgments of His mouth, O seed of Abraham His servant, You children of Jacob, His chosen ones! He is the LORD our God; His judgments are in all the earth. He remembers His covenant forever, The word which He commanded, for a thousand generations, The covenant which He made with Abraham, And His oath to Isaac, And confirmed it to Jacob for a statute, To Israel as an everlasting covenant, Saying, "To you I will give the land of Canaan As the allotment of your inheritance,"

—Psalm 105:1–11

These words may sound strange to those who never experience God's love, goodness, grace, and compassion. But to those who are in connection with God, these words are a great treasure.

Praise the Lord! I will praise the Lord with my whole heart, In the assembly of the upright and in the congregation. The works of the Lord are great, Studied by all who have pleasure in them. His work is honorable and glorious, And His righteousness endures forever. He has made His wonderful works to be remembered; The Lord is gracious and full of compassion. He has given food to those who fear Him; He will ever be mindful of His covenant. He has declared to His people the power of His works, In giving them the heritage of the nations. The works of His hands are verity and justice; All His precepts are sure. They stand fast forever and ever, And are done in truth and uprightness. He has sent redemption to His people; He has commanded His covenant forever: Holy and awesome is His name. The fear of the Lord is the beginning of wisdom; A good understanding have all those who do His commandments. His praise endures forever.

—Psalm 111:1–10

When I read these words they touched my heart very deeply. I pondered them for a long time, and I did not find a better place to be than in God's presence. A better place never was, is not, and never will be.

O LORD, You have searched me and known me. You know my sitting down and my rising up; You understand my thought afar off. You comprehend my path and my lying down, And are acquainted with all my ways. For there is not a word on my tongue, But behold, O LORD, You know it altogether. You have hedged me behind and before, And laid Your hand upon me. Such knowledge is too wonderful for me; It is high, I cannot attain it. Where can I go from Your Spirit? Or where can I flee from Your presence? If I ascend into heaven, You are there; If I make my bed in hell, behold, You are there. If I take the wings of the morning, And dwell in the uttermost parts of the sea, Even there Your hand shall lead me, And Your right hand shall hold me. If I say, "Surely the darkness shall fall on me," Even the night shall be light about me; Indeed, the darkness shall not hide from You, But the night shines as the day; The darkness and the light are both alike to You. For You formed my inward parts; You covered me in my mother's womb. I will praise You, for I am fearfully and wonderfully made; Marvelous are Your works, And that my soul knows very well. My frame was not hidden from You, When I was made in secret, And skillfully wrought in the lowest parts of the earth. Your eyes saw my substance, being yet unformed. And in Your book they all were written, The days fashioned for me, When as yet there were none of them. How precious also are Your thoughts to me, O God! How great is the sum of them! If I should count them, they would be more in number than the sand; When I awake, I am still with You.

—PSALM 139:1–18

Praise the LORD! Praise the LORD, O my soul! While I live I will praise the LORD; I will sing praises to my God while I have my being. Do not put your trust in princes, Nor in a son of man, in whom there is no help. His spirit departs, he returns to his earth; In that very day his plans perish. Happy is he who has the God of Jacob for his help, Whose hope is in the LORD his God, Who made heaven and earth, The sea, and all that is in them; Who keeps truth forever, Who executes justice for the oppressed, Who gives food to the hungry. The LORD gives freedom to the prisoners. The LORD opens the eyes of the blind; The LORD raises those who are bowed down; The LORD loves the righteous. The LORD watches over the strangers; He relieves the fatherless and widow; But the way of the wicked He turns upside down. The LORD shall reign forever—Your God, O Zion, to all generations. Praise the LORD!

—PSALM 146:1–10

Reading Psalm 148, we see that whatever Almighty God created is alive, active, and finds its way to praise its Creator.

Praise the LORD! Praise the LORD from the heavens; Praise Him in the heights! Praise Him, all His angels; Praise Him, all His hosts! Praise Him, sun and moon; Praise Him, all you stars of light! Praise Him, you heavens of heavens, And you waters above the heavens! Let them praise the name of the LORD, For He commanded and they were created. He also established them forever and ever; He made a decree which shall not pass away. Praise the LORD from the earth, You great sea creatures and all the depths; Fire and hail, snow and clouds; Stormy wind, fulfilling His word; Mountains and all hills; Fruitful trees and all cedars; Beasts and all cattle; Creeping things and flying fowl; Kings of the earth and all peoples; Princes and all judges of the earth; Both young men and maidens; Old men and children. Let them praise the name of the LORD, For His name alone is exalted; His glory is above the earth and heaven. And He has exalted the horn of His people, The praise of all His saints—Of the children of Israel, A people near to Him. Praise the LORD!

—PSALM 148:1–14

Praise the LORD! Praise God in His sanctuary; Praise Him in His mighty firmament! Praise Him for His mighty acts; Praise Him according to His excellent greatness! Praise Him with the sound of the trumpet; Praise Him with the lute and harp! Praise Him with the timbrel and dance; Praise Him with stringed instruments and flutes! Praise Him with loud cymbals; Praise Him with clashing cymbals! Let everything that has breath praise the LORD. Praise the LORD!

—PSALM 150:1–6

After reading these magnificent psalms, I think we all can bow down and praise our God and agree with Isaiah 64:6–9:

But we are all like an unclean thing, And all our righteousnesses are like filthy rags; We all fade as a leaf, And our iniquities, like the wind, Have taken us away. And there is no one who calls on Your name, Who stirs himself up to take hold of You; For You have hidden Your face from us, And have consumed us because of our iniquities. But now, O LORD, You are our Father; We are the clay, and You our potter; And all we are the work of Your hand. Do not be furious, O LORD, Nor remember iniquity forever; Indeed, please look—we all are Your people!

After this long journey through the pages of the Bible, let's return to the first people, Adam and Eve, and see what went on in the life of this young couple.

6

THE FALL OF
THE FIRST MAN

W E READ FROM THE PAGES OF THE HOLE BIBLE THAT
God created man in the likeness of Himself and assigned
him a great task. God commanded man to oversee the
world and to have dominion over the living creatures and take care
of the garden. He authorized man to be the landlord of the earth.
The psalmist David writes the following:

> You have made him to have dominion over the works of Your
> hands; You have put all things under his feet, All sheep and
> oxen—Even the beasts of the field, The birds of the air, And
> the fish of the sea That pass through the paths of the seas. O
> LORD, our Lord, How excellent is Your name in all the earth!
> —PSALM 8:6–9

Lord God gave man only one command, which was not to eat
from the tree of knowledge. God said that the consequence for
disobeying this command would be death. Let's look now at how

Adam acted and how he coped with this restriction. We'll find the answer to this in the Bible:

> Now the serpent was more cunning than any beast of the field which the LORD God had made. And he said to the woman, "Has God indeed said, 'You shall not eat of every tree of the garden'?" And the woman said to the serpent, "We may eat the fruit of the trees of the garden; but of the fruit of the tree which is in the midst of the garden, God has said, 'You shall not eat it, nor shall you touch it, lest you die.'" Then the serpent said to the woman, "You will not surely die. For God knows that in the day you eat of it your eyes will be opened, and you will be like God, knowing good and evil." So when the woman saw that the tree was good for food, that it was pleasant to the eyes, and a tree desirable to make one wise, she took of its fruit and ate. She also gave to her husband with her, and he ate. Then the eyes of both of them were opened, and they knew that they were naked; and they sewed fig leaves together and made themselves coverings.
>
> —GENESIS 3:1–7

We see, from the pages of the first book, that the first people broke the commandment. They neglected God's command. Their response to the goodness of God was disobedience.

7

THE SERPENT

W HO IS THIS serpent? This question is wise and proper. Let's stop and see who this serpent really is. This serpent, which so cunningly came to the woman and caused her to commit a crime, is Satan, God's enemy. But who is this Satan? Who is this adversary of God? Where did he come from? Why did he appear on Earth? These questions are very interesting and very important. We must know the answers to them. Even now in the twenty-first century, when we hear the name *Satan* we complain about him. At times we try to protect ourselves and blame Satan by saying, "This is the work of Satan. He is the one at fault." I think that only a few people can say who Satan really is. Only a few can describe him who does evil on this Earth. Let's see what the Bible says of him.

Before God created the world and all that is found on it, He created heaven and the beings in heaven. He created the visible and the invisible realms. Colossians writes the following about the invisible world:

For by Him all things were created that are in heaven and that are on Earth, visible and invisible, whether thrones or dominions or principalities or powers. All things were created through Him and for Him.

—COLOSSIANS 1:16

We have now learned that God created both the things visible and invisible to man's eyes. The visible world is the one that we see and includes the earth, sun, moon, stars, people, animals, and plants. The invisible world consists of the angels, seraphim, and archangels. We have heard of many references to angels, for example the angel Gabriel, the angel Michael, God's angel, and the archangel Lucifer. Lucifer was the name given to the highest-ranking angel. The name *Lucifer* means "beautiful and mighty."

Let's see what the Word of God says about Lucifer and what happened with him. The Word of God does not give us a timeline of events to guide our understanding of his fall; this could have been millions or billions of years ago, but it did indeed occur because it is recorded on the pages of God's Constitution. Let's read from the book of Ezekiel:

"Son of man, take up a lamentation for the king of Tyre, and say to him, 'Thus says the Lord GOD: "You were the seal of perfection, Full of wisdom and perfect in beauty. You were in Eden, the garden of God; Every precious stone was your covering: The sardius, topaz, and diamond, Beryl, onyx, and jasper, Sapphire, turquoise, and emerald with gold. The workmanship of your timbrels and pipes Was prepared for you on the day you were created. "You were the anointed cherub who covers; I established you; You were on the holy mountain of God; You walked back and forth in the midst of fiery stones. You were perfect in your ways from the day you were created, Till iniquity was found in you. "By the abundance of your trading You became filled with violence within, And you sinned; Therefore I cast you as a profane thing Out of the mountain of God; And I destroyed you, O covering cherub, From the midst of the fiery stones. "Your heart was lifted up because of your beauty; You corrupted your wisdom for the sake of your splendor; I cast you to the ground, I laid you before kings, That they might gaze at you."

—EZEKIEL 28:12–17

The Word of God writes that Lucifer was filled with wisdom, crowned with beauty, and anointed a cherub. The success of his activities and his beauty caused his innermost being to fill with pride, which caused him to sin. He was no longer content with his position and he wanted to take the place of the living God; he wanted to be like Him. Let's read what the prophet Isaiah wrote:

How you are fallen from heaven, O Lucifer, son of the morning! How you are cut down to the ground, You who weakened the nations! For you have said in your heart: "I will ascend into heaven, I will exalt my throne above the stars of God; I will also sit on the mount of the congregation On the farthest sides of the north; I will ascend above the heights of the clouds, I will be like the Most High."

—ISAIAH 14:12–14

Immense pride entered the heart of Lucifer, and he even called himself God.

Because your heart is lifted up, And you say, "I am a god, I sit in the seat of gods, In the midst of the seas."

—EZEKIEL 28:2

Do you know what happened in heaven? Let's read what it says in Revelation:

> And war broke out in heaven: Michael and his angels fought with the dragon; and the dragon and his angels fought, but they did not prevail, nor was a place found for them in heaven any longer. So the great dragon was cast out, that serpent of old, called the Devil and Satan, who deceives the whole world; he was cast to the earth, and his angels were cast out with him.
>
> —REVELATION 12:7–9

There is no place in the heavens for sinful creatures. When the Lord Jesus Christ was on Earth, He also spoke of the following event:

> And He said to them, "I saw Satan fall like lightning from heaven."
>
> —LUKE 10:18

The mighty cherub became Satan, an adversary of God. When he was thrown down to Earth, he took one-third of the angels with him. He and these angels were then called unclean spirits. Satan works even now on this planet. He breaks God's laws. He tries to rip people from God's will for their life by different ways, which are concealed by various outward appearances. Everything that contradicts God's laws and rules comes from Satan. It is his will to break the laws of God. Satan enters families and sows misunderstanding among family members. He brings divorce and breaks the marital bond. He sows unfriendly relations between parents and children and vice versa. Satan works among rulers also by creating conflict and disagreement. Satan works among nations and brings them to war. Satan even enters churches and teaches things that break God's laws. He permits teachings that are contradictions to God's will. He strives to change God's laws, to add one thing or to delete another, just to make it different from how God decreed it in the beginning. The Word of God writes this of Satan:

> He was a murderer from the beginning, and does not stand in the truth, because there is no truth in him.
>
> —John 8:44

> He who sins is of the devil, for the devil has sinned from the beginning. For this purpose the Son of God was manifest, that He might destroy the works of the devil.
>
> —1 John 3:8

Satan is also called a slanderer because he slanders the Christian people in front of God. This is also recorded in the Bible:

> Then I heard a loud voice saying in heaven, "Now salvation, and strength, and the kingdom of our God, and the power of His Christ have come, for the accuser of our brethren, who accused them before our God day and night, has been cast down.
>
> —Revelation 12:10

Satan will work on this earth until the appointed time. He then will be cast into the lake of fire, together with his angles, the evil spirits. The Word of God says this:

> Then He will also say to those on the left hand, "Depart from Me, you cursed, into the everlasting fire prepared for the devil and his angels."
>
> —Matthew 25:41

As long as Satan exists and works on this Earth, the Word of God tells us to deprive him of room in our lives:

Nor give place to the devil.

—Ephesians 4:27

What does it mean to not give room for the devil? It means to not sin in your life, not to do evil toward anyone but rather to do the will of God.

Therefore submit to God. Resists the devil and he will flee from you.

—James 4:7

Be sober, be vigilant; because your adversary the devil walks about like a roaring lion, seeking whom he may devour.

—1 Peter 5:8

We must fight with Satan every day, twenty-four hours per day. But how should we fight with him? Satan remains a spirit. What armor do we need to succeed? The Word of God has an answer to this question. In Ephesians, a great and powerful weapon is given to Christians to fight with the dark spirits of this earth:

Finally, my brethren, be strong in the Lord and in the power of His might. Put on the whole armor of God, that you may be able to stand against the wiles of the devil. For we do not wrestle against flesh and blood, but against principalities, against powers, against the rulers of the darkness of this age, against spiritual hosts of wickedness in the heavenly places. Therefore take up the whole armor of God, that you may be able to withstand in the evil day, and having done all, to stand. Stand therefore, having girded your waist with truth, having put on the breastplate of righteousness, and having shod your feet with the preparation of the gospel of peace; above all, taking the shield of faith with which you will be able to quench all the fiery darts of the wicked one. And take the helmet of salvation, and the sword of the Spirit, which is the word of God; praying always with all prayer and supplication in the Spirit, being watchful to this end with all perseverance and supplication for all the saints

—EPHESIANS 6:10–18

This is the armor that the mighty One gave to His chosen ones to defeat the darkness and power of the enemy. People can only defeat Satan with the Word of God, which is a spiritual sword. This is why it is very important for Christians to know the Word of God, His Holy Scriptures. When we know His Word, we are then armed with His sword, no matter what circumstances we find ourselves in.

Jesus Christ, when He was on this planet, gave the disciples great power, strength, and authority to conquer God's adversaries: the devil and his followers. Jesus Christ gives strength and power to all who ask, believe, and need this great gift, this mighty sword.

Then the seventy returned with joy, saying, "Lord, even the demons are subject to us in Your name." And He said to them, "I saw Satan fall like lightning from heaven. Behold, I give you the authority to trample on serpents and scorpions, and over all the power of the enemy, and nothing shall by any means hurt you. Nevertheless do not rejoice in this, that the spirits are subject to you, but rather rejoice because your names are written in heaven."

—LUKE 10:17–20

And as you go, preach, saying, "The kingdom of heaven is at hand." Heal the sick, cleanse the lepers, raise the dead, cast out demons. Freely you have received, freely give.

—MATTHEW 10:7–8

And these signs will follow those who believe: In My name they will cast out demons; they will speak with new tongues.
—MARK 16:17

Then He called His twelve disciples together and gave them power and authority over all demons, and to cure diseases.
—LUKE 9:1

Dear reader, listen to the Word of God because it is a spiritual sword for you. This sword will help you be victorious in the dreariest of circumstances. Read the Word of God daily and also use this sword daily:

You are of God, little children, and have overcome them, because He who is in you is greater than he who is in the world.
—1 JOHN 4:4

What a great promise God prepared for His followers! We can only say, "Glory to You, Creator of heaven and Earth, that You love your creation—mankind—and have prepared an unshakeable defense for him."

How good it is to be a believer! How good it is to know God's truth. How good it is to know the Word of God, God's Constitution, and the laws that He prepared for the human race. How good it is to have fellowship with our Father. When we know God's will and laws, we can boldly and confidently march through this earthly journey. And in our journey, we will then be able to conquer all the arrows of the enemy. When we are armed with the Word of God, we will always be victorious. It is good to be in the hands of the living God!

8

SPIRITUAL DEATH

L ET'S RETURN TO THE FIRST PEOPLE, ADAM AND EVE, AND see how their lives played out after they disobeyed God's command. We'll keep reading the third chapter of Genesis:

And they heard the sound of the LORD God walking in the garden in the cool of the day, and Adam and his wife hid themselves from the presence of the LORD God among the trees of the garden. Then the LORD God called to Adam and said to him, "Where are you?" So he said, "I heard Your voice in the garden, and I was afraid because I was naked; and I hid myself." And He said, "Who told you that you were naked? Have you eaten from the tree of which I commanded you that you should not eat?" Then the man said, "The woman whom You gave to be with me, she gave me of the tree, and I ate." And the LORD God said to the woman, "What is this you have done?" The woman said, "The serpent deceived me, and I ate."

—GENESIS 3:8–13

After reading these verses, we can see that a change occurred between God and people. The first people didn't physically die; they died spiritually. They lost friendly relations with their Maker; they lost fellowship with Him. Adam, when he heard the voice of God, his Maker, hid himself from God. He felt guilty in front of Him. He saw his nakedness and was gripped with embarrassment. Fear entered his heart and Adam began to be fearful of God, his Maker. To answer God's question—did you eat from that of which I commanded you not to eat?—Adam immediately tried to justify himself by blaming his wife, as though to rebuke God for giving her to him. Eve, to justify herself, blamed the serpent.

The first people lost fellowship with their Maker in this manner. They saw their nakedness and their hearts grew fearful. This fear of God entered all of mankind and exists to this day. The man who lacks fellowship with God also fears God. He's afraid even to listen to God's voice. I've noticed more than once that people don't like speaking on spiritual themes. You may converse with them about different subjects; you can discuss good issues and bad issues, moral and immoral, but when you begin taking about God, of His laws, of the Bible, people don't want to listen. They quickly change the subject to avoid the conversation. Some even say that these themes are not for the contemporary person. Their hearts are already filled with fear and guilt, and they try to escape reality by ignoring God and any topics about God that a believer might bring up. Modern people act just like Adam did because they feel guilty and naked in front of their Maker.

When I lived in Poland, everyone at my workplace knew that I had another faith. Sometimes my co-workers would approach me and ask me questions. They would ask, can you do this and that in your faith? I answered that our faith is based solely on the Word of God, on the Bible. When the Word of God says to do this, we do it. And when the Word of God says to not do that, then we don't do it. I would quote verses from the Bible that I had memorized by heart concerning these questions. And often, by the time I finished quoting, my co-workers were no longer next to me. They heard the voice of the living God, their Creator, and they grew afraid. They felt guilty, saw their nakedness, and hid. My friends acted just like Adam and Eve.

My husband and I went to San Francisco once to do some shopping, specifically in a Russian shop. Everything was arranged nicely in the shop, and many different products filled the shelves. Paul and I, with great amazement, took in the sight of all those Russian items. The store clerks were nice, friendly, and they smiled sweetly at us. My eyes scanned the entire store, and in one spot, I noticed a large Bible. I said, "Oh, you even carry a Bible in your shop. May I look at it?" The clerks immediately placed the precious book into my hands. This great Bible was beautifully made. As I held it, I directed my compliments to the store clerks. I said, "Oh, what great items you have in your shop, but this Bible is unique." Upon hearing my words, the faces of the clerks shone with happiness. I opened the Bible, said another compliment, and asked, "What pretty font, but what is written here in your Bible?" I then opened the book of John, the third chapter, and I slowly read, in a whisper:

> For God so loved the world that He gave His only begotten Son, that whoever believes in Him should not perish but have everlasting life. For God did not send His Son into the world to condemn the world, but that the world through Him might be saved. He who believes in Him is not condemned; but he who does not believe is condemned already, because he has not believed in the name of the only begotten Son of God.
>
> —John 3:16–18

To my amazement, when I finished reading these words I could not see a single clerk around me. The clerks, having heard the words of the living God, grew afraid and hid. They saw their spiritual situation; they saw their nakedness. Maybe these nice and friendly clerks had a religion and observed some ceremonies in their place of worship. Maybe they fulfilled the traditions of their fathers and grandfathers. But I knew that they did not know the truth. They did not have fellowship with their Creator. And when they heard the voice of the living God, they grew afraid and hid. These clerks were not afraid to order the Bible, to protect it in their shops, to take it from the shelves to show it to their customers, to sell it, but they grew afraid when they heard the words of this holy Book. This is because God Himself speaks through the words of the Bible to His creation, and for some, His words reveal the nakedness that is present in their lives.

Dear reader, do not run from the Word of God. Be a hero and read this book to its end. Do not be afraid of God's voice, your Maker's voice. Remember that your Creator loves you and wants only to bless your life on this earth. He wants to have fellowship with you because you are His creation, and you are very important to Him. Do not fear God, your Maker.

9

THE CONSEQUENCES
OF DISOBEDIENCE

G OD THE FATHER GAVE ONE COMMAND TO THE FIRST
people, and He ordained a consequence that would follow
if the command were violated. God didn't keep any secrets
from His creation. He warned the first man, Adam, what would
happen if he failed to adhere to that command. God Almighty
doesn't force anyone to fulfill His commands. He created man
in His own image, with free will, the right of choice, the right to
make decisions—to do or not do, to listen or not to listen. But God
regards His Word very highly. He cherishes His commands and
laws, and is sure to follow through with any consequences. For our
benefit, let's read from the Holy Word:

> Every word of God is pure; He is a shield to those who put their
> trust in Him.
>
> —PROVERBS 30:5

As for God, His way is perfect; The word of the LORD is proven; He is a shield to all who trust in Him.

—PSALM 18:30

Forever, O LORD, Your word is settled in heaven.

—PSALM 119:89

The grass withers, the flower fades, But the word of our God stands forever.

—ISAIAH 40:8

People who violate God's commands suffer great consequences. Let's return to our first people and see what followed their disobedience; what they suffered for being frivolous with God's will. Let's continue reading the third chapter of Genesis:

> To the woman He said: "I will greatly multiply your sorrow and your conception; in pain you shall bring forth children; your desire shall be for your husband, and he shall rule over you." Then to Adam He said, "Because you have heeded the voice of your wife, and have eaten from the tree of which I commanded you, saying, 'You shall not eat of it': Cursed is the ground for your sake; in toil you shall eat of it all the days of your life. Both thorns and thistles it shall bring forth for you, and you shall eat the herb of the field. In the sweat of your face you shall eat bread till you return to the ground, for out of it you were taken; for dust you are, and to dust you shall return." And Adam called his wife's name Eve, because she was the mother of all living. Also for Adam and his wife the LORD God made tunics of skin, and clothed them.... Therefore the Lord God sent him out of the garden of Eden to till the ground from which he was taken.
>
> —GENESIS 3:16–21, 23

What a sorrowful picture. Adam, the first man, violated God's command by eating from the tree of the knowledge of good and evil, and a great change came to the life of this couple. Adam lost everything—he lost his authority, he lost fellowship with God, and he lost paradise. Adam received a stern punishment for his actions, as did his wife, Eve. They were cast from the Garden of Eden, which was such a beautiful place. This was their consequence for disobeying God.

It's interesting to note that in the Garden of Eden, God planted the tree of life in the center. He didn't forbid Adam from eating the fruit from that tree.

An interesting situation arises after Adam and Eve sinned—let's read about it from the third chapter of Genesis.

> Then the Lord God said, "Behold, the man has become like one of Us, to know good and evil. And now, lest he put out his hand and take also of the tree of life, and eat, and live forever."...So He drove out the man; and He placed cherubim at the east of the garden of Eden and a flaming sword which turned every way, to guard the way to the tree of life.
> —GENESIS 3:22, 24

God didn't initially forbid eating the fruit from the tree of life and Adam hadn't yet eaten from the tree of life when God restricted his access to it. I think that many readers will agree with this: God intended men to live forever. And here is the answer to a big secret of why each man wants to live, and why life is priceless for each person. Father God made man to live forever, and He placed this desire into each being. This desire is alive today. Adam had the opportunity to live forever, but he broke God's command and disregarded God's Word. And with his disobedience he sinned in front of God, his Creator, and died spiritually. This means he lost fellowship with the living God. Later he died physically.

> Therefore, just as through one man sin entered the world, and death through sin, and thus death spread to all men, because all sinned.
>
> —ROMANS 5:12

But what happened with the serpent? Was he punished?

> So the LORD God said to the serpent: "Because you have done this, You are cursed more than all cattle, And more than every beast of the field; On your belly you shall go, And you shall eat dust All the days of your life."
>
> —GENESIS 3:14

My dear reader, read the above and asked the following questions: Is all lost for the life of man? Is there no opportunity to regain the lost paradise? Is there no opportunity to regain fellowship with the Creator and live happily on this earth under His management? I tell you today, yes, there is a way. God loves His creation, and He wants to have a connection with the work of His hands. He wants to have fellowship with His creation, with His people. He wants to have fellowship with me and with you, dear reader, and He therefore established a way for reconciliation.

God gave the serpent the following sentence:

> And I will put enmity Between you and the woman, And between your seed and her Seed; He shall bruise your head, And you shall bruise His heel.
>
> —GENESIS 3:15

These words describe God's plan to send a Messiah onto this Earth in order to reconcile and save the lost. This sentence is found in the beginning of the good news, the holy gospel. The following pages of this book will speak on the theme of the good news, of God's plan for salvation and reconciliation between God the Father and the sinful human race.

10
SIN ENTERED
THE WORLD

OES ADAM'S SIN HAVE ANY EFFECT ON THE REST OF mankind, especially on you and I, dear reader? Each citizen of this planet Earth should know the answer to this question. And the answer can be found only on the pages of the universal constitution. We already know that God made a man, Adam, from dust, and from his rib He made a wife for him, Eve. He commanded them to multiply and fill this earth, and He established the method for multiplying. From one man, Adam, from one blood source, God made all of mankind so that people would inhabit all of the earth. When the first man violated God's command, he sinned before his Creator and became a sinner, and the sin was passed onto all subsequent generations. The sin was passed on to me and to you, dear reader. I am a sinner, and so are you. This truth is written in the Holy Book:

> Therefore, just as through one man sin entered the world, and death through sin, and thus death spread to all men, because all sinned.... For if by the one man's offense many

died...For if by the one man's offense death reigned through the one...Therefore, as through one man's offense judgment came to all men...For as by one man's disobedience many were made sinners.

—Romans 5:12, 15, 17–19

As it is written: "There is none righteous, no, but one...They have all turned aside; They have together become unprofitable; There is none who does good, no, not one"...and all the world may become guilty before God...for all have sinned and fall short of the glory of God.

—Romans 3:10, 12, 19, 23

For the wages of sin is death.

—Romans 6:23

For as in Adam all die.

—1 Corinthians 15:22

The Word of God does not necessarily mean physical death, the death of our body, but it is referring to spiritual death. People lack contact with God because of their sin, and it is the sin that separates us from our Creator. In other words, a chasm exists between God and people. This in itself is spiritual death.

The first man neglected the first command and sinned before his Creator, thus creating the chasm. Man sinned, and the sin entered all the following generations. Through the disobedience of one man, Adam, sin began to reign on this planet. We were all born into sin; we are all sinners. I am a sinner, and you too, dear reader. Just as Adam lost fellowship with his Creator and fell short of the glory of God, so we too have lost fellowship with God.

But our good and gracious God didn't stop loving us, His creation. We wander away and hide from God, but the Creator, having immeasurable love toward His creation, has not turned away from us. He did not stop loving us because God, by definition, is love. God lovingly prepared a way for reconciliation, a path of return to our Maker. God's Constitution writes of the path. We will read the Holy Word and learn what path of reconciliation and forgiveness God prepared in the Old Testament and in the New Testament, for our generation.

11

THE HISTORY OF THE
FOLLOWING GENERATIONS

W<small>E WILL NOW TRAVEL THROUGH THE PAGES OF THE</small>
Holy Book, through the Old Testament, to learn how
God had fellowship with His people. We will see that
regardless of the fact that the first man disobeyed God's command,
God did not stop loving people. The sin of the first man allowed sin
to enter the following generations and infest the entire human race.
Sinful things began to occur immediately in the second generation.
We'll read a very sad story, the first murder in the first family:

> Now Adam knew Eve his wife, and she conceived and bore
> Cain, and said, "I have acquired a man from the Lord." Then
> she bore again, this time his brother Abel. Now Abel was a
> keeper of sheep, but Cain was a tiller of the ground. And in the
> process of time it came to pass that Cain brought an offering
> of the fruit of the ground to the Lord. Abel also brought of the
> firstborn of his flock and of their fat. And the Lord respected
> Abel and his offering, but He did not respect Cain and his

offering. And Cain was very angry, and his countenance fell. So the Lord said to Cain, "Why are you angry? And why has your countenance fallen? If you do well, will you not be accepted? And if you do not do well, sin lies at the door. And its desire is for you, but you should rule over it." Now Cain talked with Abel his brother; and it came to pass, when they were in the field, that Cain rose up against Abel his brother and killed him. Then the Lord said to Cain, "Where is Abel your brother?" He said, "I do not know. Am I my brother's keeper?" And He said, "What have you done? The voice of your brother's blood cries out to Me from the ground. So now you are cursed from the earth, which has opened its mouth to receive your brother's blood from your hand. When you till the ground, it shall no longer yield its strength to you. A fugitive and a vagabond you shall be on the earth." And Cain said to the LORD, "My punishment is greater than I can bear! Surely You have driven me out this day from the face of the ground; I shall be hidden from Your face; I shall be a fugitive and a vagabond on the earth, and it will happen that anyone who finds me will kill me."

—GENESIS 4:1–14

After reading these verses, we see that God looked after the life of His creation. He saw their actions, their good and their bad deeds. He saw the righteous and unrighteous people.

One cannot forget to mention the man by the name of Enoch and the unusual event that occurred during his time. Many times in the Bible it is written that a person lived so many years and died at a certain age. But what happened with Enoch?

Jared lived one hundred and sixty-two years, and begot Enoch. After he begot Enoch, Jared lived eight hundred years, and had sons and daughters. So all the days of Jared were nine hundred and sixty-two years; and he died. Enoch lived sixty-five years, and begot Methuselah. After he begot Methuselah, Enoch walked with God three hundred years, and had sons and daughters. So all the days of Enoch were three hundred and sixty-five years. And Enoch walked with God; and he was not, for God took him.

—GENESIS 5:18–24

The Holy Scriptures do not describe how God took Enoch. But we know that Enoch was a righteous man and that he did not die—he disappeared. We see what a tight connection existed between God the Creator and His creation.

When people began to multiply, sin increased. But God didn't forget His sinning creation. He looked after each living thing, and He observed all their actions:

Then the LORD saw that the wickedness of man was great in the earth, and that every intent of the thoughts of his heart was only evil continually. And the LORD was sorry that He had made man on the earth, and He was grieved in His heart. So the LORD said, "I will destroy man whom I have created from the face of the earth, both man and beast, creeping thing and birds of the air, for I am sorry that I have made them." But Noah found grace in the eyes of the LORD. This is the genealogy of Noah. Noah was a just man, perfect in his generations. Noah walked with God. And Noah begot three sons: Shem, Ham, and Japheth. The earth also was corrupt before God, and the earth was filled with violence. So God looked upon the earth, and indeed it was corrupt; for all flesh had corrupted their way on the earth. And God said to Noah, "The end of all flesh has come before Me, for the earth is filled with violence through them; and behold, I will destroy them with the earth. Make yourself an ark of gopherwood; make rooms in the ark, and cover it inside and outside with pitch."

—GENESIS 6:5–14

God witnessed great violence on Earth, and He set out to destroy all living things. But among the unrighteous, you can always find a righteous person, and in that time, only one man—Noah—was righteous. God decided to save Noah, his sons, and their wives. And God accomplished what He set out to do.

Then the LORD said to Noah, "Come into the ark, you and all your household, because I have seen that you are righteous before Me in this generation."

—GENESIS 7:1

When Noah, his family, and entire household obeyed God's will and entered the ark, God closed the door and it rained in such a manner that we have not seen since. The Flood killed everyone except those found in the ark.

Then God remembered Noah, and every living thing, and all the animals that were with him in the ark. And God made a wind to pass over the Earth, and the waters subsided. The fountains of the deep and windows of heaven were also stopped, and the rain from heaven was restrained.

—GENESIS 8:1–2

Then God spoke to Noah, saying, "Go out of the ark, you and your wife, and your sons and your sons' wives with you. Bring out with you every living thing of all flesh that is with you: birds and cattle and every creeping thing that creeps on the earth, so that they may abound on the earth, and be fruitful and multiply on the earth." So Noah went out, and his sons and his wife and his sons' wives with him. Every animal, every creeping thing, every bird, and whatever creeps on the earth, according to their families, went out of the ark.

—GENESIS 8:15–19

So God blessed Noah and his sons, and said to them: "Be fruitful and multiply, and fill the Earth."... Then God spoke to Noah and to his sons with him, saying: "And as for Me, behold, I establish My covenant with you and with your descendants after you, and with every living creature that is with you: the birds, the cattle, and every beast of the earth with you, of all that go out of the ark, every beast of the earth. Thus I establish My covenant with you: Never again shall all flesh be cut off by the waters of the flood; never again shall there be a flood to destroy the earth." And God said: "This is the sign of the covenant which I make between Me and you, and every living creature that is with you, for perpetual generations: I set My rainbow in the cloud, and it shall be for the sign of the covenant between Me and the earth. It shall be, when I bring a cloud over the earth, that the rainbow shall be seen in the cloud; and I will remember My covenant which is between Me and you and every living creature of all flesh; the waters shall never again become a flood to destroy all flesh."

—GENESIS 9:1, 8–15

God the Father doesn't like sin, and He eliminated all sinful fruit from the planet. Only one righteous man, Noah, along with his family, was left alive. We often see the rainbow in the sky, and the rainbow is a reminder for us that a universal flood like this will not occur again.

Time went by, and again people began to multiply. Their hearts filled with pride. In the spiritual sense, they didn't seek fellowship with their Creator. They began to try, physically, to reach the heaven. They wanted to posses it, to rule in it, and to gain the praise of future generations.

> Now the whole earth had one language and one speech. And it came to pass, as they journeyed from the east, that they found a plain in the land of Shinar, and they dwelt there. Then they said to one another, "Come, let us make bricks and bake them thoroughly." They had brick for stone, and they had asphalt for mortar. And they said, "Come, let us build ourselves a city, and a tower whose top is in the heavens; let us make a name for ourselves, lest we be scattered abroad over the face of the whole earth." But the LORD came down to see the city and the tower which the sons of men had built. And the LORD said, "Indeed the people are one and they all have one language, and this is what they begin to do; now nothing that they propose to do will be withheld from them. Come, let Us go down and there confuse their language, that they may not understand one another's speech." So the LORD scattered them abroad from there over the face of all the earth, and they ceased building the city. Therefore its name is called Babel, because there the LORD confused the language of all the earth; and from there the LORD scattered them abroad over the face of all the earth.
>
> —GENESIS 11:1–9

As we see from the reading, God looked after His creation. He set limits, which helped control their every move, every action. And when people wandered outside their limits, God held them back and stopped them. What is interesting is that we have these mixed languages to this day. The result of building the Babylonian tower—and the various languages—exists even to today, as each country has its native language. We are witnesses to this fact.

God gathered people with whom He spoke, communicated with, and revealed the future to. God gathered Abram, a man who believed in God entirely and was called a man of faith.

> Now the LORD had said to Abram: "Get out of your country, From your family And from your father's house, To a land that I will show you. I will make you a great nation; I will bless you And make your name great; And you shall be a blessing. I will bless those who bless you, And I will curse him who curses you; And in you all the families of the earth shall be blessed." So Abram departed as the LORD had spoken to him, and Lot went with him. And Abram was seventy-five years old when he departed from Haran. Then Abram took Sarai his wife and Lot his brother's son, and all their possessions that they had gathered, and the people whom they had acquired in Haran, and they departed to go to the land of Canaan. So they came to the land of Canaan.
>
> —GENESIS 12:1–5

Abram listened to the voice of the living God, his Creator, and through all the days of his life he submitted himself into God's hands. No matter what God told him to do, Abram did as he was told without complaining because he believed in his Creator. God decided to change Abram's name and to make a covenant with him. We shall see this great picture in Genesis 17:

> When Abram was ninety-nine years old, the LORD appeared to Abram and said to him, "I am Almighty God; walk before Me and be blameless. And I will make My covenant between Me and you, and will multiply you exceedingly." Then Abram

fell on his face, and God talked with him, saying: "As for Me, behold, My covenant is with you, and you shall be a father of many nations. No longer shall your name be called Abram, but your name shall be Abraham; for I have made you a father of many nations. I will make you exceedingly fruitful; and I will make nations of you, and kings shall come from you. And I will establish My covenant between Me and you and your descendants after you in their generations, for an everlasting covenant, to be God to you and your descendants after you. Also I give to you and your descendants after you the land in which you are a stranger, all the land of Canaan, as an ever-lasting possession; and I will be their God." And God said to Abraham: "As for you, you shall keep My covenant, you and your descendants after you throughout their generations. This is My covenant which you shall keep, between Me and you and your descendants after you: Every male child among you shall be circumcised; and you shall be circumcised in the flesh of your foreskins, and it shall be a sign of the covenant between Me and you. He who is eight days old among you shall be circumcised, every male child in your generations, he who is born in your house or bought with money from any foreigner who is not your descendant. He who is born in your house and he who is bought with your money must be circumcised, and My covenant shall be in your flesh for an everlasting covenant. And the uncircumcised male child, who is not circumcised in the flesh of his foreskin, that person shall be cut off from his people; he has broken My covenant." Then God said to Abraham, "As for Sarai your wife, you shall not call her name Sarai, but Sarah shall be her name. And I will bless her and also give you a son by her; then I will bless her, and she shall be a mother of nations; kings of peoples shall be from her." Then Abraham fell on his face and laughed, and said in his heart, "Shall a child be born to a man who is one hundred years old? And shall Sarah, who is ninety years old, bear a child?" And Abraham said to God, "Oh, that Ishmael might live before You!" Then God said: "No, Sarah your wife shall bear you a son, and you shall call his name Isaac; I will establish My covenant with him for an everlasting covenant, and with his descendants after him."

—GENESIS 17:1–19

God talked with Abraham in ancient times. God can talk with me and with you, dear reader, because God hasn't changed.

The occupants of Sodom and Gomorrah had done wicked deeds before our Lord. The howl of sin went up to heaven and caused God the Father to decide to send punishment. But before He did, God decided to talk with Abraham. Let's read this great dialogue:

And the LORD said, "Shall I hide from Abraham what I am doing, since Abraham shall surely become a great and mighty nation, and all the nations of the earth shall be blessed in him? For I have known him, in order that he may command his children and his household after him, that they keep the way of the Lord, to do righteousness and justice, that the LORD may bring to Abraham what He has spoken to him." And the LORD said, "Because the outcry against Sodom and Gomorrah is great, and because their sin is very grave, I will go down now and see whether they have done altogether according to the outcry against it that has come to Me; and if not, I will know." Then the men turned away from there and went toward Sodom, but Abraham still stood before the LORD. And Abraham came near and said, "Would You also destroy the righteous with the wicked? Suppose there were fifty righteous within the city; would You also destroy the place and not spare it for the fifty righteous that were in it? Far be it from You to do such a thing as this, to slay the righteous with the wicked, so that the righteous should be as the wicked; far be it from You! Shall not the Judge of all the earth do right?" So the LORD said, "If I find in Sodom fifty righteous within the city, then I will spare all the place for their sakes." Then Abraham answered and said, "Indeed now, I who am but dust and ashes have taken it upon myself to speak to the Lord: Suppose there were five less than the fifty righteous; would You destroy all of the city for lack of five?" So He said, "If I find there forty-five, I will not destroy it." And he spoke to Him yet again and said, "Suppose there should be forty found there?" So He said, "I will not do it for the sake of forty." Then he said, "Let not the Lord be angry, and I will speak: Suppose thirty should be found there?" So He said, "I will not do it if I find thirty there." And he said, "Indeed now, I have taken it upon myself to speak to the Lord: Suppose twenty should be found there?" So He said, "I will not destroy it for the sake of twenty." Then he said, "Let not the Lord be angry, and I will speak but once more: Suppose ten should be found there?" And He said, "I will not destroy it for the sake of ten." So the LORD went His way as soon as He had finished speaking with Abraham; and Abraham returned to his place.

—GENESIS 18:17–33

What touching fellowship God has with people. This fellowship expresses how much love, grace, and understanding God has toward His creation. Abraham was interceding on behalf of Sodom and Gomorrah, and Almighty God agreed with him. God the Father treasured the words of Abraham. Unfortunately though, not even ten righteous men were found, and these cities and all that was found in them were to be destroyed. But Lot, who was a righteous man, and his daughters were warned and managed to escape with their lives.

> Then the LORD rained brimstone and fire on Sodom and Gomorrah, from the LORD out of the heavens. So He overthrew those cities, all the plain, all the inhabitants of the cities, and what grew on the ground. But his wife looked back behind him, and she became a pillar of salt. And Abraham went early in the morning to the place where he had stood before the LORD. Then he looked toward Sodom and Gomorrah, and toward all the land of the plain; and he saw, and behold, the smoke of the land which went up like the smoke of a furnace.
> —GENESIS 19:24–28

God chose Isaac and Jacob. Jacob was a strong man. He fought with God to receive God's blessing for his life. Jacob knew very well that the blessing of God has great power in the life of man.

> Then Jacob was left alone; and a Man wrestled with him until the breaking of day. Now when He saw that He did not prevail against him, He touched the socket of his hip; and the socket of Jacob's hip was out of joint as He wrestled with him. And He said, "Let Me go, for the day breaks." But he said, "I will not let You go unless You bless me!" So He said to him, "What is your name?" He said, "Jacob." And He said, "Your name shall no longer be called Jacob, but Israel; for you have strug- gled with God and with men, and have prevailed."
> —GENESIS 32:24–28

I think that God loved Jacob's conduct, his heroic feat, his courage, and his persistent character. Jacob's act should be a great example to each of us on how to receive God's blessings and answers to prayers. And, by chance, if we ask and do not get a response for a long time, it'll be good to act how Jacob acted. To tell God, in simple words, "God, I will not stop praying and calling Your name. I will not stop asking until You answer me."

What was the result of Jacob's battle with God? Did God hear Jacob's prayer? Did God bless him? Did He remember his requests? We'll find the answers to these questions on the pages of the Bible:

> Then God appeared to Jacob again, when he came from Padan Aram, and blessed him. And God said to him, "Your name is Jacob; your name shall not be called Jacob anymore, but Israel shall be your name." So He called his name Israel. Also God said to him: "I am God Almighty. Be fruitful and multiply; a nation and a company of nations shall proceed from you, and kings shall come from your body. The land which I gave Abraham and Isaac I give to you; and to your descendants after you I give this land." Then God went up from him in the place where He talked with him.
>
> —Genesis 35:9–13

We see that we need to be strong and demanding. We must battle with God to receive His blessing. Sometimes God gives more than one asks. Jacob received more than he asked for, and God's blessing toward Jacob was abundant. He received a new name—Israel. God said that even kings would be born from the body of Jacob. God, through this battle, created Himself a nation that He called His chosen people, the people of God, and the nation of Israel. God loves faithful people, and each of us can be so, even in the twenty-first century. I can be a strong, persistent person of faith, as can you, dear reader, and we can be so when we entirely give our lives into the hands of the holy and great God.

Jacob had twelve sons, and one of the twelve was Joseph. Jacob loved Joseph more than the rest, and he made Joseph a colorful coat. Joseph was a man of faith, and God gave Joseph a great gift—the ability to interpret dreams. Joseph's brothers, out of jealousy, wanted to kill him.

> And Reuben said to them, "Shed no blood, but cast him into this pit which is in the wilderness, and do not lay a hand on him"—that he might deliver him out of their hands, and bring him back to his father. So it came to pass, when Joseph had come to his brothers, that they stripped Joseph of his tunic, the tunic of many colors that was on him. Then they took him and cast him into a pit. And the pit was empty; there was no water in it. And they sat down to eat a meal. Then they lifted their eyes and looked, and there was a company of Ishmaelites, coming from Gilead with their camels, bearing spices, balm, and myrrh, on their way to carry them down to Egypt. So Judah said to his brothers, "What profit is there if we kill our brother and conceal his blood? Come and let us sell him to the Ishmaelites, and let not our hand be upon him, for he is our brother and our flesh." And his brothers listened. Then Midianite traders passed by; so the brothers pulled Joseph up and lifted him out of the pit, and sold him to the Ishmaelites for twenty shekels of silver. And they took Joseph to Egypt....Now the Midianites had sold him in Egypt to Potiphar, an officer of Pharaoh and captain of the guard.
>
> —Genesis 37:22–28, 36

Joseph, as a young man, came to Egypt through great trials. But he believed in God, and his faith in God was not shaken. He heroically overcame all troubles, and God the Father was with him.

> Now Joseph had been taken down to Egypt. And Potiphar, an officer of Pharaoh, captain of the guard, an Egyptian, bought

him from the Ishmaelites who had taken him down there. The LORD was with Joseph, and he was a successful man; and he was in the house of his master the Egyptian. And his master saw that the LORD was with him and that the LORD made all he did to prosper in his hand. So Joseph found favor in his sight, and served him. Then he made him overseer of his house, and all that he had he put under his authority. So it was, from the time that he had made him overseer of his house and all that he had, that the LORD blessed the Egyptian's house for Joseph's sake; and the blessing of the LORD was on all that he had in the house and in the field.

—GENESIS 39:1–5

We see that God was with Joseph. He blessed him, as well as the entire household where Joseph was staying. But the trials did not stop here. Joseph, a handsome and attractive gentleman, found himself battling a new trial.

And it came to pass after these things that his master's wife cast longing eyes on Joseph, and she said, "Lie with me." But he refused and said to his master's wife, "Look, my master does not know what is with me in the house, and he has committed all that he has to my hand. There is no one greater in this house than I, nor has he kept back anything from me but you, because you are his wife. How then can I do this great wickedness, and sin against God?" So it was, as she spoke to Joseph day by day, that he did not heed her, to lie with her or to be with her. But it happened about this time, when Joseph went into the house to do his work, and none of the men of the house was inside, that she caught him by his garment, saying, "Lie with me." But he left his garment in her hand, and fled and ran outside. And so it was, when she saw that he had left his garment in her hand and fled outside, that she called to the men of her house and spoke to them, saying, "See, he has brought in to us a Hebrew to mock us. He came in to me to lie with me, and I cried out with a loud voice. And it happened, when he heard that I lifted my voice and cried out, that he left his garment with me, and fled and went outside." So she kept his garment with her until his master came home. Then she spoke to him with words like these, saying, "The Hebrew servant whom you brought to us came in to me to mock me; so it happened, as I lifted my voice and cried out, that he left his garment with me and fled outside." So it was, when his master heard the words which his wife spoke to him, saying, "Your servant did to me after this manner," that his anger was aroused. Then Joseph's master took him and put him into the prison, a place where the king's prisoners were confined. And he was there in the prison. But the LORD was with Joseph and showed him mercy, and He gave him favor in the sight of the keeper of the prison. And the keeper of the prison committed to Joseph's hand all the prisoners who were in the prison; whatever they did there, it was his doing. The keeper of the prison did not look into anything that was under Joseph's authority, because the LORD was with him; and whatever he did, the LORD made it prosper.

—GENESIS 39:7–23

God rewarded Joseph for his faithfulness, and He gave Joseph great wisdom. He also gave him a great gift—the ability to interpret dreams. Joseph, in the prison, interpreted the dreams of Pharaoh's wine keeper and bread carrier. And it occurred as Joseph had interpreted that it would. Pharaoh dreamed a dream as well, but no one in the land was able to interpret it. But Pharaoh heard about Joseph, and he called him into his presence.

Then Pharaoh sent and called Joseph, and they brought him quickly out of the dungeon; and he shaved, changed his clothing, and came to Pharaoh. And Pharaoh said to Joseph, "I have had a dream, and there is no one who can interpret it. But I have heard it said of you that you can understand a dream, to interpret it." So Joseph answered Pharaoh, saying, "It is not in me; God will give Pharaoh an answer of peace." Then Pharaoh said to Joseph: "Behold, in my dream I stood on the bank of the river. Suddenly seven cows came up out of the river, fine looking and fat; and they fed in the meadow. Then behold, seven other cows came up after them, poor and very ugly and gaunt, such ugliness as I have never seen in all the land of Egypt. And the gaunt and ugly cows ate up the first seven, the fat cows. When they had eaten them up, no one would have known that they had eaten them, for they were just as ugly as at the beginning. So I awoke. Also I saw in my dream, and suddenly seven heads came up on one stalk, full and good. Then behold, seven heads, withered, thin, and blighted by the east wind, sprang up after them. And the thin heads devoured the seven good heads. So I told this to the magicians, but there was no one who could explain it to me." Then Joseph said to Pharaoh, "The dreams of Pharaoh are one; God has shown Pharaoh what He is about to do: The seven good cows are seven years, and the seven good heads are seven years; the dreams are one. And the seven thin and ugly cows which came up after them are seven years, and the seven empty heads blighted by the east wind are seven years of famine. This is the thing which I have spoken to Pharaoh. God has shown Pharaoh what He is about to do. Indeed seven years of great plenty will come throughout all the land of Egypt; but after them seven years of famine will arise, and all the plenty will be forgotten in the land of Egypt; and the famine will deplete the land. So the plenty will not be known in the land because of the famine following, for it will be very severe. And the dream was repeated to Pharaoh twice because the thing is established by God, and God will shortly bring it to pass. Now therefore, let Pharaoh select a discerning and wise man, and set him over the land of Egypt. Let Pharaoh do this, and let him appoint officers over the land, to collect one-fifth of the produce of the land of Egypt in the seven plentiful years. And let them gather all the food of those good years that are coming, and store up grain under the authority of Pharaoh, and let them keep food in the cities. Then that food shall be as a reserve for the land for the seven years of famine which shall be in the land of Egypt, that the land may not perish during the famine." So the advice was good in the eyes of Pharaoh and in the eyes of all his servants. And Pharaoh said to his servants, "Can we find such a one as this, a man in whom is the Spirit of God?" Then Pharaoh said to Joseph, "Inasmuch as God has shown you all this, there is no one as discerning and wise as you. You shall be over my house, and all my people shall be ruled according to your word; only in regard to the throne will I be greater than you." And Pharaoh said to Joseph, "See, I have set you over all the land of Egypt." Then Pharaoh took his signet ring off his hand and put it on Joseph's hand; and he clothed him in garments of fine linen and put a gold chain around his neck. And he had him ride in the second chariot which he had; and they cried out before him, "Bow the knee!" So he set him over all the land of Egypt. Pharaoh also said to Joseph, "I am Pharaoh, and without your consent no man may lift his hand or foot in all the land of Egypt." And Pharaoh called Joseph's name Zaphnath-Paaneah. And he gave him as a wife Asenath, the daughter of Poti-Pherah priest of On. So Joseph went out over all the land of Egypt. Joseph was thirty years old when he stood before Pharaoh king of Egypt. And Joseph went out from the presence of Pharaoh, and went throughout all the land of Egypt. Now in the seven plentiful years the ground brought forth abundantly. So he gathered up all the food of the seven years which were in the land of Egypt, and laid up the food in the cities; he laid up in every city the food of the fields which surrounded them. Joseph gathered very much grain, as the sand of the sea, until he stopped counting, for it was immeasurable. And to Joseph were born two sons before the years of famine came, whom Asenath, the daughter of Poti-Pherah priest of On, bore to him. Joseph called the name of the firstborn Manasseh: "For God has made me forget all my toil and all my father's house." And the name of the second he called Ephraim: "For God has caused me to be fruitful in the land of my affliction." Then the seven years of plenty which were in the land of Egypt ended, and the seven years of famine began to come, as Joseph had said. The famine was in all lands, but in all the land of Egypt there was bread. So when all the land of Egypt was famished, the people cried to Pharaoh for bread. Then Pharaoh said to all the Egyptians, "Go to Joseph; whatever he says to you, do." The famine was over all the face of the earth, and Joseph opened all the storehouses and sold to the Egyptians. And the famine became severe in the land of Egypt. So all countries came to Joseph in Egypt to buy grain, because the famine was severe in all lands.

—GENESIS 41:14–57

Joseph saved all of Egypt from famine, and he helped other countries as well. People from every direction came to Joseph to buy grain—even his brothers, the very ones who sold him. Their reunion is a very interesting event, and it is worth reading. Joseph brought his father, his brothers, and their families into Egypt. There they lived, multiplied, and filled the land. Four hundred thirty years passed, and the nation of Israel had increased. During this time, the subsequent pharaohs forgot Joseph and all that he had done for Egypt, and they began to fear the people of Israel.

> And Joseph died, all his brothers, and all that generation. But the children of Israel were fruitful and increased abundantly, multiplied and grew exceedingly mighty; and the land was filled with them. Now there arose a new king over Egypt, who did not know Joseph. And he said to his people, "Look, the people of the children of Israel are more and mightier than we."
>
> —Exodus 1:6–9

And the Egyptians began to repress the nation of Israel. But God didn't forget His chosen people. God heard their cry, saw their hard life, and chose a great leader, Moses. Moses, with God's help, led the multitude of the nation of Israel out of Egypt and into the Promised Land, flowing with milk and honey.

12

THE STORY OF MOSES

EGYPTIANS ACTED CRUELLY TOWARD THE NATION OF Israel. They made their life hard with physical labor, with bricks and mortar, and other harsh work. But the more they afflicted them, the more they multiplied. They grew in such a manner that the Egyptians feared the men of Israel. The king of Egypt told the midwives to kill the male children born to the Israelites, but to spare the female children. The midwives did not do this though, and God blessed them for it. Then Pharaoh told his people to toss the male children into the river, but, again, to spare the female children. Now we will read from the pages of the Holy Book and see how a male child ended up in the house of Pharaoh's daughter:

> And a man of the house of Levi went and took as wife a daughter of Levi. So the woman conceived and bore a son. And when she saw that he was a beautiful child, she hid him three months. But when she could no longer hide him, she took an ark of bulrushes for him, daubed it with asphalt and pitch, put the child in it, and laid it in the reeds by the river's

bank. And his sister stood afar off, to know what would be done to him. Then the daughter of Pharaoh came down to bathe at the river. And her maidens walked along the riverside; and when she saw the ark among the reeds, she sent her maid to get it. And when she opened it, she saw the child, and behold, the baby wept. So she had compassion on him, and said, "This is one of the Hebrews' children." Then his sister said to Pharaoh's daughter, "Shall I go and call a nurse for you from the Hebrew women, that she may nurse the child for you?" And Pharaoh's daughter said to her, "Go." So the maiden went and called the child's mother. Then Pharaoh's daughter said to her, "Take this child away and nurse him for me, and I will give you your wages." So the woman took the child and nursed him. And the child grew, and she brought him to Pharaoh's daughter, and he became her son. So she called his name Moses, saying, "Because I drew him out of the water."

—EXODUS 2:1–10

Moses received the highest education when he was in the house of Pharaoh's daughter. He was taught according to Egyptian wisdom, and he grew strong in his words and actions. Moses was a great man in the land of Egypt, in the eyes of Pharaoh, and in the eyes of the Israelites. He held a great position in Egypt. When he turned forty, he decided to visit his brothers, the men of Israel. When he did, he saw how greatly they were being oppressed and how exhausted they were. Moses witnessed an Egyptian beating an Israelite and quickly decided to protect the Israelite. With his strength, Moses killed the Egyptian and hid him in the sand. The news of this event spread quickly, and it finally reached Pharaoh. When Pharaoh heard of this, he wanted to kill Moses, who had by then escaped into the land of Midian and became a stranger of that land. Moses remained with the priest of Midian, and he enjoyed living there. This Midian priest picked a daughter, Zipporah, as a wife for Moses. Zipporah bore a son, and Moses called him Gershom, for he said that he had been a stranger in a foreign land. Moses was highly educated and very popular in Egypt, but he served as a shepherd in Midian for a total of forty years. God spoke of Moses like this:

> Now the man Moses was very humble, more than all men who were on the face of the Earth.
>
> —NUMBERS 12:3

Time passed, years went by, but the oppression of the Israelites did not cease. They groaned with labor, and their groans were heard in heaven.

> So God heard their groaning, and God remembered His covenant with Abraham, with Isaac, and with Jacob. And God looked upon the children of Israel, and God acknowledged them.
>
> —EXODUS 2:24–25

We'll keep reading from the Holy Word, and we will learn how God helped His chosen people, the children of Israel:

> Now Moses was tending the flock of Jethro his father-in-law, the priest of Midian. And he led the flock to the back of the desert, and came to Horeb, the mountain of God. And the Angel of the LORD appeared to him in a flame of fire from the midst of a bush. So he looked, and behold, the bush was burning with fire, but the bush was not consumed. Then Moses said, "I will now turn aside and see this great sight, why the bush does not burn." So when the LORD saw that he turned aside to

look, God called to him from the midst of the bush and said, "Moses, Moses!" And he said, "Here I am." Then He said, "Do not draw near this place. Take your sandals off your feet, for the place where you stand is holy ground." Moreover He said, "I am the God of your father—the God of Abraham, the God of Isaac, and the God of Jacob." And Moses hid his face, for he was afraid to look upon God. And the LORD said: "I have surely seen the oppression of My people who are in Egypt, and have heard their cry because of their taskmasters, for I know their sorrows. So I have come down to deliver them out of the hand of the Egyptians, and to bring them up from that land to a good and large land, to a land flowing with milk and honey, to the place of the Canaanites and the Hittites and the Amorites and the Perizzites and the Hivites and the Jebusites. Now therefore, behold, the cry of the children of Israel has come to Me, and I have also seen the oppression with which the Egyptians oppress them. Come now, therefore, and I will send you to Pharaoh that you may bring My people, the children of Israel, out of Egypt." But Moses said to God, "Who am I that I should go to Pharaoh, and that I should bring the children of Israel out of Egypt?" So He said, "I will certainly be with you. And this shall be a sign to you that I have sent you: When you have brought the people out of Egypt, you shall serve God on this mountain." Then Moses said to God, "Indeed, when I come to the children of Israel and say to them, 'The God of your fathers has sent me to you,' and they say to me, 'What is His name?' what shall I say to them?" And God said to Moses, "I AM WHO I AM." And He said, "Thus you shall say to the children of Israel, 'I AM has sent me to you.'" Moreover God said to Moses, "Thus you shall say to the children of Israel: 'The LORD God of your fathers, the God of Abraham, the God of Isaac, and the God of Jacob, has sent me to you. This is My name forever, and this is My memorial to all generations.' Go and gather the elders of Israel together, and say to them, 'The Lord God of your fathers, the God of Abraham, of Isaac, and of Jacob, appeared to me, saying, "I have surely visited you and seen what is done to you in Egypt."'"

—Exodus 3:1–16

Moses didn't believe that this great mission would be accomplished, and he began to doubt, to hesitate. But God showed Moses signs and miracles that he would perform in front of Pharaoh, and Moses' confidence grew.

Then Moses answered and said, "But suppose they will not believe me or listen to my voice; suppose they say, 'The Lord has not appeared to you.'" So the Lord said to him, "What is that in your hand?" He said, "A rod." And He said, "Cast it on the ground." So he cast it on the ground, and it became a serpent; and Moses fled from it. Then the Lord said to Moses, "Reach out your hand and take it by the tail" (and he reached out his hand and caught it, and it became a rod in his hand), "that they may believe that the Lord God of their fathers, the God of Abraham, the God of Isaac, and the God of Jacob, has appeared to you." Furthermore the Lord said to him, "Now put your hand in your bosom." And he put his hand in his bosom, and when he took it out, behold, his hand was leprous, like snow. And He said, "Put your hand in your bosom again." So he put his hand in his bosom again, and drew it out of his bosom, and behold, it was restored like his other flesh. "Then it will be, if they do not believe you, nor heed the message of the first sign, that they may believe the message of the latter sign."

—Exodus 4:1–8

Moses took his wife, his kids, sat them atop of donkeys, and set out for Egypt. And he took with him the rod with which he would perform miracles for Pharaoh. Moses met with Aaron, his brother, and they gathered the elders of Israel. Aaron told the elders all the words that God had spoken to Moses, and the elders believed. Moses and Aaron met with Pharaoh and presented him with God's will—to let His people go. Pharaoh heard this request and grew resistant. Moses and Aaron performed all these miracles in front of Pharaoh, but the heart of Pharaoh was bitter and he did not let the people of Israel go from his land. Then God told Moses that He would punish the land of Egypt, and that the punishment would be the death of all the firstborn in Egypt. (See Exodus 4:20–11:4.)

> Then Moses said, "Thus says the Lord: 'About midnight I will go out into the midst of Egypt; 'and all the firstborn in the land of Egypt shall die, from the firstborn of Pharaoh who sits on his throne, even to the firstborn of the female servant who is behind the handmill, and all the firstborn of the animals. 'Then there shall be a great cry throughout all the land of Egypt, such as was not like it before, nor shall be like it again. 'But against none of the children of Israel shall a dog move its tongue, against man or beast, that you may know that the Lord does make a difference between the Egyptians and Israel.'"
> —Exodus 11:4–7

God established the Passover when He gave Moses and Aaron the power to announce to the people to take a year old lamb without blemish, kill it, and spread the blood on their doorsteps and on the beams of the door of the house where they would eat it. The lamb was to be eaten with unleavened bread and bitter spices.

> And thus you shall eat it: with a belt on your waist, your sandals on your feet, and your staff in your hand. So you shall

eat it in haste. It is the LORD's Passover. For I will pass through the land of Egypt on that night, and will strike all the first-born in the land of Egypt, both man and beast; and against all the gods of Egypt I will execute judgment: I am the LORD. Now the blood shall be a sign for you on the houses where you are. And when I see the blood, I will pass over you; and the plague shall not be on you to destroy you when I strike the land of Egypt. So this day shall be to you a memorial; and you shall keep it as a feast to the LORD throughout your genera-tions. You shall keep it as a feast by an everlasting ordinance.

—EXODUS 12:11–14

Moses gathered the elders of Israel, told them God's will, and they did as the Lord God wanted.

And it came to pass at midnight that the LORD struck all the firstborn in the land of Egypt, from the firstborn of Pharaoh who sat on his throne to the firstborn of the captive who was in the dungeon, and all the firstborn of livestock. So Pharaoh rose in the night, he, all his servants, and all the Egyptians; and there was a great cry in Egypt, for there was not a house where there was not one dead. Then he called for Moses and Aaron by night, and said, "Rise, go out from among my people, both you and the children of Israel. And go, serve the LORD as you have said. Also take your flocks and your herds, as you have said, and be gone; and bless me also." And the Egyptians urged the people, that they might send them out of the land in haste. For they said, "We shall all be dead."

—EXODUS 12:29–33

In this manner, God took His chosen people from the land of Egypt.

Then the children of Israel journeyed from Rameses to Succoth, about six hundred thousand men on foot, besides children. A mixed multitude went up with them also, and flocks and herds—a great deal of livestock. And they baked unleavened cakes of the dough which they had brought out of Egypt; for it was not leavened, because they were driven out of Egypt and could not wait, nor had they prepared provisions for themselves. Now the sojourn of the children of Israel who lived in Egypt was four hundred and thirty years. And it came to pass at the end of the four hundred and thirty years—on that very same day—it came to pass that all the armies of the LORD went out from the land of Egypt. It is a night of solemn observance to the LORD for bringing them out of the land of Egypt. This is that night of the LORD, a solemn observance for all the children of Israel throughout their generations.... And it came to pass, on that very same day, that the LORD brought the children of Israel out of the land of Egypt according to their armies.

—Exodus 12:37–42, 51

Many people traveled through the desert with Moses. They didn't have a compass, but God was with them and showed them the way.

And the LORD went before them by day in a pillar of cloud to lead the way, and by night in a pillar of fire to give them light, so as to go by day and night. He did not take away the pillar of cloud by day or the pillar of fire by night from before the people.

—EXODUS 13:21–22

The nation of Israel walked day and night, and they neared the Red Sea. The king of Egypt heard this and decided to chase the Israelites in order to capture and bring them back to his land.

Pharaoh prepared his chariot, took with him an additional six hundred—all the Egyptian chariots—and their riders, and chased after the sons of Israel. The nation of Israel looked back and saw the Egyptians approaching. They got very afraid and cried out to God. The situation of the chosen nation was not easy—the sea was before them and Pharaoh with his chariots was behind them. But God was with His nation, and with God, nothing is impossible. And God told Moses:

> But lift up your rod, and stretch out your hand over the sea and divide it. And the children of Israel shall go on dry ground through the midst of the sea. And I indeed will harden the hearts of the Egyptians, and they shall follow them. So I will gain honor over Pharaoh and over all his army, his chariots, and his horsemen. Then the Egyptians shall know that I am the Lord, when I have gained honor for Myself over Pharaoh, his chariots, and his horsemen." And the Angel of God, who went before the camp of Israel, moved and went behind them; and the pillar of cloud went from before them and stood behind them. So it came between the camp of the Egyptians and the camp of Israel. Thus it was a cloud and darkness to the one, and it gave light by night to the other, so that the one did not come near the other all that night. Then Moses stretched out his hand over the sea; and the Lord caused the sea to go back by a strong east wind all that night, and made the sea into dry land, and the waters were divided. So the children of Israel went into the midst of the sea on the dry ground, and the waters were a wall to them on their right hand and on their left. And the Egyptians pursued and went after them into the midst of the sea, all Pharaoh's horses, his chariots, and his horsemen.
>
> —Exodus 14:16–23

Then the Lord said to Moses, "Stretch out your hand over the sea, that the waters may come back upon the Egyptians, on their chariots, and on their horsemen." And Moses stretched out his hand over the sea; and when the morning appeared, the sea returned to its full depth, while the Egyptians were fleeing into it. So the Lord overthrew the Egyptians in the midst of the sea. Then the waters returned and covered the chariots, the horsemen, and all the army of Pharaoh that came into the sea after them. Not so much as one of them remained. But the children of Israel had walked on dry land in the midst of the sea, and the waters were a wall to them on their right hand and on their left. So the Lord saved Israel that day out of the hand of the Egyptians, and Israel saw the Egyptians dead on the seashore. Thus Israel saw the great work which the Lord had done in Egypt; so the people feared the Lord, and believed the Lord and His servant Moses.

—Exodus 14:26–31

The nation of Israel believed God when they saw His great miracles and the strength of His great and mighty hand. Moses and all the people of Israel rejoiced, exalted, and sang songs of praise to their God.

Then Moses and the children of Israel sang this song to the Lord, and spoke, saying: "I will sing to the Lord, For He has triumphed gloriously! The horse and its rider He has thrown into the sea! The Lord is my strength and song, And He has become my salvation; He is my God, and I will praise Him; My father's God, and I will exalt Him. The Lord is a man of war; The Lord is His name. Pharaoh's chariots and his army He has cast into the sea; His chosen captains also are drowned in the Red Sea. The depths have covered them; They sank to the bottom like a stone. Your right hand, O Lord, has become glorious in power; Your right hand, O Lord, has dashed the enemy in pieces. And in the greatness of Your excellence You have overthrown those who rose against You; You sent forth Your wrath; It consumed them like stubble. And with the blast of Your nostrils The waters were gathered together; The floods stood upright like a heap; The depths congealed in the heart of the sea. The enemy said, 'I will pursue, I will overtake, I will divide the spoil; My desire shall be satisfied on them. I will draw my sword, My hand shall destroy them.' You blew with Your wind, The sea covered them; They sank like lead in the mighty waters. Who is like You, O Lord, among the gods? Who is like You, glorious in holiness, Fearful in praises, doing wonders? You stretched out Your right hand; The earth swallowed them. You in Your mercy have led forth The people whom You have redeemed; You have guided them in Your strength To Your holy habitation."

—Exodus 15:1–13

The sons of Israel kept moving in the desert. Eventually, they began crying out to Moses and Aaron as they remembered that in Egypt they ate meat. God heard their cries and gave them manna.

Then the Lord said to Moses, "Behold, I will rain bread from heaven for you. And the people shall go out and gather a certain quota every day, that I may test them, whether they will walk in My law or not. And it shall be on the sixth day that they shall prepare what they bring in, and it shall be twice as much as they gather daily." Then Moses and Aaron said to all the children of Israel, "At evening you shall know that the Lord has brought you out of the land of Egypt. And in the morning you shall see the glory of the Lord; for He hears your complaints against the LORD. But what are we, that you complain against us?" Also Moses said, "This shall be seen when the LORD gives you meat to eat in the evening, and in the morning bread to the full; for the LORD hears your complaints which you make against Him. And what are we? Your complaints are not against us but against the LORD." Then Moses spoke to Aaron, "Say to all the congregation of the children of Israel, 'Come near before the LORD, for He has heard your complaints.'" Now it came to pass, as Aaron spoke to the whole congregation of the children of Israel, that they looked toward the wilderness, and behold, the glory of the LORD appeared in the cloud. And the LORD spoke to Moses, saying, "I have heard the complaints of the children of Israel. Speak to them, saying, 'At twilight you shall eat meat, and in the morning you shall be filled with bread. And you shall know that I am the LORD your God.'" So it was that quails came up at evening and covered the camp, and in the morning the dew lay all around the camp. And when the layer of dew lifted, there, on the surface of the wilderness, was a small round substance, as fine as frost on the ground. So when the children of Israel saw it, they said to one another, "What is it?" For they did not know what it was. And Moses said to them, "This is the bread which the LORD has given you to eat."

—Exodus 16:4–15

And the house of Israel called its name Manna. And it was like white coriander seed, and the taste of it was like wafers made with honey. Then Moses said, "This is the thing which the LORD has commanded: 'Fill an omer with it, to be kept for your generations, that they may see the bread with which I fed you in the wilderness, when I brought you out of the land of Egypt.'" And Moses said to Aaron, "Take a pot and put

an omer of manna in it, and lay it up before the LORD, to be
kept for your generations." As the LORD commanded Moses,
so Aaron laid it up before the Testimony, to be kept. And the
children of Israel ate manna forty years, until they came to an
inhabited land; they ate manna until they came to the border
of the land of Canaan.

—EXODUS 16:31–35

In the third month after the exodus from Egypt began, the men
of Israel came to the Wilderness of Sinai and set up camp.

And Moses went up to God, and the LORD called to him from
the mountain, saying, "Thus you shall say to the house of Jacob,
and tell the children of Israel: 'You have seen what I did to the
Egyptians, and how I bore you on eagles' wings and brought
you to Myself. Now therefore, if you will indeed obey My voice
and keep My covenant, then you shall be a special treasure to
Me above all people; for all the earth is Mine. And you shall
be to Me a kingdom of priests and a holy nation.' These are the
words which you shall speak to the children of Israel."

—EXODUS 19:3–6

Moses returned from the mountain and told the nation the
words that God had spoken, and the nation responded, saying that
they would do all God commanded them. In turn, Moses told God
the Israelites' response. Moses stood between God and the people
in order to inform the nation of what God spoke, and to tell God
what the nation said in response. God continued to give different
laws and teachings to His nation:

And the LORD said to Moses, "Behold, I come to you in the thick
cloud, that the people may hear when I speak with you, and believe
you forever." So Moses told the words of the people to the LORD.

Then the LORD said to Moses, "Go to the people and consecrate them today and tomorrow, and let them wash their clothes. And let them be ready for the third day. For on the third day the LORD will come down upon Mount Sinai in the sight of all the people. You shall set bounds for the people all around, saying, 'Take heed to yourselves that you do not go up to the mountain or touch its base. Whoever touches the mountain shall surely be put to death. Not a hand shall touch him, but he shall surely be stoned or shot with an arrow; whether man or beast, he shall not live.' When the trumpet sounds long, they shall come near the mountain." So Moses went down from the mountain to the people and sanctified the people, and they washed their clothes. And he said to the people, "Be ready for the third day; do not come near your wives." Then it came to pass on the third day, in the morning, that there were thunderings and lightnings, and a thick cloud on the mountain; and the sound of the trumpet was very loud, so that all the people who were in the camp trembled. And Moses brought the people out of the camp to meet with God, and they stood at the foot of the mountain. Now Mount Sinai was completely in smoke, because the LORD descended upon it in fire. Its smoke ascended like the smoke of a furnace, and the whole mountain quaked greatly. And when the blast of the trumpet sounded long and became louder and louder, Moses spoke, and God answered him by voice. Then the LORD came down upon Mount Sinai, on the top of the mountain. And the LORD called Moses to the top of the mountain, and Moses went up.

—Exodus 19:9–20

God set ten commandments for His chosen nation:

And God spoke all these words, saying: "I am the LORD your God, who brought you out of the land of Egypt, out of the house of bondage. You shall have no other gods before Me. You shall not make for yourself a carved image—any likeness of anything that is in heaven above, or that is in the earth beneath, or that is in the water under the earth; you shall not bow down to them nor serve them. For I, the LORD your God, am a jealous God, visiting the iniquity of the fathers upon the children to the third and fourth generations of those who hate Me, but showing mercy to thousands, to those who love Me and keep My commandments. You shall not take the name of the LORD your God in vain, for the LORD will not hold him guiltless who takes His name in vain. Remember the Sabbath day, to keep it holy. Six days you shall labor and do all your work, but the seventh day is the Sabbath of the LORD your God. In it you shall do no work: you, nor your son, nor your daughter, nor your male servant, nor your female servant, nor your cattle, nor your stranger who is within your gates. For in six days the LORD made the heavens and the earth, the sea, and all that is in them, and rested the seventh day. Therefore the LORD blessed the Sabbath day and hallowed it. Honor your father and your mother, that your days may be long upon the land which the LORD your God is giving you. You shall not murder. You shall not commit adultery. You shall not steal. You shall not bear false witness against your neighbor. You shall not covet your neighbor's house; you shall not covet your neighbor's wife, nor his male servant, nor his female servant, nor his ox, nor his donkey, nor anything that is your neighbor's." Now all the people witnessed the thunderings, the lightning flashes, the sound of the trumpet, and the mountain smoking; and when the people saw it, they trembled and stood afar off. Then they said to Moses, "You speak with us, and we will hear; but let not God speak with us, lest we die."

—EXODUS 20:1–19

The Lord spoke these words to His chosen people, the sons of Israel, on Mount Sinai. From the center of fire He wrote the commands on two stone tablets with His finger. The nation of Israel heard the loud voice of God, saw the smoking mountain, and stood back in the distance from the mountain.

> And when He had made an end of speaking with him on Mount Sinai, He gave Moses two tablets of the Testimony, tablets of stone, written with the finger of God.
>
> —Exodus 31:18

> Now the tablets were the work of God, and the writing was the writing of God engraved on the tablets.
>
> —Exodus 32:16

Through Moses, God gave His chosen people different commands and laws regarding sacrifices, making altars, and avoiding idol worship.

> You shall not make anything to be with Me—gods of silver or gods of gold you shall not make for yourselves.
>
> —Exodus 20:23

God laid out moral laws for His people, family-oriented laws, and laws that governed celebrations. God required, and requires, all His commands to be fulfilled.

> And in all that I have said to you, be circumspect and make no mention of the name of other gods, nor let it be heard from your mouth.
>
> —Exodus 23:13

> So you shall serve the Lord your God, and He will bless your bread and your water. And I will take sickness away from the

midst of you. No one shall suffer miscarriage or be barren in your land; I will fulfill the number of your days.

—Exodus 23:25–26

The Creator establishes and commands; creation accepts and fulfills. The link is fellowship, a relationship between God and man.

13

THE ARK OF
THE COVENANT

T HE PEOPLE OF THE NATION OF ISRAEL, EVEN AFTER SEEING
so many miracles with their own eyes and receiving so
many blessings from God for their lives, were not obedient
to their Creator. The nation did not fulfill God's will, nor did they
treasure God's goodness. They sinned in front of God the Father—
as we do often today when we do not heed God's Word, believe in
Him, or do His will. Some, before they read the Word of God, are
seized with fear. But God the Father loves us. And He directs us,
by various means, to repentance—even in these days. He wants to
have fellowship with us, just like He wanted to have fellowship with
and to be in the center of His chosen people in the Old Testament.
God's love to His creation does not have boundaries. He wants to be
linked to us, He wants to have fellowship with us and to be among
us, His people. The Israelites did not stop sinning. And God, who is
holy and righteous, could not remain among sin. Therefore, to wipe
the sin from His people, God commanded offerings to be made.

God set the following rule, "Without the shedding of blood, there is no remission" (Heb. 9:22).

God told Moses to come up on the mountain along with Aaron, Nadab, Abihu, and seventy of the elders. But only Moses was allowed to get close to God; Aaron, Nadab, Abihu and the elders could not, nor could the remainder of the Israelites. And this is what took place:

> Then Moses went up into the mountain, and a cloud covered the mountain. Now the glory of the LORD rested on Mount Sinai, and the cloud covered it six days. And on the seventh day He called to Moses out of the midst of the cloud. The sight of the glory of the LORD was like a consuming fire on the top of the mountain in the eyes of the children of Israel. So Moses went into the midst of the cloud and went up into the mountain. And Moses was on the mountain forty days and forty nights.
>
> —EXODUS 24:15–18

God began talking with Moses, and He told him to tell the sons of Israel to make an offering of gold, silver, bronze, colorful thread (blue, purple, and scarlet), acacia wood, ram, and badger skins, oil, spices, onyx stones, and other stones to set in the ephod and in the breastplate. (See Exodus 25.) God continued the conversation:

> And let them make Me a sanctuary, that I may dwell among them. According to all that I show you, that is, the pattern of the tabernacle and the pattern of all its furnishings, just so you shall make it.
>
> —EXODUS 25:8–9

When God gives a command to do something, He also provides exact instructions: what to make, how to make it, what material to use, and even the measurements. We will now travel through the pages of Exodus, and we will hear God's Word and His will in regards to the creation of the Lord's sanctuary, the place where God was to be with His people.

> And they shall make an ark of acacia wood; two and a half cubits shall be its length, a cubit and a half its width, and a cubit and a half its height. And you shall overlay it with pure gold, inside and out you shall overlay it, and shall make on it a molding of gold all around.
>
> —EXODUS 25:10–11

> And you shall put into the ark the Testimony which I will give you. You shall make a mercy seat of pure gold; two and a half cubits shall be its length and a cubit and a half its width. And you shall make two cherubim of gold; of hammered work you shall make them at the two ends of the mercy seat. Make one cherub at one end, and the other cherub at the other end; you shall make the cherubim at the two ends of it of one piece with the mercy seat.
>
> —EXODUS 25:16–19

> You shall also make a table of acacia wood; two cubits shall be its length, a cubit its width, and a cubit and a half its height. And you shall overlay it with pure gold, and make a molding of gold all around.... You shall also make a lampstand of pure gold; the lampstand shall be of hammered work. Its shaft, its branches, its bowls, its ornamental knobs, and flowers shall be of one piece.... You shall make seven lamps for it, and they shall arrange its lamps so that they give light in front of it."
>
> —EXODUS 25:23–24, 31, 37

Moreover you shall make the tabernacle with ten curtains of fine woven linen and blue, purple, and scarlet thread; with artistic designs of cherubim you shall weave them. The length of each curtain shall be twenty-eight cubits, and the width of each curtain four cubits. And every one of the curtains shall have the same measurements.... And you shall make fifty clasps of gold, and couple the curtains together with the clasps, so that it may be one tabernacle. You shall also make curtains of goats' hair, to be a tent over the tabernacle. You shall make eleven curtains. The length of each curtain shall be thirty cubits, and the width of each curtain four cubits; and the eleven curtains shall all have the same measurements.... And for the tabernacle you shall make the boards of acacia wood, standing upright. Ten cubits shall be the length of a board, and a cubit and a half shall be the width of each board.... And you shall make bars of acacia wood: five for the boards on one side of the tabernacle....You shall make a veil woven of blue, purple, and scarlet thread, and fine woven linen. It shall be woven with an artistic design of cherubim. You shall hang it upon the four pillars of acacia wood overlaid with gold. Their hooks shall be gold, upon four sockets of silver. And you shall hang the veil from the clasps. Then you shall bring the ark of the Testimony in there, behind the veil. The veil shall be a divider for you between the holy place and the Most Holy.... And you shall make for the screen five pillars of acacia wood, and overlay them with gold; their hooks shall be gold, and you shall cast five sockets of bronze for them.

—EXODUS 26:1–2, 6–8, 15–16, 26, 31–33, 37

You shall make an altar of acacia wood, five cubits long and five cubits wide—the altar shall be square—and its height shall be three cubits. You shall make its horns on its four corners; its horns shall be of one piece with it. And you shall overlay it with bronze. Also you shall make its pans to receive its ashes, and its shovels and its basins and its forks and its firepans; you shall make all its utensils of bronze.

—EXODUS 27:1–3

As we read the above words, we see that God gave a detailed description of how the sanctuary should be made for Him. God showed Moses a visual picture when He called him up onto Mount Sinai. God gave exact instructions of what and how to make, what material to use, and even what measurements to go by. God the Creator loves His creation and wants to have a link with the work of His hands, with each person individually, and with all of Earth's citizens. God even told His creation where He will be and where He will speak. He also gave commands, through Moses, for the people of Israel.

You shall put the mercy seat on top of the ark, and in the ark you shall put the Testimony that I will give you. And there I will meet with you, and I will speak with you from above the mercy seat, from between the two cherubim which are on the ark of the Testimony, about everything which I will give you in commandment to the children of Israel."

—EXODUS 25:21–22

God needs His nation to do what He says, for He is perfect. God needs the commands He lays down to be fulfilled. The Creator treasures His words, His commands, and His rules.

And see to it that you make them according to the pattern which was shown you on the mountain.

—EXODUS 25:40

God appoints individuals whom He wants to be His servants.

> Now take Aaron your brother, and his sons with him, from among the children of Israel, that he may minister to Me as priest, Aaron and Aaron's sons: Nadab, Abihu, Elemazar, and Ithamar. And you shall make holy garments for Aaron your brother, for glory and for beauty."
>
> —Exodus 28:1–2

God even described the clothes that had to be prepared for the priests that would serve the holy One. I must admit that I love reading the Old Testament.

> So you shall speak to all who are gifted artisans, whom I have filled with the spirit of wisdom, that they may make Aaron's garments, to consecrate him, that he may minister to Me as priest. And these are the garments which they shall make: a breastplate, an ephod, a robe, a skillfully woven tunic, a turban, and a sash. So they shall make holy garments for Aaron your brother and his sons, that he may minister to Me as priest. They shall take the gold, blue, purple, and scarlet thread, and the fine linen, and they shall make the ephod of gold, blue, purple, and scarlet thread, and fine woven linen, artistically worked. It shall have two shoulder straps joined at its two edges, and so it shall be joined together. And the intricately woven band of the ephod, which is on it, shall be of the same workmanship, made of gold, blue, purple, and scarlet thread, and fine woven linen. Then you shall take two onyx stones and engrave on them the names of the sons of Israel: six of their names on one stone and six names on the other stone, in order of their birth.... So Aaron shall bear the names of the sons of Israel on the breastplate of judgment over his

heart, when he goes into the holy place, as a memorial before the LORD continually.

—EXODUS 28:3–10, 29

God also chose people to create the ark of the covenant, and He filled them with wisdom, intelligence, and creativity.

Then the LORD spoke to Moses, saying: "See, I have called by name Bezalel the son of Uri, the son of Hur, of the tribe of Judah. And I have filled him with the Spirit of God, in wisdom, in understanding, in knowledge, and in all manner of workmanship, to design artistic works, to work in gold, in silver, in bronze, in cutting jewels for setting, in carving wood, and to work in all manner of workmanship. And I, indeed I, have appointed with him Aholiab the son of Ahisamach, of the tribe of Dan; and I have put wisdom in the hearts of all the gifted artisans, that they may make all that I have commanded you."

—EXODUS 31:1–6

After reading these words from the Old Testament, I see God with my own spiritual eyes. I see His abounding love toward His creation, I see His fatherly care and the link between God Himself and the work of His hands. This is the work of the holy God. When all the work was completed, the sons of Israel presented it to Moses:

Thus all the work of the tabernacle of the tent of meeting was finished. And the children of Israel did according to all that the LORD had commanded Moses; so they did...Then Moses looked over all the work, and indeed they had done it; as the Lord had commanded, just so they had done it. And Moses blessed them.

—EXODUS 39:32, 43

God promised the sons of Israel that He would remain among them, that He would open Himself up to them, and that they will be in His presence. When Moses had finished all that God commanded him, God continued speaking about the priests:

And there I will meet with the children of Israel, and the tabernacle shall be sanctified by My glory. So I will consecrate the tabernacle of meeting and the altar. I will also consecrate both Aaron and his sons to minister to Me as priests. I will dwell among the children of Israel and will be their God. And they shall know that I am the LORD their God, who brought them up out of the land of Egypt, that I may dwell among them. I am the LORD their God.

—EXODUS 29:43–46

Then you shall bring Aaron and his sons to the door of the tabernacle of meeting and wash them with water. You shall put the holy garments on Aaron, and anoint him and consecrate him, that he may minister to Me as priest. And you shall bring his sons and clothe them with tunics. You shall anoint them, as you anointed their father, that they may minister to Me as priests; for their anointing shall surely be an everlasting priesthood throughout their generations.

—EXODUS 40:12–15

He put the table in the tabernacle of meeting, on the north side of the tabernacle, outside the veil; and he set the bread in order upon it before the LORD, as the LORD had commanded Moses. He put the lampstand in the tabernacle of meeting, across from the table, on the south side of the tabernacle; and he lit the lamps before the LORD, as the LORD had commanded Moses. He put the gold altar in the tabernacle of meeting in front of the veil; and he burned sweet incense on it, as the

LORD had commanded Moses. He hung up the screen at the door of the tabernacle. And he put the altar of burnt offering before the door of the tabernacle of the tent of meeting, and offered upon it the burnt offering and the grain offering, as the LORD had commanded Moses

—EXODUS 40:22–29

And what God promised, God fulfilled:

Then the cloud covered the tabernacle of meeting, and the glory of the LORD filled the tabernacle. And Moses was not able to enter the tabernacle of meeting, because the cloud rested above it, and the glory of the LORD filled the tabernacle. Whenever the cloud was taken up from above the tabernacle, the children of Israel would go onward in all their journeys. But if the cloud was not taken up, then they did not journey till the day that it was taken up. For the cloud of the LORD was above the tabernacle by day, and fire was over it by night, in the sight of all the house of Israel, throughout all their journeys.

—EXODUS 40:34–38

The sons of Israel were not obedient to their Creator; they did not fulfill His will. That is why God required the sacrifice for sin. We will now read from the Holy Book to learn what God's will was toward sin offerings:

Now the LORD spoke to Moses, saying, "Speak to the children of Israel, saying: 'If a person sins unintentionally against any of the commandments of the LORD in anything which ought not to be done, and does any of them, if the anointed priest sins, bringing guilt on the people, then let him offer to the LORD for his sin which he has sinned a young bull without blemish as a sin offering. He shall bring the bull to the door of the tabernacle of meeting before the LORD, lay his hand on the bull's head, and kill the bull before the LORD. Then the anointed priest shall take some of the bull's blood and bring it to the tabernacle of meeting. The priest shall dip his finger in the blood and sprinkle some of the blood seven times before the LORD, in front of the veil of the sanctuary. And the priest shall put some of the blood on the horns of the altar of sweet incense before the LORD, which is in the tabernacle of meeting; and he shall pour the remaining blood of the bull at the base of the altar of the burnt offering, which is at the door of the tabernacle of meeting. He shall take from it all the fat of the bull as the sin offering. The fat that covers the entrails and all the fat which is on the entrails, the two kidneys and the fat that is on them by the flanks, and the fatty lobe attached to the liver above the kidneys, he shall remove, as it was taken from the bull of the sacrifice of the peace offering; and the priest shall burn them on the altar of the burnt offering. But the bull's hide and all its flesh, with its head and legs, its entrails and offal—the whole bull he shall carry outside the camp to a clean place, where the ashes are poured out, and burn it on wood with fire; where the ashes are poured out it shall be burned.'"

—LEVITICUS 4:1–12

This is the sacrifice for sin. This is how the sons of Israel were cleansed of their sins, and what God required of them in order to forgive them:

And according to the law almost all things are purified with blood, and without shedding of blood there is no remission.

—HEBREWS 9:22

"For the life of the flesh is in the blood, and I have given it to you upon the altar to make atonement for your souls; for it is the blood that makes atonement for the soul." Therefore I said to the children of Israel, "No one among you shall eat blood, nor shall any stranger who dwells among you eat blood."

—LEVITICUS 17:11–12

I think it will be good for me, and also for my dear reader, to read God's will in its fullest. Let's read Leviticus:

And the LORD said to Moses: "Tell Aaron your brother not to come at just any time into the Holy Place inside the veil, before the mercy seat which is on the ark, lest he die; for I will appear in the cloud above the mercy seat. Thus Aaron shall come into the Holy Place: with the blood of a young bull as a sin offering, and of a ram as a burnt offering. He shall put the holy linen tunic and the linen trousers on his body; he shall be girded with a linen sash, and with the linen turban he shall be attired. These are holy garments. Therefore he shall wash his body in water, and put them on. And he shall take from the congregation of the children of Israel two kids of the goats as a sin offering, and one ram as a burnt offering. Aaron shall offer the bull as a sin offering, which is for himself, and make atonement for himself and for his house. He shall take the two goats and present them before the LORD at the door of the tabernacle of meeting. Then Aaron shall cast lots for the two goats: one lot for the Lord and the other lot for the scapegoat. And Aaron shall bring the goat on which the LORD's lot fell, and offer it as a sin offering. But the goat on which the lot fell to be the scapegoat shall be presented alive before the LORD, to make atonement upon it, and to let it go as the scapegoat into the wilderness. And Aaron shall bring the bull of the sin offering, which is for himself, and make atonement for himself and for his house, and shall kill the bull as the sin offering which is for himself. Then he shall take a censer full of burning coals of fire from the altar before the LORD, with his hands full of sweet incense beaten fine, and bring it inside the veil. And he shall put the incense on the fire before the LORD, that the cloud of incense may cover the mercy seat that is on the Testimony, lest he die. He shall take some of the blood of the bull and sprinkle it with his finger on the mercy seat on the east side; and before the mercy seat he shall sprinkle some of the blood with his finger seven times. Then he shall kill the goat of the sin offering, which is for the people, bring its blood inside the veil, do with that blood as he did with the blood of the bull, and sprinkle it on the mercy seat and before the mercy seat. So he shall make atonement for the Holy Place, because of the uncleanness of the children of Israel, and because of their transgressions, for all their sins; and so he shall do for the tabernacle of meeting which remains among them in the midst of their uncleanness. There shall be no man in the tabernacle of meeting when he goes in to make atonement in the Holy Place, until he comes out, that he may make atonement for himself, for his household, and for all the assembly of Israel. And he shall go out to the altar that is before the LORD, and make atonement for it, and shall take some of the blood of the bull and some of the blood of the goat, and put it on the horns of the altar all around. Then he shall sprinkle some of the blood on it with his finger seven times, cleanse it, and consecrate it from the uncleanness of the children of Israel. And when he has made an end of atoning for the Holy Place, the tabernacle of meeting, and the altar, he shall bring the live goat. Aaron shall lay both his hands on the head of the live goat, confess over it all the iniquities of the children of Israel, and all their transgressions, concerning all their sins, putting them on the head of the goat, and shall send it away into the wilderness by the hand of a suitable man. The goat shall bear on itself all their iniquities to an uninhabited land; and he shall release the goat in the wilderness. Then Aaron shall come into the tabernacle of meeting, shall take off the linen garments which he put on when he went into the Holy Place, and shall leave them there. And he shall wash his body with water in a holy place, put on his garments, come out and offer his burnt offering and the burnt offering of the people, and make atonement for himself and for the people. The fat of the sin offering he shall burn on the altar. And he who released the goat as the scapegoat shall wash his clothes and bathe his body in water, and afterward he may come into the camp. The bull for the sin offering and the goat for the sin offering, whose blood was brought in to make atonement in the Holy Place, shall be carried outside the camp. And they shall burn in the fire their skins, their flesh, and their offal. Then he who burns them shall wash his clothes and bathe his body in water, and afterward he may come into the camp. This shall be a statute forever for you: In the seventh month, on the tenth day of the month, you shall afflict your souls, and do no work at all, whether a native of your own country or a stranger who dwells among you. For on that day the priest shall make atonement for you, to cleanse you, that you may be clean from all your sins before the Lord. It is a sabbath of solemn rest for you, and you shall afflict your souls. It is a statute forever."

—Leviticus 16:2–31

This is the command God laid down in the Old Testament: a living thing must die, must be killed, so that its blood could be shed for the forgiveness of the sins of man. In the Old Testament, animals were sacrificed. The sons of Israel brought bulls without blemish into the tent of the covenant where their blood was poured out. The animals were killed, and the books, priests, and the entire nation were sprinkled with blood. In this way God forgave the sins of man. During this cleansing time, the glory of God entered this place. Everything there was holy and clean. The presence of God was among the people, God forgave them their sins, and through this means, God had fellowship with His creation, with His chosen nation. This is the Old Testament.

For people who have never read the Old Testament, as I am sure there are many, God's will, commandments, and ceremonies might be incomprehensible and strange. But we must understand that these are God's decisions. God commanded the following: there is no forgiveness for sin without blood, and the consequence of sin is death. God is a Creator, and a Creator has full rights to lay down any law He wants, any He desires for His creation, His people. He is the Commander. But we, His people, are His creation and fulfillers of His will. God desires our obedience.

> But indeed, O man, who are you to reply against God? Will the thing formed say to him who formed it, "Why have you made me like this?" Does not the potter have power over the clay, from the same lump to make one vessel for honor and another for dishonor?
> —Romans 9:20–21

> But we are all like an unclean thing, And all our righteousnesses are like filthy rags; We all fade as a leaf, And our iniquities, like the wind, Have taken us away.... But now, O Lord, You are our Father; We are the clay, and You our potter; And all we are the work of Your hand. Do not be furious, O

135

LORD, Nor remember iniquity forever; Indeed, please look—
we all are Your people!
—ISAIAH 64:6, 8–9

Doubtless You are our Father, Though Abraham was ignorant
of us, And Israel does not acknowledge us. You, O LORD, are
our Father; Our Redeemer from Everlasting is Your name.
—ISAIAH 63:16

God is all-powerful. He is the Creator of heaven and Earth,
of you and me, dear reader. And we cannot contradict Him or
ask Him why He set one command and not another. We can only
fulfill His will with humility and meekness. God does not force
anyone to fulfill His commands; He only lays them out for us. And
we have full freedom, the right of choice, to be obedient and fulfill
these laws or to violate them. When we fulfill His commands
exactly, we express our trust, our faith, and our belief in God, and
also our love toward our Creator. But when we do not fulfill His
commands exactly, when we alter them by adding or subtracting,
then we neglect His words and do not express our complete faith
in our Creator.

Dear reader, engage yourself in these words and see what results
from your faith and obedience:

If you walk in My statutes and keep My commandments, and
perform them, then I will give you rain in its season, the land
shall yield its produce, and the trees of the field shall yield
their fruit. Your threshing shall last till the time of vintage,
and the vintage shall last till the time of sowing; you shall
eat your bread to the full, and dwell in your land safely. I
will give peace in the land, and you shall lie down, and none
will make you afraid; I will rid the land of evil beasts, and
the sword will not go through your land. You will chase your

enemies, and they shall fall by the sword before you. Five of you shall chase a hundred, and a hundred of you shall put ten thousand to flight; your enemies shall fall by the sword before you. For I will look on you favorably and make you fruitful, multiply you and confirm My covenant with you. You shall eat the old harvest, and clear out the old because of the new. I will set My tabernacle among you, and My soul shall not abhor you. I will walk among you and be your God, and you shall be My people.

—LEVITICUS 26:3–12

God does not force anyone to fulfill His will and commands. But people who neglect His words find themselves in circumstances that lead to unpleasant consequences.

But if you do not obey Me, and do not observe all these commandments, and if you despise My statutes, or if your soul abhors My judgments, so that you do not perform all My commandments, but break My covenant, I also will do this to you: I will even appoint terror over you, wasting disease and fever which shall consume the eyes and cause sorrow of heart. And you shall sow your seed in vain, for your enemies shall eat it. I will set My face against you, and you shall be defeated by your enemies. Those who hate you shall reign over you, and you shall flee when no one pursues you. And after all this, if you do not obey Me, then I will punish you seven times more for your sins. I will break the pride of your power; I will make your heavens like iron and your earth like bronze. And your strength shall be spent in vain; for your land shall not yield its produce, nor shall the trees of the land yield their fruit. Then, if you walk contrary to Me, and are not willing to obey Me, I will bring on you seven times more plagues, according to your sins. I will also send wild beasts among you, which shall rob you of your children, destroy your livestock, and make you few in number; and your highways shall be desolate. And if by these things you are not reformed by Me, but walk contrary to Me, then I also will walk contrary to you, and I will punish you yet seven times for your sins. And I will bring a sword against you that will execute the vengeance of the covenant; when you are gathered together within your cities I will send pestilence among you; and you shall be delivered into the hand of the enemy. When I have cut off your supply of bread, ten women shall bake your bread in one oven, and they shall bring back your bread by weight, and you shall eat and not be satisfied. And after all this, if you do not obey Me, but walk contrary to Me, then I also will walk contrary to you in fury; and I, even I, will chastise you seven times for your sins.

—LEVITICUS 26:14–28

Sometimes in life we are met with only failure. Obstacles and barriers meet us from every direction. Every door we knock on is closed. Everything we begin ends in defeat. Everything falls through our hands. There are no positive results. People seek reasons in these circumstances. They look for someone to blame, for the guilty party and the culprit. They may first blame the nation's rulers; then maybe their boss, neighbors, and family. The husband blames the wife and the wife blames the husband. But where is the root of these failures? Where can you find the cause of these defeats? I think that many readers will agree with me: you have to find the cause in yourself. You have to check your spiritual situation against God's Constitution. You have to discover what your attitude is towards your Creator, His will, and His commands. You must look into the mirror: the Bible. You have to humbly open your heart and soul and talk with your Creator. Only in this way can you find the true sources of all the setbacks and failures in your life.

When I re-read these words, and especially the Old Testament, I see God's concern for His creation. I see God's love toward man. I see God's desire to have fellowship with His nation, the work of His hands, and I experience great joy. If any of my dear readers have read the Old Testament, then it is good to read it again to remind yourself of all the details. But if you haven't read the Old Testament, then I strongly encourage and ask you to read and receive God's blessings that are always outgoing from these words.

The Old Testament is a prototype of the New Testament, and each citizen of this Earth should know that both testaments pertain to each person—to you, dear reader, and to me. I have hope that all who read the story of the Old Testament will receive God's richest blessings, because anyone who reads it will hear the voice of God, his or her very own Creator.

From what we have read of the Old Testament, we can see that God always selected people to fulfill His work here on Earth. God chose Abraham, Isaac, and Jacob. He chose Joseph to save Egypt, his father and brothers, and other nations from starvation. God chose Moses to free the sons of Israel from Egypt.

> So the LORD spoke to Moses face to face, as a man speaks to his friend.
> —EXODUS 33:11

God seeks and selects people even today with whom He wants to speak through His Word, the Holy Scriptures. He wants us to use His Word as armor when we do His will here on Earth. I think that many people reading this book will hear the words of his or her Maker and respond as the prophet Isaiah did in the following passage:

Also I heard the voice of the Lord, saying: "Whom shall I send, And who will go for Us?" Then I said, "Here am I! Send me."
—Isaiah 6:8

I also join with those who agree and pray:

Use me, Lord, for Your glory, that I may be a witness of You and Your great works to those who have not had the opportunity to hear of You. I desire to serve You, Lord, all my life until You call me home.

14

LORD GOD CONSIDERS MAN'S OPINION

ASTRONOMERS HAVE SAID THAT OUR PLANET EARTH, IN comparison with the universe, appears as a period at the end of a sentence. People who have traveled to the moon and those who have traveled in outer space say that when they looked at Earth from such a great distance it appeared as though they were looking at an object the size of a poppy seed. And this is true. Our planet is very, very small in comparison to the universe.

Now, when we look at man and compare him with the universe, mankind can say that there is no comparison. There aren't enough words to describe the comparison. But almighty God, the Creator of heaven and Earth, remembers this man. He is concerned about him, He loves him, and even considers his opinion. Who can write of the Creator's love for His creation? This love cannot be described by the human mind. God hasn't changed, even today. He is the same. He loves you, dear reader, and He loves me, too.

The nation of Israel, regardless of the fact that they witnessed so many miracles and received so many blessings from God, still sinned in front of their Creator. When Moses walked up onto Mount Sinai and didn't return for a period of time, the sons of Israel began to grumble and complain, and they committed great sin before their Maker. God the Father, after seeing great unrighteousness and the sin from His people, decided to rid them from the face of the earth. The Word of God teaches us that God is love, that He loves people, part of His Creation, with boundless love. It teaches us that God is patient, but it also teaches us that God is a powerful judge. Although He loves people, He hates sin.

> For the LORD your God is a consuming fire, a jealous God.
> —DEUTERONOMY 4:24

Moses' pleas caused our good God to change His intentions.

> Now when the people saw that Moses delayed coming down from the mountain, the people gathered together to Aaron, and said to him, "Come, make us gods that shall go before us; for as for this Moses, the man who brought us up out of the land of Egypt, we do not know what has become of him." And Aaron said to them, "Break off the golden earrings which are in the ears of your wives, your sons, and your daughters, and bring them to me." So all the people broke off the golden earrings which were in their ears, and brought them to Aaron. And he received the gold from their hand, and he fashioned it with an engraving tool, and made a molded calf. Then they said, "This is your god, O Israel, that brought you out of the land of Egypt!" So when Aaron saw it, he built an altar before it. And Aaron made a proclamation and said, "Tomorrow is a feast to the LORD." Then they rose early on the next day, offered burnt offerings, and brought peace offerings; and the people sat down to eat and drink, and rose up to play. And the LORD said to Moses, "Go, get down! For your people whom

you brought out of the land of Egypt have corrupted themselves. They have turned aside quickly out of the way which I commanded them. They have made themselves a molded calf, and worshiped it and sacrificed to it, and said, 'This is your god, O Israel, that brought you out of the land of Egypt!'" And the LORD said to Moses, "I have seen this people, and indeed it is a stiff-necked people! Now therefore, let Me alone, that My wrath may burn hot against them and I may consume them. And I will make of you a great nation." Then Moses pleaded with the LORD his God, and said: "LORD, why does Your wrath burn hot against Your people whom You have brought out of the land of Egypt with great power and with a mighty hand? Why should the Egyptians speak, and say, 'He brought them out to harm them, to kill them in the mountains, and to consume them from the face of the earth'? Turn from Your fierce wrath, and relent from this harm to Your people. Remember Abraham, Isaac, and Israel, Your servants, to whom You swore by Your own self, and said to them, 'I will multiply your descendants as the stars of heaven; and all this land that I have spoken of I give to your descendants, and they shall inherit it forever.'" So the LORD relented from the harm which He said He would do to His people. And Moses turned and went down from the mountain, and the two tablets of the Testimony were in his hand. The tablets were written on both sides; on the one side and on the other they were written. Now the tablets were the work of God, and the writing was the writing of God engraved on the tablets. And when Joshua heard the noise of the people as they shouted, he said to Moses, "There is a noise of war in the camp." But he said: "It is not the noise of the shout of victory, Nor the noise of the cry of defeat, But the sound of singing I hear." So it was, as soon as he came near the camp, that he saw the calf and the dancing. So Moses' anger became hot, and he cast the tablets out of his hands and broke them at the foot of the mountain. Then he took the calf which they had made, burned it in the fire, and ground it to powder; and he scattered it on the water and made the children of Israel drink it.

—Exodus 32:1–20

God listened to Moses' plea and changed His intentions, which He, in His fury, decided to carry out. This is a miracle. From the above, we see that our good God considers the opinion of the man who fully trusts Him.

We will now read the story of Hezekiah, and we will see God's attitude toward people:

> In those days Hezekiah was sick and near death. And Isaiah the prophet, the son of Amoz, went to him and said to him, "Thus says the LORD: 'Set your house in order, for you shall die and not live.'" Then Hezekiah turned his face toward the wall, and prayed to the LORD, and said, "Remember now, O LORD, I pray, how I have walked before You in truth and with a loyal heart, and have done what is good in Your sight." And Hezekiah wept bitterly. And the word of the LORD came to Isaiah, saying, "Go and tell Hezekiah, 'Thus says the LORD, the God of David your father: "I have heard your prayer, I have seen your tears; surely I will add to your days fifteen years. I will deliver you and this city from the hand of the king of Assyria, and I will defend this city."' And this is the sign to you from the LORD, that the LORD will do this thing which He has spoken: Behold, I will bring the shadow on the sundial, which has gone down with the sun on the sundial of Ahaz, ten degrees backward." So the sun returned ten degrees on the dial by which it had gone down. This is the writing of Heze-

kiah king of Judah, when he had been sick and had recovered from his sickness: I said, "In the prime of my life I shall go to the gates of Sheol; I am deprived of the remainder of my years." I said, "I shall not see Yah, The LORD in the land of the living; I shall observe man no more among the inhabitants of the world. My life span is gone, Taken from me like a shepherd's tent; I have cut off my life like a weaver. He cuts me off from the loom; From day until night You make an end of me. I have considered until morning—Like a lion, So He breaks all my bones; From day until night You make an end of me. Like a crane or a swallow, so I chattered; I mourned like a dove; My eyes fail from looking upward. O LORD, I am oppressed; Undertake for me! What shall I say? He has both spoken to me, And He Himself has done it. I shall walk carefully all my years In the bitterness of my soul. O Lord, by these things men live; And in all these things is the life of my spirit; So You will restore me and make me live. Indeed it was for my own peace That I had great bitterness; But You have lovingly delivered my soul from the pit of corruption, For You have cast all my sins behind Your back. For Sheol cannot thank You, Death cannot praise You; Those who go down to the pit cannot hope for Your truth. The living, the living man, he shall praise You, As I do this day; The father shall make known Your truth to the children. The LORD was ready to save me; Therefore we will sing my songs with stringed instruments All the days of our life, in the house of the LORD." Now Isaiah had said, "Let them take a lump of figs, and apply it as a poultice on the boil, and he shall recover."

—ISAIAH 38:1–21

Many of us go through tough times in our lives. And it serves us well to take an example from Hezekiah, to bow our knees and in bitter tears come to God and present Him our needs and ask for His help. Our good God saw the tears and heard Hezekiah's cry. He also sees my tears, and yours too. He will hear my cry, and yours too, dear reader. The Creator loves His creation with unending and boundless love. He waits for me, and for you, dear reader. He wants to hear my needs, and yours, too. And all we must do is come to Him, open our hearts, and present our problems.

My dear and highly respected atheist found the stories from the Old Testament were very interesting. He saw the tight connection between God and His creation. Reading the above, he saw the great love that God has for people. He saw that God wants to be in the presence of His people. He wants to forgive his or her sins and have fellowship with each person. My reader especially liked that God considers our opinions, that He treasures our opinions and that He, the Creator, listens to the suggestions of His creation.

After reading through some of the Old Testament, you may recognize yourself to be a sinner as well. You may not personally have fellowship with your Creator.

We all have sinned, and we all need our sins to be forgiven! What should we do? How can we receive forgiveness? How can we have fellowship with God? The answers can be found only on the pages of God's Holy Constitution, the Bible. We will travel further on these pages and we will find the answers.

15

THE CHANGE OF
THE OLD COVENANT

ENTURIES PASSED AND OUR GREAT AND MIGHTY GOD decided to change the covenant. He decided to change His laws and commands, which affect the chosen people and all of mankind. God can only change the Law, which He established. No man, big or small; no church, popular or unpopular; no government workers, in large or small countries, can change the commands of God or God's laws. The laws can be changed only by the One who established them—God the Father, the Creator of life and all of mankind. The pages of the Holy Scriptures describe these changes, which God spoke of Himself:

"Behold, the days are coming, says the LORD, when I will make a new covenant with the house of Israel and with the house of Judah—not according to the covenant that I made with their fathers in the day that I took them by the hand to lead them out of the land of Egypt, My covenant which they broke, though I was a husband to them, says the LORD. But this is the covenant that I will make with the house of Israel after those days, says the LORD: I will put My law in their minds, and write it on their hearts; and I will be their God, and they shall be My people. No more shall every man teach his neighbor, and every man his brother, saying, 'Know the LORD,' for they all shall know Me, from the least of them to the greatest of them, says the LORD. For I will forgive their iniquity, and their sin I will remember no more." Thus says the LORD, Who gives the sun for a light by day, The ordinances of the moon and the stars for a light by night, Who disturbs the sea, And its waves roar (The LORD of hosts is His name).

—JEREMIAH 31:31–35

This event is confirmed in the letter to the Hebrews:

For if that first covenant had been faultless, then no place would have been sought for a second…In that He says, "A new covenant," He has made the first obsolete. Now what is becoming obsolete and growing old is ready to vanish away.

—HEBREWS 8:7, 13

God the Father even decided to change the innermost being of man. Let's see what He said:

I will give you a new heart and put a new spirit within you; I will take the heart of stone out of your flesh and give you a heart of flesh. I will put My Spirit within you and cause you to walk in My statutes, and you will keep My judgments and do them.

—EZEKIEL 36:26–27

"The Redeemer will come to Zion, And to those who turn from transgression in Jacob," Says the LORD. "As for Me," says the

LORD, "this is My covenant with them: My Spirit who is upon you, and My words which I have put in your mouth, shall not depart from your mouth, nor from the mouth of your descendants, nor from the mouth of your descendants' descendants," says the Lord, "from this time and forevermore."

—ISAIAH 59:20–21

We have read from the first pages of the Holy Scriptures that when Satan entered into a serpent and tempted Eve to eat from the tree of knowledge, God said to the serpent, "And I will put enmity between you and the woman, and between your seed and her Seed; He shall bruise your head, and you shall bruise His heel" (Gen. 3:15). These are the words God spoke about the coming of the Messiah. With these words, God laid down the plan of salvation for all of mankind. We will read about the Seed from the woman in the following pages of this book.

God the Father set out to change the covenant. He decided to send a Messiah into this Earth, onto this land. Let's read from the psalm of David about this coming event:

Sacrifice and offering You did not desire; My ears You have opened. Burnt offering and sin offering You did not require. Then I said, "Behold, I come; In the scroll of the book it is written of me. I delight to do Your will, O my God, And Your law is within my heart." I have proclaimed the good news of righteousness In the great assembly; Indeed, I do not restrain my lips, O LORD, You Yourself know. I have not hidden Your righteousness within my heart; I have declared Your faithfulness and Your salvation; I have not concealed Your lovingkindness and Your truth From the great assembly.

—PSALM 40:6–10

These are the words of the Messiah Himself, who came to this Earth to fulfill the will of our Lord, God the Father. The prophet Isaiah wrote the following of the coming Messiah:

> There shall come forth a Rod from the stem of Jesse, And a Branch shall grow out of his roots. The Spirit of the LORD shall rest upon Him, The Spirit of wisdom and understanding, The Spirit of counsel and might, The Spirit of knowledge and of the fear of the LORD. His delight is in the fear of the LORD, And He shall not judge by the sight of His eyes, Nor decide by the hearing of His ears; But with righteousness He shall judge the poor, And decide with equity for the meek of the earth; He shall strike the earth with the rod of His mouth, And with the breath of His lips He shall slay the wicked. Righteousness shall be the belt of His loins, And faithfulness the belt of His waist.
>
> —ISAIAH 11:1–5

We will now hear what God, the Creator of heaven and Earth, said of the coming Messiah:

> "Behold! My Servant whom I uphold, My Elect One in whom My soul delights! I have put My Spirit upon Him; He will bring forth justice to the Gentiles. He will not cry out, nor raise His voice, Nor cause His voice to be heard in the street. A bruised reed He will not break, And smoking flax He will not quench; He will bring forth justice for truth. He will not fail nor be discouraged, Till He has established justice in the earth; And the coastlands shall wait for His law." Thus says God the LORD, Who created the heavens and stretched them out, Who spread forth the earth and that which comes from it, Who gives breath to the people on it, And spirit to those who walk on it: "I, the LORD, have called You in righteous-

ness, And will hold Your hand; I will keep You and give You as a covenant to the people, As a light to the Gentiles, To open blind eyes, To bring out prisoners from the prison, Those who sit in darkness from the prison house. I am the LORD, that is My name; And My glory I will not give to another, Nor My praise to carved images. Behold, the former things have come to pass, And new things I declare; Before they spring forth I tell you of them."

—ISAIAH 42:1–9

Again, we will read the words of the Messiah. He speaks clearly of Himself and His work here on Earth.

The Lord GOD has given Me The tongue of the learned, That I should know how to speak A word in season to him who is weary. He awakens Me morning by morning, He awakens My ear To hear as the learned. The Lord GOD has opened My ear; And I was not rebellious, Nor did I turn away. I gave My back to those who struck Me, And My cheeks to those who plucked out the beard; I did not hide My face from shame and spitting. For the Lord GOD will help Me; Therefore I will not be disgraced; Therefore I have set My face like a flint, And I know that I will not be ashamed. He is near who justifies Me; Who will contend with Me? Let us stand together. Who is My adversary? Let him come near Me. Surely the Lord GOD will help Me; Who is he who will condemn Me? Indeed they will all grow old like a garment; The moth will eat them up.

—ISAIAH 50:4–9

God the Father speaks in detail through the prophet Isaiah about how the Messiah would come into this Earth.

> Therefore the Lord Himself will give you a sign: Behold, the virgin shall conceive and bear a Son, and shall call His name Immanuel. Curds and honey He shall eat, that He may know to refuse the evil and choose the good.
>
> —ISAIAH 7:14–15

The name Immanuel means "God with us." This name describes His very being and His mission here on Earth.

Isaiah was a great prophet. Many of the teachings in the New Testament originated in Isaiah's prophecy, for example, the teachings about the Word of God, the teachings about the redemption of mankind through the Messiah, and the teachings about justification through faith and mercy. No other prophet in the Old Testament presented such exact descriptions of the Messiah and the details of His kingdom as Isaiah did. To agree with the prophesies of Isaiah, the Messiah must have been born from a virgin and must have had a name that described His inner being and His mission.

> For unto us a Child is born, Unto us a Son is given; And the government will be upon His shoulder. And His name will be called Wonderful, Counselor, Mighty God, Everlasting Father, Prince of Peace. Of the increase of His government and peace There will be no end, Upon the throne of David and over His kingdom, To order it and establish it with judgment and justice From that time forward, even forever. The zeal of the Lord of hosts will perform this.
>
> —ISAIAH 9:6–7

God the Father also speaks the following of the coming Messiah:

> Behold, My Servant shall deal prudently; He shall be exalted and extolled and be very high. Just as many were astonished

at you, So His visage was marred more than any man, And His form more than the sons of men; So shall He sprinkle many nations. Kings shall shut their mouths at Him; For what had not been told them they shall see, And what they had not heard they shall consider.

—Isaiah 52:13–15

The prophet Isaiah writes about the trials and tribulations that the coming Messiah would go through and what price He must pay for the sins of mankind—for my sins and for yours, dear reader. The Messiah was not only to be a Savior, but also our Healer. As it is written, "By His stripes we are healed" (Isa. 53:5).

The Messiah would also be an advocate for me and for you, dear reader.

Who has believed our report? And to whom has the arm of the Lord been revealed? For He shall grow up before Him as a tender plant, And as a root out of dry ground. He has no form or comeliness; And when we see Him, There is no beauty that we should desire Him. He is despised and rejected by men, A Man of sorrows and acquainted with grief. And we hid, as it were, our faces from Him; He was despised, and we did not esteem Him. Surely He has borne our griefs And carried our sorrows; Yet we esteemed Him stricken, Smitten by God, and afflicted. But He was wounded for our transgressions, He was bruised for our iniquities; The chastisement for our peace was upon Him, And by His stripes we are healed. All we like sheep have gone astray; We have turned, every one, to his own way; And the Lord has laid on Him the iniquity of us all. He was oppressed and He was afflicted, Yet He opened not His mouth; He was led as a lamb to the slaughter, And as a sheep before its shearers is silent, So He opened not His mouth. He was taken from prison and from judgment, And who will declare His generation? For He was cut off from the land of the living; For the transgressions of My people He was stricken. And they made His grave with the wicked—But with the rich at His death, Because He had done no violence, Nor was any deceit in His mouth. Yet it pleased the LORD to bruise Him; He has put Him to grief. When You make His soul an offering for sin, He shall see His seed, He shall prolong His days, And the pleasure of the LORD shall prosper in His hand. He shall see the labor of His soul, and be satisfied. By His knowledge My righteous Servant shall justify many, For He shall bear their iniquities. Therefore I will divide Him a portion with the great, And He shall divide the spoil with the strong, Because He poured out His soul unto death, And He was numbered with the transgressors, And He bore the sin of many, And made intercession for the transgressors.

—ISAIAH 53:1–12

Dear reader, maybe you have read these words for the first time in your life. Maybe these words seem strange. I ask you not to let yourself be discouraged. Do not stop reading this book, because this book found its way into your hands for a purpose. God, the Creator of the universe, remembers you, loves you, and desires to acquaint Himself with you. He wants to have personal fellowship with you. God the Father wants to present a plan of salvation for you, the plan that He prepared for mankind, His creation. And you are the work of His hands. Read these words many, many times. Even if you do not understand them, do not stop reading them. After reading these words, remember that you have read the words of the living God, your Creator. He will open up great revelations to you, and you will see how much of God there is in His words, and further, you will also see His truth.

PART II

The New Testament

16

THE COMING
OF THE MESSIAH—
THE BIRTH OF JESUS CHRIST

W HEN HEAVEN AND Earth WERE READY FOR ONE OF THE greatest events God planned for His people, the time of fulfillment arrived and God sent the Messiah. The Messiah left the heavens, the throne, and the glory, and came to Earth. He came with a plan: to save the sinful human race, reconcile people with their Creator, and establish the kingdom of God here on Earth.

The Messiah is God. He came to Earth in human flesh as the Son of God. He left the heavens to create a path to heaven for us. In the Old Testament, the Messiah was called Immanuel, which means "God with us." The Old Testament projects into the future and says that He would also be called "Wonderful, Counselor, and Mighty God." In the New Testament, the Messiah is called the King of kings, Lord of lords, Alpha and Omega, the beginning and the end, the Word of God, the Redeemer, the Savior, Jesus Christ. (See Rev. 21:6, 17:14, 19:13; Luke 2:11; Rom. 11:26; Job 19:25.)

God came to Earth and assumed a human body. The prophecy that a virgin would give birth was recorded in the Old Testament, and the fulfillment of the prophecy in Christ is described in the New Testament. God the Father appointed a virgin who did not have a husband to bring this event to pass. The young woman, Mary, was a deep believer and was blessed among women.

> Now in the sixth month the angel Gabriel was sent by God to a city of Galilee named Nazareth, to a virgin betrothed to a man whose name was Joseph, of the house of David. The virgin's name was Mary. And having come in, the angel said to her, "Rejoice, highly favored one, the Lord is with you; blessed are you among women!" But when she saw him, she was troubled at his saying, and considered what manner of greeting this was. Then the angel said to her, "Do not be afraid, Mary, for you have found favor with God. And behold, you will conceive in your womb and bring forth a Son, and shall call His name Jesus. He will be great, and will be called the Son of the Highest; and the Lord God will give Him the throne of His father David. And He will reign over the house of Jacob forever, and of His kingdom there will be no end." Then Mary said to the angel, "How can this be, since I do not know a man?" And the angel answered and said to her, "The Holy Spirit will come upon you, and the power of the Highest will overshadow you; therefore, also, that Holy One who is to be born will be called the Son of God. Now indeed, Elizabeth your relative has also conceived a son in her old age; and this is now the sixth month for her who was called barren. For with God nothing will be impossible." Then Mary said, "Behold the maidservant of the Lord! Let it be to me according to your word." And the angel departed from her.
>
> —LUKE 1:26–38

We see that Mary was a deep believer of God and she believed in God. She didn't shy away from this task, and she didn't fear. She didn't say, "What will my relatives think of me? What will those who surround me say? They can judge me and even stone me. And what will Joseph, my fiancé, say when he finds out that I am pregnant?" These thoughts apparently did not enter Mary's mind. She accepted God's news, God's will, without any sorrow and fear because she trusted God and deeply believed in the coming of the Messiah. Mary, very humbly, called herself a servant of God and displayed great readiness to accept and fulfill God's will. She was ready and did not think of the difficulties and consequences that would arise. She decided to accept God's plan to give birth to and raise a Man who would be called the Son of the Highest and whose kingdom would be unending.

Let's see about Joseph, Mary's fiancé, and what his reaction was when he found out that his future wife was pregnant. Joseph was a righteous man who thought in human terms, and he decided to release her of her obligations to him so that they could separate quietly. But God foresaw this. He knew Joseph's thoughts and spoke to Joseph through His angel.

> Now the birth of Jesus Christ was as follows: After His mother Mary was betrothed to Joseph, before they came together, she was found with child of the Holy Spirit. Then Joseph her husband, being a just man, and not wanting to make her a public example, was minded to put her away secretly. But while he thought about these things, behold, an angel of the Lord appeared to him in a dream, saying, "Joseph, son of David, do not be afraid to take to you Mary your wife, for that which is conceived in her is of the Holy Spirit. And she will bring forth a Son, and you shall call His name Jesus, for He will save His people from their sins." So all this was done that it might be

fulfilled which was spoken by the Lord through the prophet, saying: "Behold, the virgin shall be with child, and bear a Son, and they shall call His name Immanuel," which is translated, "God with us." Then Joseph, being aroused from sleep, did as the angel of the Lord commanded him and took to him his wife, and did not know her till she had brought forth her firstborn Son. And he called His name Jesus.

—Matthew 1:18–25

Luke describes the coming of Christ, as it had been foretold in the Old Testament. Angels announced the birth of Christ to the entire planet. They told the world about the happiness to come, of the birth of the Savior: Jesus Christ. The multitude of the heavenly hosts praised Jesus Christ and proclaimed peace and goodwill to all men on Earth.

And it came to pass in those days that a decree went out from Caesar Augustus that all the world should be registered. This census first took place while Quirinius was governing Syria. So all went to be registered, everyone to his own city. Joseph also went up from Galilee, out of the city of Nazareth, into Judea, to the city of David, which is called Bethlehem, because he was of the house and lineage of David, to be registered with Mary, his betrothed wife, who was with child. So it was, that while they were there, the days were completed for her to be delivered. And she brought forth her firstborn Son, and wrapped Him in swaddling cloths, and laid Him in a manger, because there was no room for them in the inn. Now there were in the same country shepherds living out in the fields, keeping watch over their flock by night. And behold, an angel of the Lord stood before them, and the glory of the Lord shone around them, and they were greatly afraid. Then the angel said to them, "Do not be afraid, for behold, I bring you good tidings of great joy which will be to all people. "For there is born to you this day in the city of David a Savior, who is Christ the Lord. "And this will be the sign to you: You will find a Babe wrapped in swaddling cloths, lying in a manger." And suddenly there was with the angel a multitude of the heavenly host praising God and saying: "Glory to God in the highest, and on Earth peace, goodwill toward men!" So it was, when the angels had gone away from them into heaven, that the shepherds said to one another, "Let us now go to Bethlehem and see this thing that has come to pass, which the Lord has made known to us." And they came with haste and found Mary and Joseph, and the Babe lying in a manger. Now when they had seen Him, they made widely known the saying which was told them concerning this Child. And all those who heard it marveled at those things which were told them by the shepherds. But Mary kept all these things and pondered them in her heart. Then the shepherds returned, glorifying and praising God for all the things that they had heard and seen, as it was told them.

—LUKE 2:1–20

Mary and Joseph believed deeply in God and were aware of the Law of Moses and therefore fulfilled all the ceremonies that related to newborns. A righteous man, Simeon, proclaimed the salvation that existed in the young Child who was to bring revelation to the Gentiles and be the glory of the nation of Israel. The prophetess Anna, when she saw the baby, praised God and declared that He was the fulfillment of God's will, that He was the Messiah.

And when eight days were completed for the circumcision of the Child, His name was called Jesus, the name given by the angel before He was conceived in the womb. Now when the days of her purification according to the law of Moses were completed, they brought Him to Jerusalem to present Him to the Lord (as it is written in the law of the Lord, "Every male who opens the womb shall be called holy to the LORD"), and to offer a sacrifice according to what is said in the law of the Lord, "A pair of turtledoves or two young pigeons." And behold, there was a man in Jerusalem whose name was Simeon, and this man was just and devout, waiting for the Consolation of Israel, and the Holy Spirit was upon him. And it had been revealed to him by the Holy Spirit that he would not see death before he had seen the Lord's Christ. So he came by the Spirit into the temple. And when the parents brought in the Child Jesus, to do for Him according to the custom of the law, he took Him up in his arms and blessed God and said: "Lord, now You are letting Your servant depart in peace, According to Your word; For my eyes have seen Your salvation Which You have prepared before the face of all peoples, A light to bring revelation to the Gentiles, And the glory of Your people Israel." And Joseph and His mother marveled at those things which were spoken of Him. Then Simeon blessed them, and said to Mary His mother, "Behold, this Child is destined for the fall and rising of many in Israel, and for a sign which will be spoken against (yes, a sword will pierce through your own soul also), that the thoughts of many hearts may be revealed." Now there was one, Anna, a prophetess, the daughter of Phanuel, of the tribe of Asher. She was of a great age, and had lived with a husband seven years from her virginity; and this woman was a widow of about eighty-four years, who did not depart from the temple, but served God with fastings and prayers night and day. And coming in that instant she gave thanks to the Lord, and spoke of Him to all those who looked for redemption in Jerusalem.

—LUKE 2:21–38

Despite the fact that Jesus was born in such poor circumstances, we see that the news of His birth spread throughout all of Judea and beyond its borders. The news even reached the farthest of places. Not only were angels, the armies of heaven, proclaiming great joy to the world, peace on Earth, and goodwill toward men, but even a star spoke about the birth of a King to the great wise men of the time. The news of Jesus' birth shook the throne of Herod and all of Israel also.

Now after Jesus was born in Bethlehem of Judea in the days of Herod the king, behold, wise men from the East came to Jerusalem, saying, "Where is He who has been born King of the Jews? For we have seen His star in the East and have come to worship Him." When Herod the king heard this, he was troubled, and all Jerusalem with him. And when he had gathered all the chief priests and scribes of the people together, he inquired of them where the Christ was to be born. So they said to him, "In Bethlehem of Judea, for thus it is written by the prophet: 'But you, Bethlehem, in the land of Judah, Are not the least among the rulers of Judah; For out of you shall come a Ruler Who will shepherd My people Israel.'" Then Herod, when he had secretly called the wise men, determined from them what time the star appeared. And he sent them to Bethlehem and said, "Go and search carefully for the young Child, and when you have found Him, bring back word to me, that I may come and worship Him also." When they heard the king, they departed; and behold, the star which they had seen in the East went before them, till it came and stood over where the young Child was. When they saw the star, they rejoiced with exceedingly great joy. And when they had come into the house, they saw the young Child with Mary His mother, and fell down and worshiped Him. And when they had opened their treasures, they presented gifts to Him: gold, frankincense, and myrrh. Then, being divinely warned in a dream that they should not return to Herod, they departed for their own country another way.

—MATTHEW 2:1–12

It is interesting to note that the wise men did not bow down to Mary, His mother, when they came into the house. They also did not worship the father. Instead, they bowed before the Child. The wise men knew that this was Messiah, God in human flesh, and they knew that only God deserves praise. But when the wise men did not return to Herod to give him a report of where the Child was, Herod grew fearful of losing his political power. In hopes of eliminating his competition, Herod ordered all male children less than two years of age to be killed. But God the Father looked after His Son, and through an angel He told Joseph how to save the life of the Child. Joseph, a righteous and God-fearing man, fulfilled the orders of the angels.

Now when they had departed, behold, an angel of the Lord appeared to Joseph in a dream, saying, "Arise, take the young Child and His mother, flee to Egypt, and stay there until I bring you word; for Herod will seek the young Child to destroy Him." When he arose, he took the young Child and His mother by night and departed for Egypt, and was there until the death of Herod, that it might be fulfilled which was spoken by the Lord through the prophet, saying, "Out of Egypt I called My Son." Then Herod, when he saw that he was deceived by the wise men, was exceedingly angry; and he sent forth and put to death all the male children who were in Bethlehem and in all its districts, from two years old and under, according to the time which he had determined from the wise men. Then was fulfilled what was spoken by Jeremiah the prophet, saying: "A voice was heard in Ramah, Lamentation, weeping, and great mourning, Rachel weeping for her children, Refusing to be comforted, Because they are no more." Now when Herod was dead, behold, an angel of the Lord appeared in a dream to Joseph in Egypt, saying, "Arise, take the young Child and His mother, and go to the land of Israel, for those who sought the young Child's life are dead." Then he arose, took the young Child and His mother, and came into the land of Israel. But when he heard that Archelaus was reigning over Judea instead of his father Herod, he was afraid to go there. And being warned by God in a dream, he turned aside into the region of Galilee. And he came and dwelt in a city called Nazareth, that it might be fulfilled which was spoken by the prophets, "He shall be called a Nazarene."

—MATTHEW 2:13–23

Time passed, and the Child grew. It is written on the pages of the Holy Bible that at age twelve, Jesus went with His parents to Jerusalem for the Feast of the Passover. As His parents began the journey home, He remained there in the temple among the teachers and displayed great wisdom to them with both His questions and answers.

And the Child grew and became strong in spirit, filled with wisdom; and the grace of God was upon Him. His parents went to Jerusalem every year at the Feast of the Passover. And when He was twelve years old, they went up to Jerusalem according to the custom of the feast. When they had finished the days, as they returned, the Boy Jesus lingered behind in Jerusalem. And Joseph and His mother did not know it; but supposing Him to have been in the company, they went a day's journey, and sought Him among their relatives and acquaintances. So when they did not find Him, they returned to Jerusalem, seeking Him. Now so it was that after three days they found Him in the temple, sitting in the midst of the teachers, both listening to them and asking them questions. And all who heard Him were astonished at His understanding and answers. So when they saw Him, they were amazed; and His mother said to Him, "Son, why have You done this to us? Look, Your father and I have sought You anxiously." And He said to them, "Why did you seek Me? Did you not know that I must be about My Father's business?" But they did not understand the statement which He spoke to them. Then He went down with them and came to Nazareth, and was subject to them, but His mother kept all these things in her heart. And Jesus increased in wisdom and stature, and in favor with God and men.

—LUKE 2:40–52

Mary, His mother, knew that He was the Messiah and treasured all this in her heart.

And Mary said: "My soul magnifies the Lord, And my spirit has rejoiced in God my Savior. For He has regarded the lowly state of His maidservant; For behold, henceforth all generations will call me blessed. For He who is mighty has done great things for me, And holy is His name. And His mercy is on those who fear Him From generation to generation.

—LUKE 1:46–50

Mary, chosen by God and blessed among women, was given a great assignment: to give birth and to raise the Son of Man, Messiah, the Savior—Jesus Christ. Mary respectfully accepted this task and thanked God for everything He had done for her.

17

BAPTISM AND THE
START OF GOD'S WORK

A S WE READ IN THE PREVIOUS CHAPTER, JESUS STAYED IN the temple as His parents returned home after the Passover. And when they came searching for Him, He asked why they did not know that He was about His Father's business. Aside from this event, the Bible does not record events about Jesus' life from the time of His birth up to age thirty. John the Baptist publicly presented Jesus as the One who would baptize with the Holy Spirit and with fire. John also baptized Jesus Christ with water, and afterwards, John heard a voice from above saying, "This is my Son, whom I love." John the Baptist also presented Jesus as the Lamb of God, the One who was taking the sins of the world upon Himself.

In those days John the Baptist came preaching in the wilderness of Judea, and saying, "Repent, for the kingdom of heaven is at hand!" For this is he who was spoken of by the prophet Isaiah, saying: "The voice of one crying in the wilderness:

'Prepare the way of the LORD; Make His paths straight.'"
Now John himself was clothed in camel's hair, with a leather
belt around his waist; and his food was locusts and wild
honey. Then Jerusalem, all Judea, and all the region around
the Jordan went out to him and were baptized by him in the
Jordan, confessing their sins. But when he saw many of the
Pharisees and Sadducees coming to his baptism, he said to
them, "Brood of vipers! Who warned you to flee from the
wrath to come? Therefore bear fruits worthy of repentance,
and do not think to say to yourselves, 'We have Abraham as
our father.' For I say to you that God is able to raise up children to Abraham from these stones. And even now the ax is
laid to the root of the trees. Therefore every tree which does
not bear good fruit is cut down and thrown into the fire. I
indeed baptize you with water unto repentance, but He who
is coming after me is mightier than I, whose sandals I am not
worthy to carry. He will baptize you with the Holy Spirit and
fire. His winnowing fan is in His hand, and He will thor-
oughly clean out His threshing floor, and gather His wheat
into the barn; but He will burn up the chaff with unquench-
able fire." Then Jesus came from Galilee to John at the Jordan
to be baptized by him. And John tried to prevent Him, saying,
"I need to be baptized by You, and are You coming to me?"
But Jesus answered and said to him, "Permit it to be so now,
for thus it is fitting for us to fulfill all righteousness." Then
he allowed Him. When He had been baptized, Jesus came up
immediately from the water; and behold, the heavens were
opened to Him, and He saw the Spirit of God descending like
a dove and alighting upon Him. And suddenly a voice came
from heaven, saying, "This is My beloved Son, in whom I am
well pleased."

—MATTHEW 3:1–17

In the Gospel of John, the author presents God as the Word that has been in the beginning, the Word that was with God and was God. This Word became flesh and dwelt among the people of God in order to reveal God to them. The author also presents Him (the Word) as the Creator of everything, as the life that gives light to all of Creation. The author presents the fact that whoever shall believe in Him and His name will be given the right to be called the sons of God.

> In the beginning was the Word, and the Word was with God, and the Word was God. He was in the beginning with God. All things were made through Him, and without Him nothing was made that was made. In Him was life, and the life was the light of men. And the light shines in the darkness, and the darkness did not comprehend it. There was a man sent from God, whose name was John. This man came for a witness, to bear witness of the Light, that all through him might believe. He was not that Light, but was sent to bear witness of that Light. That was the true Light which gives light to every man coming into the world. He was in the world, and the world was made through Him, and the world did not know Him. He came to His own, and His own did not receive Him. But as many as received Him, to them He gave the right to become children of God, to those who believe in His name: who were born, not of blood, nor of the will of the flesh, nor of the will of man, but of God. And the Word became flesh and dwelt among us, and we beheld His glory, the glory as of the only begotten of the Father, full of grace and truth. John bore witness of Him and cried out, saying, "This was He of whom I said, 'He who comes after me is preferred before me, for He was before me.'" And of His fullness we have all received, and grace for grace. For the law was given through Moses, but

grace and truth came through Jesus Christ. No one has seen God at any time. The only begotten Son, who is in the bosom of the Father, He has declared Him. Now this is the testimony of John, when the Jews sent priests and Levites from Jerusalem to ask him, "Who are you?" He confessed, and did not deny, but confessed, "I am not the Christ." And they asked him, "What then? Are you Elijah?" He said, "I am not." "Are you the Prophet?" And he answered, "No." Then they said to him, "Who are you, that we may give an answer to those who sent us? What do you say about yourself?" He said: "I am 'The voice of one crying in the wilderness: "Make straight the way of the LORD,"' as the prophet Isaiah said." Now those who were sent were from the Pharisees. And they asked him, saying, "Why then do you baptize if you are not the Christ, nor Elijah, nor the Prophet?" John answered them, saying, "I baptize with water, but there stands One among you whom you do not know. It is He who, coming after me, is preferred before me, whose sandal strap I am not worthy to loose." These things were done in Bethabara beyond the Jordan, where John was baptizing. The next day John saw Jesus coming toward him, and said, "Behold! The Lamb of God who takes away the sin of the world! This is He of whom I said, 'After me comes a Man who is preferred before me, for He was before me.' I did not know Him; but that He should be revealed to Israel, therefore I came baptizing with water." And John bore witness, saying, "I saw the Spirit descending from heaven like a dove, and He remained upon Him. I did not know Him, but He who sent me to baptize with water said to me, 'Upon whom you see the Spirit descending, and remaining on Him, this is He who baptizes with the Holy Spirit.' And I have seen and testified that this is the Son of God." Again, the next day, John stood with two of his disciples. And looking at Jesus as He walked, he said, "Behold the Lamb of God!"

—JOHN 1:1–36

After the baptism, Jesus was tempted by Satan. One interesting question remains for me, and I think for the reader also: why was Jesus tempted? Maybe it was because the Messiah chose the human path, became the Son of Man, and was under the laws of man. But the question of why He was tempted isn't as important as the fact that He overcame all temptations without sinning. Jesus heroically responded to Satan with words from the scriptures, and He overcame him. All of Satan's temptations can be overcome with this mighty power: the Word of God.

Then Jesus, being filled with the Holy Spirit, returned from the Jordan and was led by the Spirit into the wilderness, being tempted for forty days by the devil. And in those days He ate nothing, and afterward, when they had ended, He was hungry. And the devil said to Him, "If You are the Son of God, command this stone to become bread." But Jesus answered him, saying, "It is written, 'Man shall not live by bread alone, but by every word of God.'" Then the devil, taking Him up on a high mountain, showed Him all the kingdoms of the world in a moment of time. And the devil said to Him, "All this authority I will give You, and their glory; for this has been delivered to me, and I give it to whomever I wish. Therefore, if You will worship before me, all will be Yours." And Jesus answered and said to him, "Get behind Me, Satan! For it is written, 'You shall worship the Lord your God, and Him only you shall serve.'" Then he brought Him to Jerusalem, set Him on the pinnacle of the temple, and said to Him, "If You are the Son of God, throw Yourself down from here. For it is written:

'He shall give His angels charge over you, To keep you,' and, 'In their hands they shall bear you up, Lest you dash your foot against a stone.'" And Jesus answered and said to him, "It has been said, 'You shall not tempt the Lord your God.'" Now when the devil had ended every temptation, he departed from Him until an opportune time. Then Jesus returned in the power of the Spirit to Galilee, and news of Him went out through all the surrounding region.

—LUKE 4:1–14

Jesus Christ began His work when He was thirty years old. Once, when He came to Nazareth, the place where He was raised, He went into a synagogue and read the following:

"The Spirit of the LORD is upon Me, Because He has anointed Me To preach the gospel to the poor; He has sent Me to heal the brokenhearted, To proclaim liberty to the captives And recovery of sight to the blind, To set at liberty those who are oppressed; To proclaim the acceptable year of the LORD." Then He closed the book, and gave it back to the attendant and sat down. And the eyes of all who were in the synagogue were fixed on Him. And He began to say to them, "Today this Scripture is fulfilled in your hearing." So all bore witness to Him, and marveled at the gracious words which proceeded out of His mouth. And they said, "Is this not Joseph's son?"

—LUKE 4:18–22

As we see, the prediction of the prophet Isaiah was fulfilled.

Then Jesus Christ gathered twelve followers, whom He called the apostles.

Simon, whom He also named Peter, and Andrew his brother; James and John; Philip and Bartholomew; Matthew and

> Thomas; James the son of Alphaeus, and Simon called the
> Zealot; Judas the son of James, and Judas Iscariot who also
> became a traitor.
> —LUKE 6:14–16

Jesus taught people in synagogues and was admired by all. He walked throughout the cities, proclaimed the gospel of Christ, and healed people from many diseases.

> When evening had come, they brought to Him many who
> were demon-possessed. And He cast out the spirits with a
> word, and healed all who were sick, that it might be fulfilled
> which was spoken by Isaiah the prophet, saying: "He Himself
> took our infirmities And bore our sicknesses."
> —MATTHEW 8:16–17

Jesus raised the dead, cleansed the cursed, healed the possessed, and fed the hungry. The masses followed Jesus and His apostles everywhere they went, and Jesus tried to teach them.

My dear and very attentive reader, with great interest, wants to know what Jesus taught the people. What themes, what aspects of human life did His words touch? We will read together one of Jesus' sermons to see what the Son of God taught His people while on this planet:

> And seeing the multitudes, He went up on a mountain, and
> when He was seated His disciples came to Him. Then He
> opened His mouth and taught them, saying: "Blessed are the
> poor in spirit, For theirs is the kingdom of heaven. Blessed are
> those who mourn, For they shall be comforted. Blessed are the
> meek, For they shall inherit the earth. Blessed are those who
> hunger and thirst for righteousness, For they shall be filled.
> Blessed are the merciful, For they shall obtain mercy. Blessed

are the pure in heart, For they shall see God. Blessed are the peacemakers, For they shall be called sons of God. Blessed are those who are persecuted for righteousness' sake, For theirs is the kingdom of heaven. Blessed are you when they revile and persecute you, and say all kinds of evil against you falsely for My sake. Rejoice and be exceedingly glad, for great is your reward in heaven, for so they persecuted the prophets who were before you. You are the salt of the earth; but if the salt loses its flavor, how shall it be seasoned? It is then good for nothing but to be thrown out and trampled underfoot by men. You are the light of the world. A city that is set on a hill cannot be hidden. Nor do they light a lamp and put it under a basket, but on a lampstand, and it gives light to all who are in the house. Let your light so shine before men, that they may see your good works and glorify your Father in heaven. Do not think that I came to destroy the Law or the Prophets. I did not come to destroy but to fulfill. For assuredly, I say to you, till heaven and earth pass away, one jot or one tittle will by no means pass from the law till all is fulfilled. Whoever therefore breaks one of the least of these commandments, and teaches men so, shall be called least in the kingdom of heaven; but whoever does and teaches them, he shall be called great in the kingdom of heaven. For I say to you, that unless your righteousness exceeds the righteousness of the scribes and Pharisees, you will by no means enter the kingdom of heaven. You have heard that it was said to those of old, 'You shall not murder, and whoever murders will be in danger of the judgment.' But I say to you that whoever is angry with his brother without a cause shall be in danger of the judgment. And whoever says to his brother, 'Raca!' shall be in danger of the council. But whoever says, 'You fool!' shall be in danger of hell fire. Therefore if you bring your gift to the altar, and there remember that your brother has something against you, leave your gift there before the altar, and go your way. First be reconciled to your brother, and then come and offer your gift. Agree with your adversary quickly, while you are on the way with him, lest your adversary deliver you to the judge, the judge hand you over to the officer, and you be thrown into prison. Assuredly, I say to you, you will by no means get out of there till you have paid the last penny. You have heard that it was said to those of old, 'You shall not commit adultery.' But I say to you that whoever looks at a woman to lust for her has already committed adultery with her in his heart. If your right eye causes you to sin, pluck it out and cast it from you; for it is more profitable for you that one of your members perish, than for your whole body to be cast into hell. And if your right hand causes you to sin, cut it off and cast it from you; for it is more profitable for you that one of your members perish, than for your whole body to be cast into hell. Furthermore it has been said, 'Whoever divorces his wife, let him give her a certificate of divorce.' But I say to you that whoever divorces his wife for any reason except sexual immorality causes her to commit adultery; and whoever marries a woman who is divorced commits adultery. Again you have heard that it was said to those of old, 'You shall not swear falsely, but shall perform your oaths to the Lord.' But I say to you, do not swear at all: neither by heaven, for it is God's throne; nor by the earth, for it is His footstool; nor by Jerusalem, for it is the city of the great King. Nor shall you swear by your head, because you cannot make one hair white or black. But let your 'Yes' be 'Yes,' and your 'No,' 'No.' For whatever is more than these is from the evil one. You have heard that it was said, 'An eye for an eye and a tooth for a tooth.' But I tell you not to resist an evil person. But whoever slaps you on your right cheek, turn the other to him also. If anyone wants to sue you and take away your tunic, let him have your cloak also. And whoever compels you to go one mile, go with him two. Give to him who asks you, and from him who wants to borrow from you do not turn away. You have heard that it was said, 'You shall love your neighbor and hate your enemy.' But I say to you, love your enemies, bless those who curse you, do good to those who hate you, and pray for those who spitefully use you and persecute you, that you may be sons of your Father in heaven; for He makes His sun rise on the evil and on the good, and sends rain on the just and on the unjust. For if you love those who love you, what reward have you? Do not even the tax collectors do the same? And if you greet your brethren only, what do you do more than others? Do not even the tax collectors do so? Therefore you shall be perfect, just as your Father in heaven is perfect.

—MATTHEW 5:1–48

"Take heed that you do not do your charitable deeds before men, to be seen by them. Otherwise you have no reward from your Father in heaven. Therefore, when you do a charitable deed, do not sound a trumpet before you as the hypocrites do in the synagogues and in the streets, that they may have glory from men. Assuredly, I say to you, they have their reward. But when you do a charitable deed, do not let your left hand know what your right hand is doing, that your charitable deed may be in secret; and your Father who sees in secret will Himself reward you openly. And when you pray, you shall not be like the hypocrites. For they love to pray standing in the synagogues and on the corners of the streets, that they may be seen by men. Assuredly, I say to you, they have their reward. But you, when you pray, go into your room, and when you have shut your door, pray to your Father who is in the secret place; and your Father who sees in secret will reward you openly. And when you pray, do not use vain repetitions as the heathen do. For they think that they will be heard for their many words. Therefore do not be like them. For your Father knows the things you have need of before you ask Him. In this manner, therefore, pray: Our Father in heaven, Hallowed be Your name. Your kingdom come. Your will be done On earth as it is in heaven. Give us this day our daily bread. And forgive us our debts, As we forgive our debtors. And do not lead us into temptation, But deliver us from the evil one. For Yours is the kingdom and the power and the glory forever. Amen. For if you forgive men their trespasses, your heavenly Father will also forgive you. But if you do not forgive men their trespasses, neither will your Father forgive your trespasses. Moreover, when you fast, do not be like the hypocrites, with a sad countenance. For they disfigure their faces that they may appear to men to be fasting. Assuredly, I say to you, they have their reward. But you, when you fast, anoint your head and wash your face, so that you do not appear to men to be fasting, but to your Father who is in the secret place; and your Father who sees in secret will reward you openly. Do not lay up for yourselves treasures on earth, where moth and rust destroy and where thieves break in and steal; but lay up for yourselves treasures in heaven, where neither moth nor rust destroys and where thieves do not break in and steal. For where your treasure is, there your heart will be also. The lamp of the body is the eye. If therefore your eye is good, your whole body will be full of light. But if your eye is bad, your whole body will be full of darkness. If therefore the light that is in you is darkness, how great is that darkness! No one can serve two masters; for either he will hate the one and love the other, or else he will be loyal to the one and despise the other. You cannot serve God and mammon. Therefore I say to you, do not worry about your life, what you will eat or what you will drink; nor about your body, what you will put on. Is not life more than food and the body more than clothing? Look at the birds of the air, for they neither sow nor reap nor gather into barns; yet your heavenly Father feeds them. Are you not of more value than they? Which of you by worrying can add one cubit to his stature? So why do you worry about clothing? Consider the lilies of the field, how they grow: they neither toil nor spin; and yet I say to you that even Solomon in all his glory was not arrayed like one of these. Now if God so clothes the grass of the field, which today is, and tomorrow is thrown into the oven, will He not much more clothe you, O you of little faith? Therefore do not worry, saying, 'What shall we eat?' or 'What shall we drink?' or 'What shall we wear?' For after all these things the Gentiles seek. For your heavenly Father knows that you need all these things. But seek first the kingdom of God and His righteousness, and all these things shall be added to you. Therefore do not worry about tomorrow, for tomorrow will worry about its own things. Sufficient for the day is its own trouble.

—MATTHEW 6:1–34

"Judge not, that you be not judged. For with what judgment you judge, you will be judged; and with the measure you use, it will be measured back to you. And why do you look at the speck in your brother's eye, but do not consider the plank in your own eye? Or how can you say to your brother, 'Let me remove the speck from your eye'; and look, a plank is in your own eye? Hypocrite! First remove the plank from your own eye, and then you will see clearly to remove the speck from your brother's eye. Do not give what is holy to the dogs; nor cast your pearls before swine, lest they trample them under their feet, and turn and tear you in pieces. Ask, and it will be given to you; seek, and you will find; knock, and it will be opened to you. For everyone who asks receives, and he who seeks finds, and to him who knocks it will be opened. Or what man is there among you who, if his son asks for bread, will give him a stone? Or if he asks for a fish, will he give him a serpent? If you then, being evil, know how to give good gifts to your children, how much more will your Father who is in heaven give good things to those who ask Him! Therefore, whatever you want men to do to you, do also to them, for this is the Law and the Prophets. Enter by the narrow gate; for wide is the gate and broad is the way that leads to destruction, and there are many who go in by it. Because narrow is the gate and difficult is the way which leads to life, and there are few who find it. Beware of false prophets, who come to you in sheep's clothing, but inwardly they are ravenous wolves. You will know them by their fruits. Do men gather grapes from thornbushes or figs from thistles? Even so, every good tree bears good fruit, but a bad tree bears bad fruit. A good tree cannot bear bad fruit, nor can a bad tree bear good fruit. Every tree that does not bear good fruit is cut down and thrown into the fire. Therefore by their fruits you will know them. Not everyone who says to Me, 'Lord, Lord,' shall enter the kingdom of heaven, but he who does the will of My Father in heaven. Many will say to Me in that day, 'Lord, Lord, have we not prophesied in Your name, cast out demons in Your name, and done many wonders in Your name?' And then I will declare to them, 'I never knew you; depart from Me, you who practice lawlessness!' Therefore whoever hears these sayings of Mine, and does them, I will liken him to a wise man who built his house on the rock: and the rain descended, the floods came, and the winds blew and beat on that house; and it did not fall, for it was founded on the rock. But everyone who hears these sayings of Mine, and does not do them, will be like a foolish man who built his house on the sand: and the rain descended, the floods came, and the winds blew and beat on that house; and it fell. And great was its fall." And so it was, when Jesus had ended these sayings, that the people were astonished at His teaching, for He taught them as one having authority, and not as the scribes.

—MATTHEW 7:1–29

The teachings of Jesus Christ are of great interest. During His time on Earth, He preached the kingdom of God and called people to repentance. He also performed many great miracles.

And Jesus went about all Galilee, teaching in their synagogues, preaching the gospel of the kingdom, and healing all kinds of sickness and all kinds of disease among the people. Then His fame went throughout all Syria; and they brought to Him all sick people who were afflicted with various diseases and torments, and those who were demon-possessed, epileptics, and paralytics; and He healed them. Great multitudes followed Him—from Galilee, and from Decapolis, Jerusalem, Judea, and beyond the Jordan.

—MATTHEW 4:23–25

After one of His sermons, Jesus Christ healed a man who had stood far from those gathered to listen to Jesus. The man had a contagious disease, and it was forbidden for such people to be among the healthy.

When He had come down from the mountain, great multitudes followed Him. And behold, a leper came and worshiped Him, saying, "Lord, if You are willing, You can make me clean." Then

> Jesus put out His hand and touched him, saying, "I am willing; be cleansed." Immediately his leprosy was cleansed.
>
> —MATTHEW 8:1–3

Let's travel through the pages of the New Testament to learn more about the work of the Son of God and His actions here on Earth:

> When Jesus departed from there, two blind men followed Him, crying out and saying, "Son of David, have mercy on us!" And when He had come into the house, the blind men came to Him. And Jesus said to them, "Do you believe that I am able to do this?" They said to Him, "Yes, Lord." Then He touched their eyes, saying, "According to your faith let it be to you." And their eyes were opened. And Jesus sternly warned them, saying, "See that no one knows it." But when they had departed, they spread the news about Him in all that country.
>
> —MATTHEW 9:27–31

> And again He entered Capernaum after some days, and it was heard that He was in the house. Immediately many gathered together, so that there was no longer room to receive them, not even near the door. And He preached the word to them. Then they came to Him, bringing a paralytic who was carried by four men. And when they could not come near Him because of the crowd, they uncovered the roof where He was. So when they had broken through, they let down the bed on which the paralytic was lying. When Jesus saw their faith, He said to the paralytic, "Son, your sins are forgiven you." And some of the scribes were sitting there and reasoning in their hearts, "Why does this Man speak blasphemies like this? Who can forgive sins but God alone?" But immediately, when Jesus perceived in His spirit that they reasoned thus within themselves, He said to them, "Why do you reason about these things in your hearts?

Which is easier, to say to the paralytic, 'Your sins are forgiven you,' or to say, 'Arise, take up your bed and walk'? But that you may know that the Son of Man has power on earth to forgive sins"—He said to the paralytic, "I say to you, arise, take up your bed, and go to your house." Immediately he arose, took up the bed, and went out in the presence of them all, so that all were amazed and glorified God, saying, "We never saw anything like this!" Then He went out again by the sea; and all the multitude came to Him, and He taught them.

—MARK 2:1–13

Now a certain woman had a flow of blood for twelve years, and had suffered many things from many physicians. She had spent all that she had and was no better, but rather grew worse. When she heard about Jesus, she came behind Him in the crowd and touched His garment. For she said, "If only I may touch His clothes, I shall be made well." Immediately the fountain of her blood was dried up, and she felt in her body that she was healed of the affliction. And Jesus, immediately knowing in Himself that power had gone out of Him, turned around in the crowd and said, "Who touched My clothes?" But His disciples said to Him, "You see the multitude thronging You, and You say, 'Who touched Me?'" And He looked around to see her who had done this thing. But the woman, fearing and trembling, knowing what had happened to her, came and fell down before Him and told Him the whole truth. And He said to her, "Daughter, your faith has made you well. Go in peace, and be healed of your affliction."

—MARK 5:25–34

Again, departing from the region of Tyre and Sidon, He came through the midst of the region of Decapolis to the Sea of Galilee. Then they brought to Him one who was deaf and had an impediment in his speech, and they begged Him to put His hand on him. And He took him aside from the multitude, and put His fingers in his ears, and He spat and touched his tongue. Then, looking up to heaven, He sighed, and said to him, "Ephphatha," that is, "Be opened." Immediately his ears were opened, and the impediment of his tongue was loosed, and he spoke plainly. Then He commanded them that they should tell no one; but the more He commanded them, the more widely they proclaimed it. And they were astonished beyond measure, saying, "He has done all things well. He makes both the deaf to hear and the mute to speak."

—MARK 7:31–37

Now they came to Jericho. As He went out of Jericho with His disciples and a great multitude, blind Bartimaeus, the son of Timaeus, sat by the road begging. And when he heard that it was Jesus of Nazareth, he began to cry out and say, "Jesus, Son of David, have mercy on me!" Then many warned him to be quiet; but he cried out all the more, "Son of David, have mercy on me!" So Jesus stood still and commanded him to be called. Then they called the blind man, saying to him, "Be of good cheer. Rise, He is calling you." And throwing aside his garment, he rose and came to Jesus. So Jesus answered and said to him, "What do you want Me to do for you?" The blind man said to Him, "Rabboni, that I may receive my sight." Then Jesus said to him, "Go your way; your faith has made you well." And immediately he received his sight and followed Jesus on the road.

—MARK 10:46–52

Now it happened as He went to Jerusalem that He passed through the midst of Samaria and Galilee. Then as He entered a certain village, there met Him ten men who were lepers, who stood afar off. And they lifted up their voices and said, "Jesus,

Master, have mercy on us!" So when He saw them, He said to them, "Go, show yourselves to the priests." And so it was that as they went, they were cleansed. And one of them, when he saw that he was healed, returned, and with a loud voice glorified God, and fell down on his face at His feet, giving Him thanks. And he was a Samaritan. So Jesus answered and said, "Were there not ten cleansed? But where are the nine? Were there not any found who returned to give glory to God except this foreigner?" And He said to him, "Arise, go your way. Your faith has made you well."

—LUKE 17:11–19

Now as Jesus passed by, He saw a man who was blind from birth. And His disciples asked Him, saying, "Rabbi, who sinned, this man or his parents, that he was born blind?" Jesus answered, "Neither this man nor his parents sinned, but that the works of God should be revealed in him. I must work the works of Him who sent Me while it is day; the night is coming when no one can work. As long as I am in the world, I am the light of the world." When He had said these things, He spat on the ground and made clay with the saliva; and He anointed the eyes of the blind man with the clay. And He said to him, "Go, wash in the pool of Siloam" (which is translated, Sent). So he went and washed, and came back seeing. Therefore the neighbors and those who previously had seen that he was blind said, "Is not this he who sat and begged?" Some said, "This is he." Others said, "He is like him." He said, "I am he." Therefore they said to him, "How were your eyes opened?" He answered and said, "A Man called Jesus made clay and anointed my eyes and said to me, 'Go to the pool of Siloam and wash.' So I went and washed, and I received sight."

—JOHN 9:1–11

The news of Jesus spread quickly on the earth. Seeing His works and listening to His teachings, many people believed in Him and followed Him. The Pharisees and the scribes did not like this, and they observed Him to see if He would heal on the Sabbath. If He did, they hoped to accuse Him of breaking the Law.

> At that time Jesus went through the grainfields on the Sabbath. And His disciples were hungry, and began to pluck heads of grain and to eat. And when the Pharisees saw it, they said to Him, "Look, Your disciples are doing what is not lawful to do on the Sabbath!" But He said to them, "Have you not read what David did when he was hungry, he and those who were with him: how he entered the house of God and ate the showbread which was not lawful for him to eat, nor for those who were with him, but only for the priests? Or have you not read in the law that on the Sabbath the priests in the temple profane the Sabbath, and are blameless? Yet I say to you that in this place there is One greater than the temple. But if you had known what this means, 'I desire mercy and not sacrifice,' you would not have condemned the guiltless. For the Son of Man is Lord even of the Sabbath." Now when He had departed from there, He went into their synagogue. And behold, there was a man who had a withered hand. And they asked Him, saying, "Is it lawful to heal on the Sabbath?"—that they might accuse Him. Then He said to them, "What man is there among you who has one sheep, and if it falls into a pit on the Sabbath, will not lay hold of it and lift it out? Of how much more value then is a man than a sheep? Therefore it is lawful to do good on the Sabbath." Then He said to the man, "Stretch out your hand." And he stretched it out, and it was restored as whole as the other. Then the Pharisees went out and plotted against Him, how they might destroy

Him. But when Jesus knew it, He withdrew from there. And great multitudes followed Him, and He healed them all.

—MATTHEW 12:1–15

Now He was teaching in one of the synagogues on the Sabbath. And behold, there was a woman who had a spirit of infirmity eighteen years, and was bent over and could in no way raise herself up. But when Jesus saw her, He called her to Him and said to her, "Woman, you are loosed from your infirmity." And He laid His hands on her, and immediately she was made straight, and glorified God. But the ruler of the synagogue answered with indignation, because Jesus had healed on the Sabbath; and he said to the crowd, "There are six days on which men ought to work; therefore come and be healed on them, and not on the Sabbath day." The Lord then answered him and said, "Hypocrite! Does not each one of you on the Sabbath loose his ox or donkey from the stall, and lead it away to water it? So ought not this woman, being a daughter of Abraham, whom Satan has bound—think of it—for eighteen years, be loosed from this bond on the Sabbath?" And when He said these things, all His adversaries were put to shame; and all the multitude rejoiced for all the glorious things that were done by Him.

—LUKE 13:10–17

After this there was a feast of the Jews, and Jesus went up to Jerusalem. Now there is in Jerusalem by the Sheep Gate a pool, which is called in Hebrew, Bethesda, having five porches. In these lay a great multitude of sick people, blind, lame, paralyzed, waiting for the moving of the water. For an angel went down at a certain time into the pool and stirred up the water; then whoever stepped in first, after the stirring of the water, was made well of whatever disease he had. Now a certain man was there who had an infirmity thirty-eight years. When Jesus saw him lying there, and knew that he already had been in that condition a long time, He said to him, "Do you want to be made well?" The sick man answered Him, "Sir, I have no man to put me into the pool when the water is stirred up; but while I am coming, another steps down before me." Jesus said to him, "Rise, take up your bed and walk." And immediately the man was made well, took up his bed, and walked. And that day was the Sabbath. The Jews therefore said to him who was cured, "It is the Sabbath; it is not lawful for you to carry your bed." He answered them, "He who made me well said to me, 'Take up your bed and walk.'" Then they asked him, "Who is the Man who said to you, 'Take up your bed and walk'?" But the one who was healed did not know who it was, for Jesus had withdrawn, a multitude being in that place. Afterward Jesus found him in the temple, and said to him, "See, you have been made well. Sin no more, lest a worse thing come upon you." The man departed and told the Jews that it was Jesus who had made him well. For this reason the Jews persecuted Jesus, and sought to kill Him, because He had done these things on the Sabbath. 17 But Jesus answered them, "My Father has been working until now, and I have been working." Therefore the Jews sought all the more to kill Him, because He not only broke the Sabbath, but also said that God was His Father, making Himself equal with God.

—John 5:1–18

Not only were there many sick among the general population, but disease also struck the home of Jesus' disciple Peter.

Now when Jesus had come into Peter's house, He saw his wife's mother lying sick with a fever. So He touched her hand, and the fever left her. And she arose and served them. When evening had come, they brought to Him many who were demon-possessed. And He cast out the spirits with a word, and healed all who were sick, that it might be fulfilled which was spoken by Isaiah the prophet, saying: "He Himself took our infirmities And bore our sicknesses."

—MATTHEW 8:14–17

We must give some additional attention to the seventeenth verse, where it is written that the prophecy of Isaiah was fulfilled. The fulfillments of this prophecy support the fact that Jesus Christ is the Messiah. Let's read of some additional miracles that Jesus performed while on Earth:

Jesus departed from there, skirted the Sea of Galilee, and went up on the mountain and sat down there. Then great multitudes came to Him, having with them the lame, blind, mute, maimed, and many others; and they laid them down at Jesus' feet, and He healed them. So the multitude marveled when they saw the mute speaking, the maimed made whole, the lame walking, and the blind seeing; and they glorified the God of Israel.

—MATTHEW 15:29–31

When they had crossed over, they came to the land of Gennesaret and anchored there. And when they came out of the boat, immediately the people recognized Him, ran through that whole surrounding region, and began to carry about on beds those who were sick to wherever they heard He was. Wherever He entered, into villages, cities, or the country, they laid the sick in the marketplaces, and begged Him that they might just touch the hem of His garment. And as many as touched Him were made well.

—MARK 6:53–56

Unclean spirits obeyed Jesus and left the people they inhabited when Jesus commanded them to.

> Then they came to the other side of the sea, to the country of the Gadarenes. And when He had come out of the boat, immediately there met Him out of the tombs a man with an unclean spirit, who had his dwelling among the tombs; and no one could bind him, not even with chains, because he had often been bound with shackles and chains. And the chains had been pulled apart by him, and the shackles broken in pieces; neither could anyone tame him. And always, night and day, he was in the mountains and in the tombs, crying out and cutting himself with stones. When he saw Jesus from afar, he ran and worshiped Him. And he cried out with a loud voice and said, "What have I to do with You, Jesus, Son of the Most High God? I implore You by God that You do not torment me." For He said to him, "Come out of the man, unclean spirit!" Then He asked him, "What is your name?" And he answered, saying, "My name is Legion; for we are many." Also he begged Him earnestly that He would not send them out of the country. Now a large herd of swine was feeding there near the mountains. So all the demons begged Him, saying, "Send us to the swine, that we may enter them." And at once Jesus gave them permission. Then the unclean spirits went out and entered the swine (there were about two thousand); and the herd ran violently down the steep place into the sea, and drowned in the sea. So those who fed the swine fled, and they told it in the city and in the country. And they went out to see what it was that had happened. Then they came to Jesus, and saw the one who had been demon-possessed and had the legion, sitting and clothed and in his right mind. And they were afraid. And those who saw it told them how it happened to him who had been demon-possessed,

and about the swine. Then they began to plead with Him to depart from their region. And when He got into the boat, he who had been demon-possessed begged Him that he might be with Him. However, Jesus did not permit him, but said to him, "Go home to your friends, and tell them what great things the Lord has done for you, and how He has had compassion on you." And he departed and began to proclaim in Decapolis all that Jesus had done for him; and all marveled.

—MARK 5:1–20

From there He arose and went to the region of Tyre and Sidon. And He entered a house and wanted no one to know it, but He could not be hidden. For a woman whose young daughter had an unclean spirit heard about Him, and she came and fell at His feet. The woman was a Greek, a Syro-Phoenician by birth, and she kept asking Him to cast the demon out of her daughter. But Jesus said to her, "Let the children be filled first, for it is not good to take the children's bread and throw it to the little dogs." And she answered and said to Him, "Yes, Lord, yet even the little dogs under the table eat from the children's crumbs." Then He said to her, "For this saying go your way; the demon has gone out of your daughter." And when she had come to her house, she found the demon gone out, and her daughter lying on the bed.

—MARK 7:24–30

And when He came to the disciples, He saw a great multitude around them, and scribes disputing with them. Immediately, when they saw Him, all the people were greatly amazed, and running to Him, greeted Him. And He asked the scribes, "What are you discussing with them?" Then one of the crowd answered and said, "Teacher, I brought You my son, who has a mute spirit. And wherever it seizes him, it throws him down; he foams at the mouth, gnashes his teeth, and becomes rigid. So I spoke to Your disciples, that they should cast it out, but they could not." He answered him and said, "O faithless generation, how long shall I be with you? How long shall I bear with you? Bring him to Me." Then they brought him to Him. And when he saw Him, immediately the spirit convulsed him, and he fell on the ground and wallowed, foaming at the mouth. So He asked his father, "How long has this been happening to him?" And he said, "From childhood. 22 And often he has thrown him both into the fire and into the water to destroy him. But if You can do anything, have compassion on us and help us." Jesus said to him, "If you can believe, all things are possible to him who believes." Immediately the father of the child cried out and said with tears, "Lord, I believe; help my unbelief!" When Jesus saw that the people came running together, He rebuked the unclean spirit, saying to it, "Deaf and dumb spirit, I command you, come out of him and enter him no more!" Then the spirit cried out, convulsed him greatly, and came out of him. And he became as one dead, so that many said, "He is dead." But Jesus took him by the hand and lifted him up, and he arose. And when He had come into the house, His disciples asked Him privately, "Why could we not cast it out?" So He said to them, "This kind can come out by nothing but prayer and fasting."

—MARK 9:14–29

No matter where Jesus Christ turned, He always healed the sick. He did not send away anyone who drew closer to Him. He did not deny, neglect, or exclude anyone. His love and mercy extended to everyone. Not only did Jesus Christ heal, but He raised the dead also.

Now it happened, the day after, that He went into a city called Nain; and many of His disciples went with Him, and a large crowd. And when He came near the gate of the city, behold, a dead man was being carried out, the only son of his mother; and she was a widow. And a large crowd from the city was with her. When the Lord saw her, He had compassion on her and said to her, "Do not weep." Then He came and touched the open coffin, and those who carried him stood still. And He said, "Young man, I say to you, arise." So he who was dead sat up and began to speak. And He presented him to his mother. Then fear came upon all, and they glorified God, saying, "A great prophet has risen up among us"; and, "God has visited His people."

—Luke 7:11–16

Now when Jesus had crossed over again by boat to the other side, a great multitude gathered to Him; and He was by the sea. And behold, one of the rulers of the synagogue came, Jairus by name. And when he saw Him, he fell at His feet and begged Him earnestly, saying, "My little daughter lies at the point of death. Come and lay Your hands on her, that she may be healed, and she will live." So Jesus went with him, and a great multitude followed Him and thronged Him.... While He was still speaking, some came from the ruler of the synagogue's house who said, "Your daughter is dead. Why trouble the Teacher any further?" As soon as Jesus heard the word that was spoken, He said to the ruler of the synagogue, "Do not be afraid; only believe." And He permitted no one to follow Him except Peter, James, and John the brother of James. Then He came to the house of the ruler of the synagogue, and saw a tumult and those who wept and wailed loudly. When He came in, He said to them, "Why make this commotion and weep? The child is not dead, but sleeping." And they ridiculed Him. But when He had put them all outside, He took the father and the mother of the child, and those who were with Him, and entered where the child was lying. Then He took the child by the hand, and said to her, "Talitha, cumi," which is translated, "Little girl, I say to you, arise." Immediately the girl arose and walked, for she was twelve years of age. And they were overcome with great amazement. But He commanded them strictly that no one should know it, and said that something should be given her to eat.

—MARK 5:21–24, 35–43

Now a certain man was sick, Lazarus of Bethany, the town of Mary and her sister Martha. It was that Mary who anointed the Lord with fragrant oil and wiped His feet with her hair, whose brother Lazarus was sick. Therefore the sisters sent to Him, saying, "Lord, behold, he whom You love is sick." When Jesus heard that, He said, "This sickness is not unto death, but for the glory of God, that the Son of God may be glorified through it." Now Jesus loved Martha and her sister and Lazarus. So, when He heard that he was sick, He stayed two more days in the place where He was. Then after this He said to the disciples, "Let us go to Judea again." The disciples said to Him, "Rabbi, lately the Jews sought to stone You, and are You going there again?" Jesus answered, "Are there not twelve hours in the day? If anyone walks in the day, he does not stumble, because he sees the light of this world. But if one walks in the night, he stumbles, because the light is not in him." These things He said, and after that He said to them, "Our friend Lazarus sleeps, but I go that I may wake him up." Then His disciples said, "Lord, if he sleeps he will get well." However, Jesus spoke of his death, but they thought that He was speaking about taking rest in sleep. Then Jesus said to them plainly, "Lazarus is dead. And I am glad for your sakes that I was not there, that you may believe. Nevertheless let us go to him." Then Thomas, who is called the Twin, said to his fellow disciples, "Let us also go, that we may die with Him." So when Jesus came, He found that he had already been in the tomb four days. Now Bethany was near Jerusalem, about two miles away. And many of the Jews had joined the women around Martha and Mary, to comfort them concerning their brother. Now Martha, as soon as she heard that Jesus was coming, went and met Him, but Mary was sitting in the house. Now Martha said to Jesus, "Lord, if You had been here, my brother would not have died. But even now I know that whatever You ask of God, God will give You." Jesus said to her, "Your brother will rise again." Martha said to Him, "I know that he will rise again in the resurrection at the last day." Jesus said to her, "I am the resurrection and the life. He who believes in Me, though he may die, he shall live. And whoever lives and believes in Me shall never die. Do you believe this?" She said to Him, "Yes, Lord, I believe that You are the Christ, the Son of God, who is to come into the world." And when she had said these things, she went her way and secretly called Mary her sister, saying, "The Teacher has come and is calling for you." As soon as she heard that, she arose quickly and came to Him. Now Jesus had not yet come into the town, but was in the place where Martha met Him. Then the Jews who were with her in the house, and comforting her, when they saw that Mary rose up quickly and went out, followed her, saying, "She is going to the tomb to weep there." Then, when Mary came where Jesus was, and saw Him, she fell down at His feet, saying to Him, "Lord, if You had been here, my brother would not have died." Therefore, when Jesus saw her weeping, and the Jews who came with her weeping, He groaned in the spirit and was troubled. And He said, "Where have you laid him?"

They said to Him, "Lord, come and see." Jesus wept. Then the Jews said, "See how He loved him!" And some of them said, "Could not this Man, who opened the eyes of the blind, also have kept this man from dying?" Then Jesus, again groaning in Himself, came to the tomb. It was a cave, and a stone lay against it. Jesus said, "Take away the stone." Martha, the sister of him who was dead, said to Him, "Lord, by this time there is a stench, for he has been dead four days." Jesus said to her, "Did I not say to you that if you would believe you would see the glory of God?" Then they took away the stone from the place where the dead man was lying. And Jesus lifted up His eyes and said, "Father, I thank You that You have heard Me. And I know that You always hear Me, but because of the people who are standing by I said this, that they may believe that You sent Me." Now when He had said these things, He cried with a loud voice, "Lazarus, come forth!" And he who had died came out bound hand and foot with graveclothes, and his face was wrapped with a cloth. Jesus said to them, "Loose him, and let him go." Then many of the Jews who had come to Mary, and had seen the things Jesus did, believed in Him.

—JOHN 11:1–45

Only He who is Life can give life to a dead person. This person is Jesus Christ. All nature, all water, wind, and storms also listened to God and were obedient to Him, just as they are now.

On the same day, when evening had come, He said to them, "Let us cross over to the other side." Now when they had left the multitude, they took Him along in the boat as He was. And other little boats were also with Him. And a great windstorm arose, and the waves beat into the boat, so that it was already filling. But He was in the stern, asleep on a pillow. And they awoke Him and said to Him, "Teacher, do You not care that we are perishing?" Then He arose and rebuked the wind, and said to the sea, "Peace, be still!" And the wind ceased and there was a great calm. But He said to them, "Why are you so fearful? How is it that you have no faith?" And they feared exceedingly, and said to one another, "Who can this be, that even the wind and the sea obey Him!"

—MARK 4:35–41

Immediately Jesus made His disciples get into the boat and go before Him to the other side, while He sent the multitudes away. And when He had sent the multitudes away, He went up on the mountain by Himself to pray. Now when evening came, He was alone there. But the boat was now in the middle of the sea, tossed by the waves, for the wind was contrary. Now in the fourth watch of the night Jesus went to them, walking on the sea. And when the disciples saw Him walking on the sea, they were troubled, saying, "It is a ghost!" And they cried out for fear. But immediately Jesus spoke to them, saying, "Be of good cheer! It is I; do not be afraid." And Peter answered Him and said, "Lord, if it is You, command me to come to You on the water." So He said, "Come." And when Peter had come down out of the boat, he walked on the water to go to Jesus. But when he saw that the wind was boisterous, he was afraid; and beginning to sink he cried out, saying, "Lord, save me!" And immediately Jesus stretched out His hand and caught him, and said to him, "O you of little faith, why did you doubt?" And when they got into the boat, the wind ceased. Then those who were in the boat came and worshiped Him, saying, "Truly You are the Son of God."

—MATTHEW 14:22–33

So it was, as the multitude pressed about Him to hear the word of God, that He stood by the Lake of Gennesaret, and saw two boats standing by the lake; but the fishermen had gone from them and were washing their nets. Then He got into one of the boats, which was Simon's, and asked him to put out a little from the land. And He sat down and taught the multitudes from the boat. When He had stopped speaking, He said to Simon, "Launch out into the deep and let down your nets for a catch." But Simon answered and said to Him, "Master, we have toiled all night and caught nothing; nevertheless at Your word I will let down the net." And when they had done this, they caught a great number of fish, and their net was breaking. So they signaled to their partners in the other boat to come and help them. And they came and filled both the boats, so that they began to sink.

—Luke 5:1–7

Jesus Christ not only fed the people with spiritual food, but He knew and understood the physical needs of man.

And Jesus, when He came out, saw a great multitude and was moved with compassion for them, because they were like sheep not having a shepherd. So He began to teach them many things. When the day was now far spent, His disciples came to Him and said, "This is a deserted place, and already the hour is late. Send them away, that they may go into the surrounding country and villages and buy themselves bread; for they have nothing to eat." But He answered and said to them, "You give them something to eat." And they said to Him, "Shall we go and buy two hundred denarii worth of bread and give them something to eat?" But He said to them, "How many loaves do you have? Go and see." And when they found out they said,

"Five, and two fish." Then He commanded them to make them all sit down in groups on the green grass. So they sat down in ranks, in hundreds and in fifties. And when He had taken the five loaves and the two fish, He looked up to heaven, blessed and broke the loaves, and gave them to His disciples to set before them; and the two fish He divided among them all. So they all ate and were filled. And they took up twelve baskets full of fragments and of the fish. Now those who had eaten the loaves were about five thousand men.

—MARK 6:34–44

Now Jesus called His disciples to Himself and said, "I have compassion on the multitude, because they have now continued with Me three days and have nothing to eat. And I do not want to send them away hungry, lest they faint on the way." Then His disciples said to Him, "Where could we get enough bread in the wilderness to fill such a great multitude?" Jesus said to them, "How many loaves do you have?" And they said, "Seven, and a few little fish." So He commanded the multitude to sit down on the ground. And He took the seven loaves and the fish and gave thanks, broke them and gave them to His disciples; and the disciples gave to the multitude. So they all ate and were filled, and they took up seven large baskets full of the fragments that were left. Now those who ate were four thousand men, besides women and children. And He sent away the multitude, got into the boat, and came to the region of Magdala.

—MATTHEW 15:32–39

Jesus Christ did many miracles while on Earth, and in the Gospel of John, the following is written:

> And there are also many other things that Jesus did, which if
> they were written one by one, I suppose that even the world itself
> could not contain the books that would be written. Amen.
>
> —JOHN 21:25

Not only did Jesus Christ do many miracles Himself, He gave the
right to His followers to do the same.

> And as you go, preach, saying, "The kingdom of heaven is at
> hand." Heal the sick, cleanse the lepers, raise the dead, cast out
> demons. Freely you have received, freely give.
>
> —MATTHEW 10:7–8

> And He called the twelve to Himself, and began to send them
> out two by two, and gave them power over unclean spirits.... So
> they went out and preached that people should repent. And they
> cast out many demons, and anointed with oil many who were
> sick, and healed them.
>
> —MARK 6:7, 12–13

After these things the Lord appointed seventy others also, and
sent them two by two before His face into every city and place
where He Himself was about to go.

> Then He said to them, "The harvest truly is great, but the
> laborers are few; therefore pray the Lord of the harvest to
> send out laborers into His harvest. Go your way; behold, I
> send you out as lambs among wolves.... He who hears you
> hears Me, he who rejects you rejects Me, and he who rejects
> Me rejects Him who sent Me." Then the seventy returned with
> joy, saying, "Lord, even the demons are subject to us in Your
> name." And He said to them, "I saw Satan fall like lightning
> from heaven. Behold, I give you the authority to trample on

serpents and scorpions, and over all the power of the enemy, and nothing shall by any means hurt you. Nevertheless do not rejoice in this, that the spirits are subject to you, but rather rejoice because your names are written in heaven."

—LUKE 10:2–3, 16–20

Is anyone among you sick? Let him call for the elders of the church, and let them pray over him, anointing him with oil in the name of the Lord. And the prayer of faith will save the sick, and the Lord will raise him up. And if he has committed sins, he will be forgiven. Confess your trespasses to one another, and pray for one another, that you may be healed. The effective, fervent prayer of a righteous man avails much.

—JAMES 5:14–16

What great power Jesus Christ gave to His followers. And yet, He even said that greater works will be done than what He did.

Most assuredly, I say to you, he who believes in Me, the works that I do he will do also; and greater works than these he will do, because I go to My Father.

—JOHN 14:12

Jesus Christ taught His followers that He came to Earth to serve people—and He did in fact do this.

Yet it shall not be so among you; but whoever desires to become great among you, let him be your servant. And whoever desires to be first among you, let him be your slave—just as the Son of Man did not come to be served, but to serve, and to give His life a ransom for many.

—MATTHEW 20:26–28

The Pharisees and the scribes listened to His teachings, saw His great work, witnessed the great multitudes that followed Him and how He drank and ate with sinners and tax collectors, and wondered how it was that He could do so. But Jesus Christ upheld His mission with the following words:

> As He passed by, He saw Levi the son of Alphaeus sitting at the tax office. And He said to him, "Follow Me." So he arose and followed Him. Now it happened, as He was dining in Levi's house, that many tax collectors and sinners also sat together with Jesus and His disciples; for there were many, and they followed Him. And when the scribes and Pharisees saw Him eating with the tax collectors and sinners, they said to His disciples, "How is it that He eats and drinks with tax collectors and sinners?" When Jesus heard it, He said to them, "Those who are well have no need of a physician, but those who are sick. I did not come to call the righteous, but sinners, to repentance."
>
> —MARK 2:14–17

> For the Son of Man has come to seek and to save that which was lost.
>
> —LUKE 19:10

The purpose of Jesus being on this earth was to save the sinful mankind, to find and save the lost, to serve people, and to give His life for the salvation of many—for your salvation, dear reader, and mine. This indeed is proof that God loves His people; this is the true love of the Creator for His creation.

18

PREDICTION OF DEATH AND THE DIGNIFIED ENTRANCE TO JERUSALEM

JESUS CHRIST UNDERSTOOD HIS MISSION WELL; HE KNEW WHY He came to Earth. He knew that He came to die for sinners—for the human race. He, the Son of God, who was sinless, came to take upon Himself all the sins of the world. He knew that only He could be the Lamb of God who could be killed for our salvation. Jesus Christ told His disciples of His future, of His mission, but they did not understand Him. Jesus taught His disciples that the Son of Man first had to suffer much and be rejected by the elders, priests, intellectuals, and then be killed.

Jesus asked His disciples to tell Him what people thought about Him, about who He was. Some said they thought He was John the Baptist. Others said He was Elijah, and others still said He was Jeremiah or another prophet. Jesus turned to His disciples and asked them what they thought of Him. Peter said the following:

"Lord, to whom shall we go? You have the words of eternal life. Also we have come to believe and know that You are the Christ, the Son of the living God."

—JOHN 6:68–69

From that time Jesus began to show to His disciples that He must go to Jerusalem, and suffer many things from the elders and chief priests and scribes, and to be killed, and be raised the third day.

—MATTHEW 16:21

Jesus Christ reminded His disciples of His mission for a second time.

Now while they were staying in Galilee, Jesus said to them, "The Son of Man is about to be betrayed into the hands of men, and they will kill Him, and the third day He will be raised up." And they were exceedingly sorrowful.

—MATTHEW 17:22–23

Jesus Christ, amid His disciples, called Himself a pastor and described what a good pastor should do for His sheep:

"I am the good shepherd. The good shepherd gives His life for the sheep.

—JOHN 10:11

The Passover was approaching, and Jesus decided to go to Jerusalem with His disciples. Along the way, He reminded His disciples of His mission for the third time.

Then He took the twelve aside and said to them, "Behold, we are going up to Jerusalem, and all things that are written by the prophets concerning the Son of Man will be accomplished.

For He will be delivered to the Gentiles and will be mocked
and insulted and spit upon. They will scourge Him and kill
Him. And the third day He will rise again." But they understood none of these things; this saying was hidden from them,
and they did not know the things which were spoken.

—LUKE 18:31–34

Jesus performed many miracles and taught the nation of God
many truths. Many people followed Him, which the priests and
Pharisees did not like. The Pharisees and the priests therefore
plotted to kill Him.

Then many of the Jews who had come to Mary, and had seen
the things Jesus did, believed in Him. But some of them went
away to the Pharisees and told them the things Jesus did. Then
the chief priests and the Pharisees gathered a council and said,
"What shall we do? For this Man works many signs. If we let
Him alone like this, everyone will believe in Him, and the
Romans will come and take away both our place and nation."
And one of them, Caiaphas, being high priest that year, said
to them, "You know nothing at all, nor do you consider that
it is expedient for us that one man should die for the people,
and not that the whole nation should perish." Now this he did
not say on his own authority; but being high priest that year
he prophesied that Jesus would die for the nation, and not for
that nation only, but also that He would gather together in one
the children of God who were scattered abroad. Then, from
that day on, they plotted to put Him to death. Therefore Jesus
no longer walked openly among the Jews, but went from there
into the country near the wilderness, to a city called Ephraim,
and there remained with His disciples. And the Passover of
the Jews was near, and many went from the country up to

Jerusalem before the Passover, to purify themselves. Then they sought Jesus, and spoke among themselves as they stood in the temple, "What do you think—that He will not come to the feast?" Now both the chief priests and the Pharisees had given a command, that if anyone knew where He was, he should report it, that they might seize Him.

—JOHN 11:45–57

Jesus made His trip into Jerusalem on a small donkey.

Now when they drew near Jerusalem, and came to Bethphage, at the Mount of Olives, then Jesus sent two disciples, saying to them, "Go into the village opposite you, and immediately you will find a donkey tied, and a colt with her. Loose them and bring them to Me. And if anyone says anything to you, you shall say, 'The Lord has need of them,' and immediately he will send them." All this was done that it might be fulfilled which was spoken by the prophet, saying: "Tell the daughter of Zion, 'Behold, your King is coming to you, Lowly, and sitting on a donkey, A colt, the foal of a donkey.'" So the disciples went and did as Jesus commanded them. They brought the donkey and the colt, laid their clothes on them, and set Him on them. And a very great multitude spread their clothes on the road; others cut down branches from the trees and spread them on the road. Then the multitudes who went before and those who followed cried out, saying: "Hosanna to the Son of David! 'Blessed is He who comes in the name of the Lord!' Hosanna in the highest!" And when He had come into Jerusalem, all the city was moved, saying, "Who is this?" So the multitudes said, "This is Jesus, the prophet from Nazareth of Galilee." Then Jesus went into the temple of God and drove out all those who bought and sold in the temple, and overturned the tables of the money changers and the seats of those who sold doves. And He said to them, "It is written, 'My house shall be called a house of prayer,' but you have made it a 'den of thieves.'" Then the blind and the lame came to Him in the temple, and He healed them. But when the chief priests and scribes saw the wonderful things that He did, and the children crying out in the temple and saying, "Hosanna to the Son of David!" they were indignant and said to Him, "Do You hear what these are saying?" And Jesus said to them, "Yes. Have you never read, 'Out of the mouth of babes and nursing infants You have perfected praise'?"

—MATTHEW 21:1–16

Many prophesies from the Old Testament were fulfilled. Great multitudes proclaimed Jesus Christ as King of peace and as just and righteous.

19

THE LAST SUPPER AND THE ESTABLISHMENT OF THE NEW COVENANT

IN BETHANY, JESUS RAISED LAZARUS, THE BROTHER OF Martha and Mary. Mary, as you might recall, was the one who washed His feet with myrrh and wiped them with her hair. After the resurrection of Lazarus, the word of Jesus spread across the surrounding regions and abroad. Many of the Jews, seeing what Jesus had done, believed in Him. The news of Jesus, of His actions and miracles, reached the Pharisees and the chief priests.

> Then the chief priests and the Pharisees gathered a council and said, "What shall we do? For this Man works many signs. If we let Him alone like this, everyone will believe in Him, and the Romans will come and take away both our place and nation." And one of them, Caiaphas, being high priest that year, said to them, "You know nothing at all, nor do you consider that it is expedient for us that one man should die for the people, and not that the whole nation should perish." Now this he did

not say on his own authority; but being high priest that year he prophesied that Jesus would die for the nation, and not for that nation only, but also that He would gather together in one the children of God who were scattered abroad. Then, from that day on, they plotted to put Him to death.

—JOHN 11:47–53

In Jerusalem, Jesus Christ taught people in the house of God and performed many miracles, but the priests and scribes did not attempt to seize Him during the day.

Now it came to pass, when Jesus had finished all these sayings, that He said to His disciples, "You know that after two days is the Passover, and the Son of Man will be delivered up to be crucified." Then the chief priests, the scribes, and the elders of the people assembled at the palace of the high priest, who was called Caiaphas, and plotted to take Jesus by trickery and kill Him. But they said, "Not during the feast, lest there be an uproar among the people."

—MATTHEW 26:1–5

And the chief priests and the scribes sought how they might kill Him, for they feared the people. Then Satan entered Judas, surnamed Iscariot, who was numbered among the twelve. So he went his way and conferred with the chief priests and captains, how he might betray Him to them.

—LUKE 22:2–4

And [Judas] said, "What are you willing to give me if I deliver Him to you?" And they counted out to him thirty pieces of silver.

—MATTHEW 26:15

Judas agreed to this price—thirty pieces of silver—and the chief priests rejoiced when they heard his words. From that moment, Judas sought out a good time in which to sell Jesus—a time when Jesus was not among the masses.

The day of the Passover came, as did the day when a lamb had to be killed. The disciples asked Jesus where He wanted to eat the Passover meal, and He directed them to a place. When evening came and the Passover was ready, Jesus and His twelve disciples gathered around the table and ate. Jesus understood His mission well, and He knew that only He could be the Lamb for the sacrifice. He knew that He would be sold and killed, and He also knew who would betray Him.

> Now as they were eating, He said, "Assuredly, I say to you, one of you will betray Me." And they were exceedingly sorrowful, and each of them began to say to Him, "Lord, is it I?" He answered and said, "He who dipped his hand with Me in the dish will betray Me. The Son of Man indeed goes just as it is written of Him, but woe to that man by whom the Son of Man is betrayed! It would have been good for that man if he had not been born." Then Judas, who was betraying Him, answered and said, "Rabbi, is it I?" He said to him, "You have said it."
> —MATTHEW 26:21–25

This was our Savior's last supper, and He shared it with His disciples. During the supper, Jesus established a new covenant, a new law for the sons of man, for each citizen of this planet. Three writers of the Gospels testify of this event, and we shall read the words that Christ Himself spoke:

> And as they were eating, Jesus took bread, blessed and broke it, and gave it to the disciples and said, "Take, eat; this is My

body." Then He took the cup, and gave thanks, and gave it to them, saying, "Drink from it, all of you. For this is My blood of the new covenant, which is shed for many for the remission of sins. But I say to you, I will not drink of this fruit of the vine from now on until that day when I drink it new with you in My Father's kingdom."

—MATTHEW 26:26–29

And as they were eating, Jesus took bread, blessed and broke it, and gave it to them and said, "Take, eat; this is My body." Then He took the cup, and when He had given thanks He gave it to them, and they all drank from it. And He said to them, "This is My blood of the new covenant, which is shed for many. Assuredly, I say to you, I will no longer drink of the fruit of the vine until that day when I drink it new in the kingdom of God."

—MARK 14:22–25

Then He said to them, "With fervent desire I have desired to eat this Passover with you before I suffer; for I say to you, I will no longer eat of it until it is fulfilled in the kingdom of God." Then He took the cup, and gave thanks, and said, "Take this and divide it among yourselves; for I say to you, I will not drink of the fruit of the vine until the kingdom of God comes." And He took bread, gave thanks and broke it, and gave it to them, saying, "This is My body which is given for you; do this in remembrance of Me." Likewise He also took the cup after supper, saying, "This cup is the new covenant in My blood, which is shed for you.

—LUKE 22:15–20

Jesus Christ established this new law, commandment, and, ultimately, covenant symbolically and literally, first during this supper and then when He shed His blood during His crucifixion. This was a historical event in the spiritual realm, and it began a new era. Now new questions arise: When did this new covenant go into effect? When did it acquire value and importance?

20

THE CRUCIFIXION AND DEATH OF CHRIST

AFTER THE LAST SUPPER, JESUS AND HIS DISCIPLES WENT to the Mount of Olives, where Jesus told them what He soon was going to endure:

> Then Jesus said to them, "All of you will be made to stumble because of Me this night, for it is written: 'I will strike the Shepherd, And the sheep will be scattered.' But after I have been raised, I will go before you to Galilee." Peter said to Him, "Even if all are made to stumble, yet I will not be." Jesus said to him, "Assuredly, I say to you that today, even this night, before the rooster crows twice, you will deny Me three times." But he spoke more vehemently, "If I have to die with You, I will not deny You!" And they all said likewise.
>
> —MARK 14:27–31

Jesus' spirit was sorrowful. He walked a little way away, fell on His face, and prayed to His Father.

He went a little farther and fell on His face, and prayed, saying, "O My Father, if it is possible, let this cup pass from Me; nevertheless, not as I will, but as You will." Then He came to the disciples and found them sleeping, and said to Peter, "What! Could you not watch with Me one hour? Watch and pray, lest you enter into temptation. The spirit indeed is willing, but the flesh is weak." Again, a second time, He went away and prayed, saying, "O My Father, if this cup cannot pass away from Me unless I drink it, Your will be done." And He came and found them asleep again, for their eyes were heavy. So He left them, went away again, and prayed the third time, saying the same words.

—Matthew 26:39–44

The Gospel of Luke describes how fervently Jesus prayed:

And being in agony, He prayed more earnestly. Then His sweat became like great drops of blood falling down to the ground.

—Luke 22:44

Judas, His betrayer, knew the place where Jesus came for prayer because Jesus often gathered there with His disciples. Judas took soldiers, the servants of the chief priests, and the Pharisees and went there, armed with weapons, to meet Jesus. Then Jesus turned to His disciples and said the following:

Then He came to His disciples and said to them, "Are you still sleeping and resting? Behold, the hour is at hand, and the Son of Man is being betrayed into the hands of sinners. Rise, let us be going. See, My betrayer is at hand." And while He was still speaking, behold, Judas, one of the twelve, with a great multitude with swords and clubs, came from the chief priests and elders of the people. Now His betrayer had given them a sign, saying, "Whomever I kiss, He is the One; seize Him." Immediately he went up to Jesus and said, "Greetings, Rabbi!" and kissed Him. But Jesus said to him, "Friend, why have you come?" Then they came and laid hands on Jesus and took Him.

—MATTHEW 26:45–50

Jesus turned to the mass of people and said the following:

Then Jesus said to the chief priests, captains of the temple, and the elders who had come to Him, "Have you come out, as against a robber, with swords and clubs? When I was with you daily in the temple, you did not try to seize Me. But this is your hour, and the power of darkness."

—LUKE 22:52–53

Jesus, the Son of God, fell into the hands of the ungodly, into the hands of sinners. All of His disciples left Him, and He was alone among them. Soldiers, the church rulers, and their servants took Jesus and restrained Him. They took Him to the father-in-law of Caiaphas, the first chief priest. Caiaphas, as you might recall, was the one who told the Jews that it would be best for one man (Jesus) to die instead of an entire nation. (See John 11:49–50.) Many elders and intellectuals gathered at the chief priest's house. They sought out people to bear false witnesses against Jesus in order to have a reason to send Him to death, but they found none. Many witnessed for Him, but their witnessing was not enough. Peter followed Jesus into the courtyard of the chief priest. He entered and sat with the people in order to witness the end.

Now when they had kindled a fire in the midst of the court-yard and sat down together, Peter sat among them. And a certain servant girl, seeing him as he sat by the fire, looked intently at him and said, "This man was also with Him." But he denied Him, saying, "Woman, I do not know Him." And after a little while another saw him and said, "You also are of them." But Peter said, "Man, I am not!" Then after about an hour had passed, another confidently affirmed, saying, "Surely this fellow also was with Him, for he is a Galilean." But Peter said, "Man, I do not know what you are saying!" Immediately, while he was still speaking, the rooster crowed. And the Lord turned and looked at Peter. Then Peter remembered the word of the Lord, how He had said to him, "Before the rooster crows, you will deny Me three times." So Peter went out and wept bitterly.

—Luke 22:55–62

Now the chief priests and all the council sought testimony against Jesus to put Him to death, but found none.... Then some rose up and bore false witness against Him, saying, "We heard Him say, 'I will destroy this temple made with hands, and within three days I will build another made without hands.'" But not even then did their testimony agree.

—Mark 14:55, 57–59

Many witnessed against Him and asked Him many questions, but the Son of God answered with silence.

And the high priest stood up in the midst and asked Jesus, saying, "Do You answer nothing? What is it these men testify against You?" But He kept silent and answered nothing. Again the high priest asked Him, saying to Him, "Are You the Christ, the Son of the Blessed?" Jesus said, "I am. And you will see the Son of Man sitting at the right hand of the Power, and coming with the clouds of heaven." Then the high priest tore his clothes and said, "What further need do we have of witnesses?

You have heard the blasphemy! What do you think?" And they all condemned Him to be deserving of death. Then some began to spit on Him, and to blindfold Him, and to beat Him, and to say to Him, "Prophesy!" And the officers struck Him with the palms of their hands.

—MARK 14:60–65

When morning came, the chief priests, the elders, and the entire council held a meeting in which they decided to send Jesus to Pilate, the ruler of Rome. But what happened with the betrayer of Jesus, with Judas Iscariot?

Then Judas, His betrayer, seeing that He had been condemned, was remorseful and brought back the thirty pieces of silver to the chief priests and elders, saying, "I have sinned by betraying innocent blood." And they said, "What is that to us? You see to it!" Then he threw down the pieces of silver in the temple and departed, and went and hanged himself. But the chief priests took the silver pieces and said, "It is not lawful to put them into the treasury, because they are the price of blood." And they consulted together and bought with them the potter's field, to bury strangers in. Therefore that field has been called the Field of Blood to this day. Then was fulfilled what was spoken by Jeremiah the prophet, saying, "And they took the thirty pieces of silver, the value of Him who was priced, whom they of the children of Israel priced, and gave them for the potter's field, as the Lord directed me."

—MATTHEW 27:3–10

Jesus Christ, the Son of the living God, found Himself in the hands of Pilate.

Pilate then went out to them and said, "What accusation do you bring against this Man?" They answered and said to him, "If He were not an evildoer, we would not have delivered Him up to you." Then Pilate said to them, "You take Him and judge Him according to your law." Therefore the Jews said to him, "It is not lawful for us to put anyone to death," that the saying of Jesus might be fulfilled which He spoke, signifying by what death He would die. Then Pilate entered the Praetorium again, called Jesus, and said to Him, "Are You the King of the Jews?" Jesus answered him, "Are you speaking for yourself about this, or did others tell you this concerning Me?" Pilate answered, "Am I a Jew? Your own nation and the chief priests have delivered You to me. What have You done?" Jesus answered, "My kingdom is not of this world. If My kingdom were of this world, My servants would fight, so that I should not be delivered to the Jews; but now My kingdom is not from here." Pilate therefore said to Him, "Are You a king then?" Jesus answered, "You say rightly that I am a king. For this cause I was born, and for this cause I have come into the world, that I should bear witness to the truth. Everyone who is of the truth hears My voice." Pilate said to Him, "What is truth?" And when he had said this, he went out again to the Jews, and said to them, "I find no fault in Him at all.

—JOHN 18:29–38

The chief priests and the elders blamed Jesus for many things, and many of them bore false witness. But He answered with silence. Pilate was amazed at this and knew that they wrongfully had Him in custody.

Pilate's wife spoke some very true words.

While he was sitting on the judgment seat, his wife sent to him, saying, "Have nothing to do with that just Man, for I have suffered many things today in a dream because of Him."

—MATTHEW 27:19

Pilate, when he could not find any fault in Jesus, knew that Jesus of Galilee was innocent. Pilate then decided to send Him to Herod.

Now when Herod saw Jesus, he was exceedingly glad; for he had desired for a long time to see Him, because he had heard many things about Him, and he hoped to see some miracle done by Him. Then he questioned Him with many words, but He answered him nothing. And the chief priests and scribes stood and vehemently accused Him. Then Herod, with his men of war, treated Him with contempt and mocked Him, arrayed Him in a gorgeous robe, and sent Him back to Pilate. That very day Pilate and Herod became friends with each other, for previously they had been at enmity with each other.

—LUKE 23:8–12

Like Pilot, Herod could not find any fault with Jesus—he could not find any basis for the accusations made by the chief priests and elders. But even still, the people demanded the death of Jesus.

Pilate said to them, "What then shall I do with Jesus who is called Christ?" They all said to him, "Let Him be crucified!" Then the governor said, "Why, what evil has He done?" But they cried out all the more, saying, "Let Him be crucified!" When Pilate saw that he could not prevail at all, but rather that a tumult was rising, he took water and washed his hands before the multitude, saying, "I am innocent of the blood of this just Person. You see to it." And all the people answered and said, "His blood be on us and on our children."

—MATTHEW 27:22–25

There was a ritual in Judah. During the Passover, the ruler released any prisoner that the people voted for. There was a man, Barabbas, who was imprisoned both for murder and organizing rebellions and revolts. Pilate asked the people if they wanted the King of the Jews to be released. But the chief priests and elders encouraged the people to vote for the release of Barabbas and the death of Jesus.

> Pilate, therefore, wishing to release Jesus, again called out to them. But they shouted, saying, "Crucify Him, crucify Him!" Then he said to them the third time, "Why, what evil has He done? I have found no reason for death in Him. I will therefore chastise Him and let Him go." But they were insistent, demanding with loud voices that He be crucified. And the voices of these men and of the chief priests prevailed. So Pilate gave sentence that it should be as they requested. And he released to them the one they requested, who for rebellion and murder had been thrown into prison; but he delivered Jesus to their will.
>
> —LUKE 23:20–25

Jesus, the Son of God, was judged by a sinful world and was crucified.

> Then the soldiers of the governor took Jesus into the Praetorium and gathered the whole garrison around Him. And they stripped Him and put a scarlet robe on Him. When they had twisted a crown of thorns, they put it on His head, and a reed in His right hand. And they bowed the knee before Him and

mocked Him, saying, "Hail, King of the Jews!" Then they spat on Him, and took the reed and struck Him on the head. And when they had mocked Him, they took the robe off Him, put His own clothes on Him, and led Him away to be crucified.

—MATTHEW 27:27–31

They constructed a cross and forced Jesus to carry it for His own crucifixion. Jesus was beaten, tired, and He kept falling under the weight of the cross. They then found Simeon in the crowd, and they forced him to carry the cross for Jesus. They led the Son of God to Golgotha, which in Hebrew means "the place of the skull." A great multitude followed Jesus, and many women wept for Him. Jesus turned His attention to them and said:

But Jesus, turning to them, said, "Daughters of Jerusalem, do not weep for Me, but weep for yourselves and for your children. For indeed the days are coming in which they will say, 'Blessed are the barren, wombs that never bore, and breasts which never nursed!' Then they will begin 'to say to the mountains, "Fall on us!" and to the hills, "Cover us!"' For if they do these things in the green wood, what will be done in the dry?"

—LUKE 23:28–31

Two thieves were also crucified with Jesus on Golgotha, one on either side of Him.

So the Scripture was fulfilled which says, "And He was numbered with the transgressors."

—MARK 15:28

And those who passed by blasphemed Him, wagging their heads and saying, "You who destroy the temple and build it in three days, save Yourself! If You are the Son of God, come down from the cross." Likewise the chief priests also, mocking with the scribes and elders, said, "He saved others; Himself He cannot save. If He is the King of Israel, let Him now come down from the cross, and we will believe Him. He trusted in God; let Him deliver Him now if He will have Him; for He said, 'I am the Son of God.'"

—Matthew 27:39–43

The soldiers also mocked Him, coming and offering Him sour wine, and saying, "If You are the King of the Jews, save Yourself."

—Luke 23:36–37

Jesus, seeing how everyone mocked Him, said, "Father, forgive them for they do not know what they are doing" (Luke 23:34). But how did the thieves, who were also crucified, act? How did they perceive Jesus?

Then one of the criminals who were hanged blasphemed Him, saying, "If You are the Christ, save Yourself and us." But the other, answering, rebuked him, saying, "Do you not even fear God, seeing you are under the same condemnation? And we indeed justly, for we receive the due reward of our deeds; but this Man has done nothing wrong." Then he said to Jesus, "Lord, remember me when You come into Your kingdom." And Jesus said to him, "Assuredly, I say to you, today you will be with Me in Paradise."

—Luke 23:39–43

Pilate put the following sign on the cross of Jesus—King of the Jews.

Then many of the Jews read this title, for the place where Jesus was crucified was near the city; and it was written in Hebrew, Greek, and Latin. Therefore the chief priests of the Jews said to Pilate, "Do not write, 'The King of the Jews,' but, 'He said, "I am the King of the Jews."'" Pilate answered, "What I have written, I have written."

—JOHN 19:20–22

The soldiers divided Jesus' clothing after they had crucified Him.

Then the soldiers, when they had crucified Jesus, took His garments and made four parts, to each soldier a part, and also the tunic. Now the tunic was without seam, woven from the top in one piece. They said therefore among themselves, "Let us not tear it, but cast lots for it, whose it shall be," that the Scripture might be fulfilled which says: "They divided My garments among them, And for My clothing they cast lots." Therefore the soldiers did these things.

—JOHN 19:23–24

Many women, who had followed Him throughout Galilee and Jerusalem, observed everything from a distance. Among them was His mother, whom Jesus did not forget as He hung on the cross.

Now there stood by the cross of Jesus His mother, and His mother's sister, Mary the wife of Clopas, and Mary Magdalene. When Jesus therefore saw His mother, and the disciple whom He loved standing by, He said to His mother, "Woman, behold your son!" Then He said to the disciple, "Behold your mother!" And from that hour that disciple took her to his own home.

—JOHN 19:25–27

In the sixth hour, the sun grew dark and darkness fell.

> And at the ninth hour Jesus cried out with a loud voice, saying,
> "Eloi, Eloi, lama sabachthani?" which is translated, "My God,
> My God, why have You forsaken Me?"
>
> —MARK 15:34

> After this, Jesus, knowing that all things were now accom-
> plished, that the Scripture might be fulfilled, said, "I thirst!"
> Now a vessel full of sour wine was sitting there; and they filled
> a sponge with sour wine, put it on hyssop, and put it to His
> mouth. So when Jesus had received the sour wine, He said, "It
> is finished!" And bowing His head, He gave up His spirit.
>
> —JOHN 19:28–30

Salvation was established for the human race. The Son of God
was killed; He served as the Lamb sacrificed for our sins. The
people who were physically present at the crucifixion were not the
only witnesses to this, but nature confirmed this also.

> Then, behold, the veil of the temple was torn in two from top
> to bottom; and the earth quaked, and the rocks were split,
> and the graves were opened; and many bodies of the saints
> who had fallen asleep were raised; and coming out of the
> graves after His resurrection, they went into the holy city and
> appeared to many. So when the centurion and those with him,
> who were guarding Jesus, saw the earthquake and the things
> that had happened, they feared greatly, saying, "Truly this was
> the Son of God!"
>
> —MATTHEW 27:51–54

The crucifixions were on Friday, and in order to bury them by
the Sabbath, the soldiers asked Pilate for permission to break their

legs. Permission was granted, but Jesus' legs were not broken, as He had already died.

> Then the soldiers came and broke the legs of the first and of the other who was crucified with Him. But when they came to Jesus and saw that He was already dead, they did not break His legs. But one of the soldiers pierced His side with a spear, and immediately blood and water came out. And he who has seen has testified, and his testimony is true; and he knows that he is telling the truth, so that you may believe. For these things were done that the Scripture should be fulfilled, "Not one of His bones shall be broken." And again another Scripture says, "They shall look on Him whom they pierced."
> —JOHN 19:32–37

Among those present were Joseph from Arimathea, a righteous disciple of Jesus who awaited the kingdom of heaven, and Nicodemus, who brought a mixture of myrrh and aloes. After asking Pilate for Jesus' body, Joseph and Nicodemus took it from the cross, wrapped it with linen and spices, and placed it into the grave. The grave was in a garden, not far from Golgotha, and no one had yet lain in it.

It is interesting to read of how the chief priests and elders felt after the death of Jesus. Let's read from the Holy Scriptures.

> On the next day, which followed the Day of Preparation, the chief priests and Pharisees gathered together to Pilate, saying, "Sir, we remember, while He was still alive, how that deceiver said, 'After three days I will rise.' Therefore command that the tomb be made secure until the third day, lest His disciples come by night and steal Him away, and say to the people, 'He has risen from the dead.' So the last deception will be worse

than the first." Pilate said to them, "You have a guard; go your way, make it as secure as you know how." So they went and made the tomb secure, sealing the stone and setting the guard.

—Matthew 27:62–66

And so the grave was sealed with a large, heavy stone. We have read of how Jesus, the Son of the living God, was crucified, how He shed His blood, and how He died just for us. He paid a high price for our salvation, dear reader. His crucifixion fulfilled the words of Isaiah:

Who has believed our report? And to whom has the arm of the Lord been revealed? For He shall grow up before Him as a tender plant, And as a root out of dry ground. He has no form or comeliness; And when we see Him, There is no beauty that we should desire Him. He is despised and rejected by men, A Man of sorrows and acquainted with grief. And we hid, as it were, our faces from Him; He was despised, and we did not esteem Him. Surely He has borne our griefs And carried our sorrows; Yet we esteemed Him stricken, Smitten by God, and afflicted. But He was wounded for our transgressions, He was bruised for our iniquities; The chastisement for our peace was upon Him, And by His stripes we are healed. All we like sheep have gone astray; We have turned, every one, to his own way; And the Lord has laid on Him the iniquity of us all. He was oppressed and He was afflicted, Yet He opened not His mouth; He was led as a lamb to the slaughter, And as a sheep before its shearers is silent, So He opened not His mouth. He was taken from prison and from judgment, And who will declare His generation? For He was cut off from the land of the living; For the transgressions of My people He was stricken. And they made His grave with the wicked—But with the rich at His death, Because He had done no violence, Nor was any deceit in His mouth. Yet it pleased the Lord to bruise Him; He has put Him to grief. When You make His soul an offering for sin, He shall see His seed, He shall prolong His days, And the pleasure of the LORD shall prosper in His hand. He shall see the labor of His soul, and be satisfied. By His knowledge My righteous Servant shall justify many, For He shall bear their iniquities. Therefore I will divide Him a portion with the great, And He shall divide the spoil with the strong, Because He poured out His soul unto death, And He was numbered with the transgressors, And He bore the sin of many, And made intercession for the transgressors.

—ISAIAH 53:1–12

Jesus was crucified and His body was placed into a grave, which was sealed with a giant stone. Soldiers were positioned around the grave to secure His body. It seemed that all was finished, that the mission of Jesus was fulfilled. My dear reader, as you hear of this great and tragic event, questions may grow in your heart: Is this really true? Is it really finished? Is it true that the end has come? Dear reader, this is not the end. Rather, it is only the beginning of the good news, which we will read about on the following pages.

21

JESUS HAS RISEN

A FTER THE CRUCIFIXION ON FRIDAY, SATURDAY PASSED peacefully. The pages of the Hole Bible do not record any unusual events on Saturday. But what happened on Sunday, the third day after the death of the Son of God?

Now after the Sabbath, as the first day of the week began to dawn, Mary Magdalene and the other Mary came to see the tomb. And behold, there was a great earthquake; for an angel of the Lord descended from heaven, and came and rolled back the stone from the door, and sat on it. His countenance was like lightning, and his clothing as white as snow. And the guards shook for fear of him, and became like dead men. But the angel answered and said to the women, "Do not be afraid, for I know that you seek Jesus who was crucified. He is not here; for He is risen, as He said. Come, see the place where the Lord lay. And go quickly and tell His disciples that He is risen from the dead, and indeed He is going before you into Galilee; there you will see Him. Behold, I have told you." So they went out quickly from the tomb with fear and great joy, and ran to bring His disciples word.

—MATTHEW 28:1–8

The grave was empty. Jesus Christ had risen from the dead. The words of the prophets were fulfilled. Death had no power over the Son of God—death had no authority. The Earth again shook, but how did the guards of the grave react? The soldiers, after seeing and hearing all that transpired, grew afraid. They went and told everything to the chief priests and scribes, who found a way to hide the truth from the people.

> When they had assembled with the elders and consulted together, they gave a large sum of money to the soldiers, saying, "Tell them, 'His disciples came at night and stole Him away while we slept.' And if this comes to the governor's ears, we will appease him and make you secure." So they took the money and did as they were instructed; and this saying is commonly reported among the Jews until this day.
>
> —MATTHEW 28:12–15

Jesus first appeared to Mary Magdalene, then to two apostles as they were making their way to Emmaus, and also to the eleven when they had gathered together.

> Then, the same day at evening, being the first day of the week, when the doors were shut where the disciples were assembled, for fear of the Jews, Jesus came and stood in the midst, and said to them, "Peace be with you." When He had said this, He showed them His hands and His side. Then the disciples were glad when they saw the Lord. So Jesus said to them again, "Peace to you! As the Father has sent Me, I also send you." And when He had said this, He breathed on them,

and said to them, "Receive the Holy Spirit. If you forgive the sins of any, they are forgiven them; if you retain the sins of any, they are retained." Now Thomas, called the Twin, one of the twelve, was not with them when Jesus came. The other disciples therefore said to him, "We have seen the Lord." So he said to them, "Unless I see in His hands the print of the nails, and put my finger into the print of the nails, and put my hand into His side, I will not believe." And after eight days His disciples were again inside, and Thomas with them. Jesus came, the doors being shut, and stood in the midst, and said, "Peace to you!" Then He said to Thomas, "Reach your finger here, and look at My hands; and reach your hand here, and put it into My side. Do not be unbelieving, but believing." And Thomas answered and said to Him, "My Lord and my God!" Jesus said to him, "Thomas, because you have seen Me, you have believed. Blessed are those who have not seen and yet have believed." And truly Jesus did many other signs in the presence of His disciples, which are not written in this book; but these are written that you may believe that Jesus is the Christ, the Son of God, and that believing you may have life in His name.

—JOHN 20:19–31

And there are also many other things that Jesus did, which if they were written one by one, I suppose that even the world itself could not contain the books that would be written. Amen.

—JOHN 21:25

Jesus appeared to His apostles for the third time by the sea of Tiberias. Seven apostles were fishing all night, and by morning they had failed to catch anything. But Jesus appeared and told them to cast their net to the other side of the boat. After hearing and obeying these words, they were unable to bring their net out of the water because they had caught so many fish.

During the forty days following the resurrection, Jesus appeared to His disciples and spoke to them about the kingdom of heaven. The apostle Paul writes in 1 Corinthians that Jesus appeared to him also:

> For I delivered to you first of all that which I also received: that Christ died for our sins according to the Scriptures, and that He was buried, and that He rose again the third day according to the Scriptures, and that He was seen by Cephas, then by the twelve. After that He was seen by over five hundred brethren at once, of whom the greater part remain to the present, but some have fallen asleep. After that He was seen by James, then by all the apostles. Then last of all He was seen by me also, as by one born out of due time. For I am the least of the apostles, who am not worthy to be called an apostle, because I persecuted the church of God.
>
> —1 CORINTHIANS 15:3–9

When Jesus Christ was with His apostles, He told them about the kingdom of God and about Himself. He also gave them rules to follow in order to fulfill God's will. For our benefit, let's read the following, which He left for His chosen people and for all citizens on this planet:

> Then He said to them, "Thus it is written, and thus it was necessary for the Christ to suffer and to rise from the dead the third day, and that repentance and remission of sins should be preached in His name to all nations, beginning at Jerusalem. And you are witnesses of these things. Behold, I send

the Promise of My Father upon you; but tarry in the city of Jerusalem until you are endued with power from on high."

—Luke 24:46–49

And Jesus came and spoke to them, saying, "All authority has been given to Me in heaven and on earth. Go therefore and make disciples of all the nations, baptizing them in the name of the Father and of the Son and of the Holy Spirit, teaching them to observe all things that I have commanded you; and lo, I am with you always, even to the end of the age." Amen.

—Matthew 28:18–20

And He said to them, "Go into all the world and preach the gospel to every creature. He who believes and is baptized will be saved; but he who does not believe will be condemned. And these signs will follow those who believe: In My name they will cast out demons; they will speak with new tongues; they will take up serpents; and if they drink anything deadly, it will by no means hurt them; they will lay hands on the sick, and they will recover."

—Mark 16:15–18

And being assembled together with them, He commanded them not to depart from Jerusalem, but to wait for the Promise of the Father, "which," He said, "you have heard from Me; for John truly baptized with water, but you shall be baptized with the Holy Spirit not many days from now.... But you shall receive power when the Holy Spirit has come upon you; and you shall be witnesses to Me in Jerusalem, and in all Judea and Samaria, and to the end of the earth."

—Acts 1:4–5, 8

Jesus ascended to heaven while they watched, and the clouds covered Him from their sight.

> So then, after the Lord had spoken to them, He was received up into heaven, and sat down at the right hand of God. And they went out and preached everywhere, the Lord working with them and confirming the word through the accompanying signs. Amen.
>
> —MARK 16:19–20

Jesus Christ arose from the dead, rose into heaven, and sits on the right side of God. He intercedes for us.

> For Christ has not entered the holy places made with hands, which are copies of the true, but into heaven itself, now to appear in the presence of God for us.
>
> —HEBREW 9:24

22

THE NEW COVENANT
CAME INTO EFFECT

On Thursday evening, before the Son of God had to suffer and be crucified on Golgotha, He shared the last meal with His disciples. During this supper, the King of heaven and Earth established a new law, described in the New Testament.

Jesus Christ took the bread, broke it, and gave it to His disciples, saying "Take, eat, this is My body, which has been given for you. Do this in remembrance of Me." He then took the cup and said, "Drink from it, all of you. For this is My blood of the new covenant, which is shed for many for the remission of sins" (Matt. 26:27–18). The Son of God established the new covenant when He gave His body to be crucified and when His innocent blood was shed on the cross. Jesus commanded all those who love Him, who believe in Him and accept Him as their own personal Savior, to fulfill it. Those who do the above also accept His teachings, communicate with Him, and walk in His way in the path He created. Jesus Christ knew His fate very well. He knew why He came to Earth, He knew that He would be crucified on the cross, and He knew that He would shed His holy blood. And when He taught in the synagogues, He spoke freely of His mission, of the fate that awaited Him. He knew that only He is the Lamb of God, the only One who could suffer and be killed in order to take the sins of the world. He knew that He had to establish a new covenant for us, and He invites us to use His sacrifice for our benefit.

> "I am the bread of life.... I am the living bread which came down from heaven. If anyone eats of this bread, he will live forever; and the bread that I shall give is My flesh, which I shall give for the life of the world."... Then Jesus said to them, "Most assuredly, I say to you, unless you eat the flesh of the Son of Man and drink His blood, you have no life in you. Whoever eats My flesh and drinks My blood has eternal life, and I will raise him up at the last day. For My flesh is food indeed, and My blood is drink indeed. He who eats My flesh and drinks My blood abides in Me, and I in him. As the living Father sent Me, and I live because of the Father, so he who feeds on Me will live because of Me. This is the bread which came down from heaven—not as your fathers ate the manna, and are dead. He who eats this bread will live forever."
> —JOHN 6:48, 51, 53–58

Those who heard these words did not understand them. These words were strange, new, and rather hard to comprehend. Jesus Christ gave these commands so that His followers, while eating and drinking the bread and wine, would remember His suffering, His patience, His sacrifice, His death, and most importantly, the new covenant.

When Jesus Christ establishes commands for His creation, He also gives exact directions on how to accomplish those commands.

He gives simple and practical ways to fulfill them. And in return, He requires that we fulfill His will exactly. Only when we fulfill God's will entirely can we confirm our obedience to Him and our belief in Him, our Creator. The followers of Jesus Christ must partake of Jesus' Last Supper. We must eat the bread and drink the wine to remember His suffering and death, for this is His will.

The apostle Paul also encourages Christians to partake of the Last Supper, to take part in the act that relives His death until His Second Coming:

> For I received from the Lord that which I also delivered to you: that the Lord Jesus on the same night in which He was betrayed took bread; and when He had given thanks, He broke it and said, "Take, eat; this is My body which is broken for you; do this in remembrance of Me." In the same manner He also took the cup after supper, saying, "This cup is the new covenant in My blood. This do, as often as you drink it, in remembrance of Me." For as often as you eat this bread and drink this cup, you proclaim the Lord's death till He comes.
> —1 CORINTHIANS 11:23–26

The Word of God teaches us that where there is a will, there should also be a testator who had prepared the will before their death. It is also this way in our earthly life. When a will is made, it only becomes effective upon the death of the person who created it. What is left for someone else becomes theirs only when the original owner passes away. The document only has power after the death of the author. Whoever is named in the will has no right to any of the property while the creator of the will lives; they cannot legally claim anything before the owner's death. It is the same in our spiritual life, as the Word of God says:

> For where there is a testament, there must also of necessity be
> the death of the testator. For a testament is in force after men
> are dead, since it has no power at all while the testator lives.
> —HEBREWS 9:16–17

Salvation was established for the sinful human race at that moment. From then on—that precise moment—the new covenant was in effect. A new era began in our history. God the Father established a new covenant with His creation, and a new word came to life: Christianity.

When the first people broke God's command and sinned before their Creator, their eyes were opened. They noticed their nakedness and their sinful nature, and they grew afraid and tried to cover their sin using leaves.

> Then the eyes of both of them were opened, and they knew
> that they were naked; and they sewed fig leaves together and
> made themselves coverings.
> —GENESIS 3:7

But God the Father established the following: the shedding of blood is required for the forgiveness of sin. After the disobedience and fall of the first people, Adam and Eve, God required blood to hide their nakedness, and subsequently, our nakedness.

> Also for Adam and his wife the LORD God made tunics of
> skin, and clothed them.
> —GENESIS 3:21

In order to make leather clothing, some living animal had to die, had to shed its blood. The Old Testament further shows that blood is required for forgiveness, and I do not think it will hurt us to read the following passage.

For when Moses had spoken every precept to all the people according to the law, he took the blood of calves and goats, with water, scarlet wool, and hyssop, and sprinkled both the book itself and all the people, saying, "This is the blood of the covenant which God has commanded you." Then likewise he sprinkled with blood both the tabernacle and all the vessels of the ministry. And according to the law almost all things are purified with blood, and without shedding of blood there is no remission.

—Hebrews 9:19–22

The blood of Jesus Christ upholds the covenant, and the Bible writes much about the meaning of His blood. I think that it will be good for me, and for each dear reader, to read a few verses that speak about His blood and the power it has for all of mankind.

For all have sinned and fall short of the glory of God, being justified freely by His grace through the redemption that is in Christ Jesus, whom God set forth as a propitiation by His blood, through faith, to demonstrate His righteousness, because in His forbearance God had passed over the sins that were previously committed.

—Romans 3:23–25

But God demonstrates His own love toward us, in that while we were still sinners, Christ died for us. Much more then, having now been justified by His blood, we shall be saved from wrath through Him.

—Romans 5:8–9

Having predestined us to adoption as sons by Jesus Christ to Himself, according to the good pleasure of His will, to the praise of the glory of His grace, by which He made us accepted in the Beloved. In Him we have redemption through His blood, the forgiveness of sins, according to the riches of His grace.

—EPHESIANS 1:5–7

But now in Christ Jesus you who once were far off have been brought near by the blood of Christ.

—EPHESIANS 2:13

Giving thanks to the Father who has qualified us to be partakers of the inheritance of the saints in the light. He has delivered us from the power of darkness and conveyed us into the kingdom of the Son of His love, in whom we have redemption through His blood, the forgiveness of sins. He is the image of the invisible God, the firstborn over all creation. For by Him all things were created that are in heaven and that are on earth, visible and invisible, whether thrones or dominions or principalities or powers. All things were created through Him and for Him. And He is before all things, and in Him all things consist. And He is the head of the body, the church, who is the beginning, the firstborn from the dead, that in all things He may have the preeminence. For it pleased the Father that in Him all the fullness should dwell, and by Him to reconcile all things to Himself, by Him, whether things on earth or things in heaven, having made peace through the blood of His cross. And you, who once were alienated and enemies in your mind by wicked works, yet now He has reconciled in the body of His flesh through death, to present you holy, and blameless, and above reproach in His sight—

—COLOSSIANS 1:12–22

Knowing that you were not redeemed with corruptible things, like silver or gold, from your aimless conduct received by tradition from your fathers, but with the precious blood of Christ, as of a lamb without blemish and without spot. He indeed was foreordained before the foundation of the world, but was manifest in these last times for you.

—1 Peter 1:18–20

Therefore take heed to yourselves and to all the flock, among which the Holy Spirit has made you overseers, to shepherd the church of God which He purchased with His own blood.

—Acts 20:28

And from Jesus Christ, the faithful witness, the firstborn from the dead, and the ruler over the kings of the earth. To Him who loved us and washed us from our sins in His own blood, and has made us kings and priests to His God and Father, to Him be glory and dominion forever and ever. Amen.

—Revelation 1:5–6

And they sang a new song, saying: "You are worthy to take the scroll, And to open its seals; For You were slain, And have redeemed us to God by Your blood Out of every tribe and tongue and people and nation, And have made us kings and priests to our God; And we shall reign on the earth."

—Revelation 5:9–10

Then one of the elders answered, saying to me, "Who are these arrayed in white robes, and where did they come from?" And I said to him, "Sir, you know." So he said to me, "These are the ones who come out of the great tribulation, and washed their robes and made them white in the blood of the Lamb. Therefore they are before the throne of God, and serve Him day and night in His temple. And He who sits on the throne will dwell among them. They shall neither hunger anymore nor thirst anymore; the sun shall not strike them, nor any heat; for the Lamb who is in the midst of the throne will shepherd them and lead them to living fountains of waters. And God will wipe away every tear from their eyes."

—REVELATION 7:13–17

Now I saw heaven opened, and behold, a white horse. And He who sat on him was called Faithful and True, and in righteousness He judges and makes war. His eyes were like a flame of fire, and on His head were many crowns. He had a name written that no one knew except Himself. He was clothed with a robe dipped in blood, and His name is called The Word of God.

—REVELATION 19:11–13

After reading these words and thinking a bit about them, we see that they refer to when Jesus shed His blood for us. I think that each reader will support the fact that salvation is only possible through the blood of the Lamb, the Son of God, and that this is the only way. God the Father established one path for salvation, and the path is the same for the entire human race, for all tribes and all generations. The path is possible only because of the sacrifice of God's only Son. Only the blood of the Lamb of God can wash away our sins.

But if we walk in the light as He is in the light, we have fellow-ship with one another, and the blood of Jesus Christ His Son cleanses us from all sin.

—1 JOHN 1:7

Jesus Christ told us to remember His suffering, His sacrifice, and His blood that He shed. We can do so when we take part in communion, in the eating and drinking of the bread and the wine.

The bread is a symbol of His body, which was broken for us, for our physical healing. The wine is a symbol of the blood, of His blood, which washes us from all our sin. This is the new covenant, and in the twenty-first century it is alive, active, and effective, something for which we should praise God.

23

RECONCILIATION

DAM, THE FIRST MAN, THROUGH HIS DISOBEDIENCE AND disregard of God's law, made it necessary for God to send His only begotten Son, Jesus Christ, into the world. Adam's disobedience caused him to lose contact and fellowship with his God and Creator. His sin created a chasm between heaven and Earth, between man and God. Jesus Christ came into this world to reunite the creation with the Creator and to do away with the chasm.

Sin entered the world through one man, Adam, and with sin came death. But through one man, the Son of Man and Son of God, blessing and eternal life came to Earth.

> Therefore, just as through one man sin entered the world, and death through sin, and thus death spread to all men, because all sinned...But the free gift is not like the offense. For if by the one man's offense many died, much more the grace of God and the gift by the grace of the one Man, Jesus Christ, abounded to many. And the gift is not like that which came through the one who sinned. For the judgment which came

from one offense resulted in condemnation, but the free gift which came from many offenses resulted in justification. For if by the one man's offense death reigned through the one, much more those who receive abundance of grace and of the gift of righteousness will reign in life through the One, Jesus Christ.) Therefore, as through one man's offense judgment came to all men, resulting in condemnation, even so through one Man's righteous act the free gift came to all men, resulting in justification of life. For as by one man's disobedience many were made sinners, so also by one Man's obedience many will be made righteous. Moreover the law entered that the offense might abound. But where sin abounded, grace abounded much more, so that as sin reigned in death, even so grace might reign through righteousness to eternal life through Jesus Christ our Lord.

—ROMANS 5:12, 15–21

But now having been set free from sin, and having become slaves of God, you have your fruit to holiness, and the end, everlasting life. For the wages of sin is death, but the gift of God is eternal life in Christ Jesus our Lord.

—ROMANS 6:22–23

For since by man came death, by Man also came the resurrection of the dead. For as in Adam all die, even so in Christ all shall be made alive.

—1 CORINTHIANS 15:21–22

The death of Jesus Christ united heaven with Earth and established a path for reconciliation for all mankind, for all nations, races, and generations. He united those from the north and south, the east and west, those who are near and those who are far into one family, and He gave them a way to heaven. This is the good news. Let's read from the pages of the Holy Constitution about how this was accomplished and fulfilled in the spiritual realm:

> Giving thanks to the Father who has qualified us to be partakers of the inheritance of the saints in the light. He has delivered us from the power of darkness and conveyed us into the kingdom of the Son of His love, in whom we have redemption through His blood, the forgiveness of sins. He is the image of the invisible God, the firstborn over all creation. For by Him all things were created that are in heaven and that are on earth, visible and invisible, whether thrones or dominions or principalities or powers. All things were created through Him and for Him. And He is before all things, and in Him all things consist. And He is the head of the body, the church, who is the beginning, the firstborn from the dead, that in all things He may have the preeminence. For it pleased the Father that in Him all the fullness should dwell, and by Him to reconcile all things to Himself, by Him, whether things on earth or things in heaven, having made peace through the blood of His cross. And you, who once were alienated and enemies in your mind by wicked works, yet now He has reconciled in the body of His flesh through death, to present you holy, and blameless, and above reproach in His sight—if indeed you continue in the faith, grounded and steadfast, and are not moved away from the hope of the gospel which you heard, which was preached to every creature under heaven, of which I, Paul, became a minister.
>
> —Colossians 1:12–23

Therefore remember that you, once Gentiles in the flesh—who are called Uncircumcision by what is called the Circumcision made in the flesh by hands—that at that time you were without Christ, being aliens from the commonwealth of Israel and strangers from the covenants of promise, having no hope and without God in the world. But now in Christ Jesus you who once were far off have been brought near by the blood of Christ. For He Himself is our peace, who has made both one, and has broken down the middle wall of separation, having abolished in His flesh the enmity, that is, the law of commandments contained in ordinances, so as to create in Himself one new man from the two, thus making peace, and that He might reconcile them both to God in one body through the cross, thereby putting to death the enmity. And He came and preached peace to you who were afar off and to those who were near. For through Him we both have access by one Spirit to the Father. Now, therefore, you are no longer strangers and foreigners, but fellow citizens with the saints and members of the household of God, having been built on the foundation of the apostles and prophets, Jesus Christ Himself being the chief cornerstone, in whom the whole building, being fitted together, grows into a holy temple in the Lord, in whom you also are being built together for a dwelling place of God in the Spirit.

—Ephesians 2:11–22

All those who believe and trust in Jesus accepted His sacrifice and declare Him their personal Savior. Their next step of obedience is water baptism, at which point they accept the will of God for their life. They make Jesus the God of their lives. The Word of God calls these people the children of God:

Therefore, if anyone is in Christ, he is a new creation; old things have passed away; behold, all things have become new. Now all things are of God, who has reconciled us to Himself

through Jesus Christ, and has given us the ministry of reconciliation, that is, that God was in Christ reconciling the world
to Himself, not imputing their trespasses to them, and has
committed to us the word of reconciliation. Now then, we are
ambassadors for Christ, as though God were pleading through
us: we implore you on Christ's behalf, be reconciled to God.
For He made Him who knew no sin to be sin for us, that we
might become the righteousness of God in Him.

—2 CORINTHIANS 5:17–21

In the Word of God, we find two categories of people. The first
includes those who are in Adam. The second includes those who
are in Christ. The Word of God makes an interesting comparison
and a very deep difference between the two categories, and all citizens of this earth should be aware of this.

And so it is written, "The first man Adam became a living
being." The last Adam became a life-giving spirit. However,
the spiritual is not first, but the natural, and afterward the
spiritual. The first man was of the earth, made of dust; the
second Man is the Lord from heaven. As was the man of dust,
so also are those who are made of dust; and as is the heavenly Man, so also are those who are heavenly. And as we have
borne the image of the man of dust, we shall also bear the
image of the heavenly Man.

—1 CORINTHIANS 15:45–49

Jesus Christ, the Son of the living God, is the only One who
stands between man and God. He is the only peacemaker between
heaven and Earth, and there will never be another intercessor.

For there is one God and one Mediator between God and men, the Man Christ Jesus, who gave Himself a ransom for all, to be testified in due time.

—1 TIMOTHY 2:5–6

Jesus said to him, "I am the way, the truth, and the life. No one comes to the Father except through Me."

—JOHN 14:6

24

JESUS CHRIST, THE HIGH PRIEST OF THE NEW TESTAMENT

I N THE OLD TESTAMENT, THERE WERE CHIEF PRIESTS CHOSEN from among the Israelites. Though ordinary people, they were selected to present the entire nation before God. Their job was to bring gifts and sacrifices for the sins of the people, and also for their personal sins. Because the priests were regular people, they understood human problems, hardships, and sins. They went through similar situations and experienced similar events in their lives as compared to the masses. We must admit that no one can become a priest simply because they want to—they must also be chosen. In the Word of God, God Himself found and gathered His servants. God picked the chief priests. For example, Aaron was chosen by God, as was Jesus Christ.

So also Christ did not glorify Himself to become High Priest, but it was He who said to Him: "You are My Son, Today I have begotten You." As He also says in another place: "You are a priest forever According to the order of Melchizedek."

—HEBREWS 5:5–6

Jesus Christ, sent by God, assumed a human body and walked with the people of the earth. His presence among the people was a requirement for becoming the Son of Man. He had to be our first chief priest before our God the Father. When He was on this earth, Jesus Christ went through the same temptations we experience, and for this reason He understands our problems. He understands my hardships and shortcomings and yours also, dear reader. The Word of God says the following:

> Therefore, in all things He had to be made like His brethren, that He might be a merciful and faithful High Priest in things pertaining to God, to make propitiation for the sins of the people. For in that He Himself has suffered, being tempted, He is able to aid those who are tempted.
>
> —HEBREWS 2:17–18

Even though Jesus Christ was the Son of God, He had to go through much suffering in order to understand obedience. After He victoriously passed through these trials, He became the giver of eternal life for all those who listen, give their life into His hands, and believe Him and in Him. The Word of God says this:

> Though He was a Son, yet He learned obedience by the things which He suffered. And having been perfected, He became the author of eternal salvation to all who obey Him, called by God as High Priest "according to the order of Melchizedek."
>
> —HEBREWS 5:8–10

Many chief priests had to exist so that when one died, another would be present as a replacement. Jesus Christ, our Chief Priest, is everlasting, and we do not have need for any other. He lives eternally and is able to save those who come to God through Him. He is the perpetual Intercessor for us.

> But He, because He continues forever, has an unchangeable priesthood. Therefore He is also able to save to the uttermost those who come to God through Him, since He always lives to make intercession for them.
> —HEBREWS 7:24–25

The chief priests were charged with bringing gifts and sacrifices, and Jesus also had to bring His sacrifice. He did this by bringing Himself, on the cross. His sacrifice was different from the previous ones that were brought by the rest of the priests.

> But now He has obtained a more excellent ministry, inasmuch as He is also Mediator of a better covenant, which was established on better promises.
> —HEBREWS 8:6

In the Old Testament the priest was in the church daily, bringing offerings repeatedly. The sacrifices never could erase sin completely, forever. It was impossible for the blood of animals to wipe away the sins of man. God the Father changed the need for these Old Testament sacrifices by sending His only begotten Son into the world. Let's read of how this change happened:

> Therefore, when He came into the world, He said: "Sacrifice and offering You did not desire, But a body You have prepared for Me. In burnt offerings and sacrifices for sin You had no pleasure. Then I said, 'Behold, I have come—In the volume

of the book it is written of Me—To do Your will, O God.'"
Previously saying, "Sacrifice and offering, burnt offerings,
and offerings for sin You did not desire, nor had pleasure in
them " (which are offered according to the law), then He said,
"Behold, I have come to do Your will, O God." He takes away
the first that He may establish the second. By that will we
have been sanctified through the offering of the body of Jesus
Christ once for all. And every priest stands ministering daily
and offering repeatedly the same sacrifices, which can never
take away sins. But this Man, after He had offered one sacrifice for sins forever, sat down at the right hand of God,

—HEBREWS 10:5–12

This world requires such a priest. Even now, in the twenty-first
century, a priest such as this is needed by each of us. I need Him,
and you do too, dear reader.

For such a High Priest was fitting for us, who is holy, harmless, undefiled, separate from sinners, and has become higher
than the heavens; who does not need daily, as those high
priests, to offer up sacrifices, first for His own sins and then
for the people's, for this He did once for all when He offered
up Himself.

—HEBREWS 7:26–27

In the Old Testament, the priests were in the tabernacle as they
carried out their service. The tabernacle was made by people who
followed the instructions God gave to Moses. To remind ourselves
of how the tabernacle looked and how the service was carried out,
let's read a few verses:

For a tabernacle was prepared: the first part, in which was the
lampstand, the table, and the showbread, which is called the

sanctuary; and behind the second veil, the part of the tabernacle which is called the Holiest of All, which had the golden
censer and the ark of the covenant overlaid on all sides with
gold, in which were the golden pot that had the manna, Aaron's
rod that budded, and the tablets of the covenant; and above it
were the cherubim of glory overshadowing the mercy seat. Of
these things we cannot now speak in detail. Now when these
things had been thus prepared, the priests always went into
the first part of the tabernacle, performing the services. But
into the second part the high priest went alone once a year,
not without blood, which he offered for himself and for the
people's sins committed in ignorance.

—HEBREWS 9:2–7

Let's now read from the New Testament and see what service
the Son of God, our Savior, performed:

But Christ came as High Priest of the good things to come,
with the greater and more perfect tabernacle not made with
hands, that is, not of this creation. Not with the blood of goats
and calves, but with His own blood He entered the Most Holy
Place once for all, having obtained eternal redemption. For if
the blood of bulls and goats and the ashes of a heifer, sprinkling the unclean, sanctifies for the purifying of the flesh,
how much more shall the blood of Christ, who through the
eternal Spirit offered Himself without spot to God, cleanse
your conscience from dead works to serve the living God?
And for this reason He is the Mediator of the new covenant,
by means of death, for the redemption of the transgressions
under the first covenant, that those who are called may receive
the promise of the eternal inheritance.... For Christ has not
entered the holy places made with hands, which are copies of

the true, but into heaven itself, now to appear in the presence
of God for us.

—HEBREWS 9:11–15, 24

Now this is the main point of the things we are saying: We
have such a High Priest, who is seated at the right hand of
the throne of the Majesty in the heavens, a Minister of the
sanctuary and of the true tabernacle which the Lord erected,
and not man.

—HEBREWS 8:1–2

Jesus Christ, the Son of the living God and our High Priest,
returned to heaven after His resurrection to sit at the right side
of God and to intercede for us. For this reason, we cannot stop
believing in Him. He understands our weaknesses, our infirmities,
and shortcomings. He sees the trials we go through because He
also went through suffering and temptation. The only difference
between Him and us is that He was without sin after all His trials.

Seeing then that we have a great High Priest who has passed
through the heavens, Jesus the Son of God, let us hold fast
our confession. For we do not have a High Priest who cannot
sympathize with our weaknesses, but was in all points tempted
as we are, yet without sin. Let us therefore come boldly to the
throne of grace, that we may obtain mercy and find grace to
help in time of need.

—HEBREWS 4:14–16

Jesus Christ came to this earth to bring us to God, and He
suffered once and for all for our sins. He, a righteous and sinless
Man, died for us, an unrighteous and sinful race. When He comes
for the second time, He will come in glory as the King of kings.

He will come again to gather and take His faithful ones to be with Him in heaven.

> And as it is appointed for men to die once, but after this the judgment, so Christ was offered once to bear the sins of many. To those who eagerly wait for Him He will appear a second time, apart from sin, for salvation.
>
> —HEBREWS 9:27–28

This is good news! This is good news for all generations, for all people, nations, tribes, and tongues.

25

THE NAMES AND TITLES
OF JESUS CHRIST

T HE NAMES OF JESUS REFLECT HIS PERSONALITY, CHARACTER, godliness, actions, and His purpose for coming to Earth. From the Holy Scriptures, His personality is remembered. In the third chapter of Genesis, He is called the seed of woman:

> And I will put enmity Between you and the woman, And between your seed and her Seed; He shall bruise your head, And you shall bruise His heel.
> —GENESIS 3:15

In The Old Testament, the Israelites ate manna, a food substance that God provided for His people for forty years.

> And the house of Israel called its name Manna. And it was like white coriander seed, and the taste of it was like wafers made with honey.... And the children of Israel ate manna forty

years, until they came to an inhabited land; they ate manna until they came to the border of the land of Canaan.

—Exodus 16:31, 35

In the New Testament, Jesus Christ calls Himself the Bread of Life, the Living Bread, which only comes from the heavens.

"Our fathers ate the manna in the desert; as it is written, 'He gave them bread from heaven to eat.'"...And Jesus said to them, "I am the bread of life. He who comes to Me shall never hunger, and he who believes in Me shall never thirst."

—John 6:31, 35

His name is unique. There is only one Jesus Christ.

And the Lord shall be King over all the earth. In that day it shall be—"The Lord is one," And His name one.

—Zechariah 14:9

Yet for us there is one God, the Father, of whom are all things, and we for Him; and one Lord Jesus Christ, through whom are all things, and through whom we live.

—1 Corinthians 8:6

Jesus Christ is the ruler, lawmaker, and leader.

For the Lord is our Judge, The Lord is our Lawgiver, The Lord is our King; He will save us.

—Isaiah 33:22

But you, Bethlehem Ephrathah, Though you are little among the thousands of Judah, Yet out of you shall come forth to Me

The One to be Ruler in Israel, Whose goings forth are from of old, From everlasting.

—MICAH 5:2

"'But you, Bethlehem, in the land of Judah, Are not the least among the rulers of Judah; For out of you shall come a Ruler Who will shepherd My people Israel.'"

—MATTHEW 2:6

There is one Lawgiver, who is able to save and to destroy.

—JAMES 4:12

Jesus Christ is the root and the branch of David.

In that day the Branch of the LORD shall be beautiful and glorious; And the fruit of the earth shall be excellent and appealing For those of Israel who have escaped.

—ISAIAH 4:2

There shall come forth a Rod from the stem of Jesse, And a Branch shall grow out of his roots. The Spirit of the LORD shall rest upon Him, The Spirit of wisdom and understanding, The Spirit of counsel and might, The Spirit of knowledge and of the fear of the LORD.... Righteousness shall be the belt of His loins, And faithfulness the belt of His waist.... And in that day there shall be a Root of Jesse, Who shall stand as a banner to the people; For the Gentiles shall seek Him, And His resting place shall be glorious."

—ISAIAH 11:1–2, 5, 10

"Behold, the days are coming," says the LORD, "That I will raise to David a Branch of righteousness; A King shall reign and prosper, And execute judgment and righteousness in the Earth."

—JEREMIAH 23:5

Then speak to him, saying, "Thus says the LORD of hosts, saying: 'Behold, the Man whose name is the BRANCH! From His place He shall branch out, And He shall build the temple of the LORD; Yes, He shall build the temple of the LORD. He shall bear the glory, And shall sit and rule on His throne; So He shall be a priest on His throne, And the counsel of peace shall be between them both.'"

—ZECHARIAH 6:12–13

But one of the elders said to me, "Do not weep. Behold, the Lion of the tribe of Judah, the Root of David, has prevailed to open the scroll and to loose its seven seals."

—REVELATION 5:5

I, Jesus, have sent My angel to testify to you these things in the churches. I am the Root and the Offspring of David, the Bright and Morning Star.

—REVELATION 22:16

Jesus Christ is the heir of all that exists.

Has in these last days spoken to us by His Son, whom He has appointed heir of all things, through whom also He made the worlds.

—HEBREWS 1:2

Jesus Christ is the hiding place, strength, and the Rock for the nation of God.

The LORD is my rock and my fortress and my deliverer; My God, my strength, in whom I will trust; My shield and the horn of my salvation, my stronghold. I will call upon the

Lord, who is worthy to be praised; So shall I be saved from my enemies.

—Psalm 18:2–3

For You are my rock and my fortress; Therefore, for Your name's sake, Lead me and guide me. Pull me out of the net which they have secretly laid for me, For You are my strength. Into Your hand I commit my spirit; You have redeemed me, O Lord God of truth.

—Psalm 31:3–5

The Lord is good, A stronghold in the day of trouble; And He knows those who trust in Him.

—Nahum 1:7

Jesus Christ is our hope.

O the Hope of Israel, his Savior in time of trouble, Why should You be like a stranger in the land, And like a traveler who turns aside to tarry for a night?

—Jeremiah 14:8

Blessed is the man who trusts in the Lord, And whose hope is the Lord. For he shall be like a tree planted by the waters, Which spreads out its roots by the river, And will not fear when heat comes; But its leaf will be green, And will not be anxious in the year of drought, Nor will cease from yielding fruit.

—Jeremiah 17:7–8

O Lord, the hope of Israel, All who forsake You shall be ashamed.

—Jeremiah 17:13

Paul, an apostle of Jesus Christ, by the commandment of God
our Savior and the Lord Jesus Christ, our hope.

—1 Timothy 1:1

**Only Jesus can be our hope today. Jesus Christ is the source of
living water; He is the source of life.**

For with You is the fountain of life; in Your light we see light.

—Psalm 36:9

For My people have committed two evils: They have forsaken
Me, the fountain of living waters, And hewn themselves
cisterns—broken cisterns that can hold no water.

—Jeremiah 2:13

O Lord, the hope of Israel, All who forsake You shall be
ashamed. "Those who depart from Me Shall be written in the
earth, Because they have forsaken the Lord, The fountain of
living waters."

—Jeremiah 17:13

But whoever drinks of the water that I shall give him will
never thirst. But the water that I shall give him will become
in him a fountain of water springing up into everlasting life.

—John 4:14

And He said to me, "It is done! I am the Alpha and the Omega,
the Beginning and the End. I will give of the fountain of the
water of life freely to him who thirsts.

—Revelation 21:6

On the last day, that great day of the feast, Jesus stood and
cried out, saying, "If anyone thirsts, let him come to Me and

drink. He who believes in Me, as the Scripture has said, out of his heart will flow rivers of living water.

–John 7:37–38

The name Immanuel is the name of Jesus.

Therefore the Lord Himself will give you a sign: Behold, the virgin shall conceive and bear a Son, and shall call His name Immanuel.

—Isaiah 7:14

"And she will bring forth a Son, and you shall call His name JESUS, for He will save His people from their sins." So all this was done that it might be fulfilled which was spoken by the Lord through the prophet, saying: "Behold, the virgin shall be with child, and bear a Son, and they shall call His name Immanuel," which is translated, "God with us."

—Matthew 1:21-23

For unto us a Child is born, Unto us a Son is given; And the government will be upon His shoulder. And His name will be called Wonderful, Counselor, Mighty God, Everlasting Father, Prince of Peace. Of the increase of His government and peace There will be no end, Upon the throne of David and over His kingdom, To order it and establish it with judgment and justice From that time forward, even forever. The zeal of the Lord of hosts will perform this.

—Isaiah 9:6–7

Then the angel said to them, "Do not be afraid, for behold, I bring you good tidings of great joy which will be to all people. For there is born to you this day in the city of David a Savior, who is Christ the Lord. And this will be the sign to you: You will find a Babe wrapped in swaddling cloths, lying in a manger."

—LUKE 2:10–12

Jesus Christ is from Nazareth.

And He came and dwelt in a city called Nazareth, that it might be fulfilled which was spoken by the prophets, "He shall be called a Nazarene."

—MATTHEW 2:23

So the multitudes said, "This is Jesus, the prophet from Nazareth of Galilee."

—MATTHEW 21:11

So I answered, "Who are You, Lord?" And He said to me, "I am Jesus of Nazareth, whom you are persecuting."

—ACTS 22:8

Jesus Christ is holy.

And one cried to another and said: "Holy, holy, holy is the LORD of hosts; The whole earth is full of His glory!"

—ISAIAH 6:3

[A man with an unclean spirit cried out] "Let us alone! What have we to do with You, Jesus of Nazareth? Did You come to destroy us? I know who You are—the Holy One of God!"

—MARK 1:24

Also with the lute I will praise You—and Your faithfulness, O my God! To You I will sing with the harp, O holy One of Israel.

—PSALM 71:22

But you denied the holy One and the Just, and asked for a murderer to be granted to you.

—ACTS 3:14

And to the angel of the church in Philadelphia write, "These things says He who is holy, He who is true, 'He who has the key of David, He who opens and no one shuts, and shuts and no one opens.'"

—REVELATION 3:7

The four living creatures, each having six wings, were full of eyes around and within. And they do not rest day or night, saying: "Holy, holy, holy, Lord God Almighty, Who was and is and is to come!"

—REVELATION 4:8

Jesus Christ is the firstborn, the begotten Son, the Son of the Highest, the Son of God.

And I will pour on the house of David and on the inhabitants of Jerusalem the Spirit of grace and supplication; then they will look on Me whom they pierced; they will mourn for Him as one mourns for his only son, and grieve for Him as one grieves for a firstborn.

—ZECHARIAH 12:10

He said to them, "But who do you say that I am?" Simon Peter answered and said, "You are the Christ, the Son of the living God."

—MATTHEW 16:15–16

While he was still speaking, behold, a bright cloud over-shadowed them; and suddenly a voice came out of the cloud, saying, "This is My beloved Son, in whom I am well pleased. Hear Him!"

—MATTHEW 17:5

And the Word became flesh and dwelt among us, and we beheld His glory, the glory as of the only begotten of the Father, full of grace and truth.... Nathanael answered and said to Him, "Rabbi, You are the Son of God! You are the King of Israel!"

—JOHN 1:14, 49

She said to Him, "Yes, Lord, I believe that You are the Christ, the Son of God, who is to come into the world."

—JOHN 11:27

And behold, you will conceive in your womb and bring forth a Son, and shall call His name JESUS. He will be great, and will be called the Son of the Highest; and the Lord God will give Him the throne of His father David. And He will reign over the house of Jacob forever, and of His kingdom there will be no end.

—LUKE 1:31–33

For to which of the angels did He ever say: "You are My Son, Today I have begotten You"? And again: "I will be to Him a Father, And He shall be to Me a Son"?

—HEBREWS 1:5

Jesus Christ is the Creator of the universe.

In the beginning was the Word, and the Word was with God, and the Word was God. He was in the beginning with God. All things were made through Him, and without Him nothing was made that was made.

—JOHN 1:1–3

For by Him all things were created that are in heaven and that are on earth, visible and invisible, whether thrones or dominions or principalities or powers. All things were created through Him and for Him. And He is before all things, and in Him all things consist.

—COLOSSIANS 1:16–17

But to the Son He says: "Your throne, O God, is forever and ever; A scepter of righteousness is the scepter of Your kingdom. You have loved righteousness and hated lawlessness; Therefore God, Your God, has anointed You With the oil of gladness more than Your companions." And: "You, LORD, in the beginning laid the foundation of the earth, And the heavens are the work of Your hands. They will perish, but You remain; And they will all grow old like a garment; Like a cloak You will fold them up, And they will be changed. But You are the same, And Your years will not fail."

—HEBREWS 1:8–12

For every house is built by someone, but He who built all things is God.

—HEBREWS 3:4

Jesus Christ is the Son of Man.

When Jesus came into the region of Caesarea Philippi, He asked His disciples, saying, "Who do men say that I, the Son of Man, am?"

—MATTHEW 16:13

For as Jonah was three days and three nights in the belly of the great fish, so will the Son of Man be three days and three nights in the heart of the earth.

—MATTHEW 12:40

Behold, we are going up to Jerusalem, and the Son of Man will be betrayed to the chief priests and to the scribes; and they will condemn Him to death and deliver Him to the Gentiles....For even the Son of Man did not come to be served, but to serve, and to give His life a ransom for many.

—MARK 10: 33, 45

For the Son of Man did not come to destroy men's lives but to save them.

—LUKE 9:56

For the Son of Man has come to seek and to save that which was lost.

—LUKE 19:10

Then they will see the Son of Man coming in a cloud with power and great glory...."Watch therefore, and pray always that you may be counted worthy to escape all these things that will come to pass, and to stand before the Son of Man."

—LUKE 21:27, 36

Jesus Christ, the Son of God, is the Lord of the Sabbath.

And He said to them, "The Sabbath was made for man, and not man for the Sabbath. Therefore the Son of Man is also Lord of the Sabbath."

—MARK 2:27–28

Jesus Christ is the image of God.

> He is the image of the invisible God, the firstborn over all creation.
>
> —Colossians 1:15

> Whose minds the god of this age has blinded, who do not believe, lest the light of the gospel of the glory of Christ, who is the image of God, should shine on them.
>
> —2 Corinthians 4:4

> Jesus said to him, "Have I been with you so long, and yet you have not known Me, Philip? He who has seen Me has seen the Father; so how can you say, 'Show us the Father'?
>
> —John 14:9

> For in Him dwells all the fullness of the Godhead bodily.
>
> —Colossians 2:9

Jesus Christ is wisdom and is above wisdom.

> I, wisdom, dwell with prudence, And find out knowledge and discretion. The fear of the Lord is to hate evil; Pride and arrogance and the evil way And the perverse mouth I hate. Counsel is mine, and sound wisdom; I am understanding, I have strength.
>
> —Proverbs 8:12–14

> And the Child grew and became strong in spirit, filled with wisdom; and the grace of God was upon Him.... And Jesus increased in wisdom and stature, and in favor with God and men.
>
> —Luke 2:40, 52

And when the Sabbath had come, He began to teach in the synagogue. And many hearing Him were astonished, saying, "Where did this Man get these things? And what wisdom is this which is given to Him, that such mighty works are performed by His hands!

—MARK 6:2

But of Him you are in Christ Jesus, who became for us wisdom from God—and righteousness and sanctification and redemption.

—1 CORINTHIANS 1:30

That their hearts may be encouraged, being knit together in love, and attaining to all riches of the full assurance of understanding, to the knowledge of the mystery of God, both of the Father and of Christ, in whom are hidden all the treasures of wisdom and knowledge.

—COLOSSIANS 2:2–3

Oh, the depth of the riches both of the wisdom and knowledge of God! How unsearchable are His judgments and His ways past finding out! "For who has known the mind of the LORD? Or who has become His counselor?" "Or who has first given to Him And it shall be repaid to him?" For of Him and through Him and to Him are all things, to whom be glory forever. Amen.

—ROMANS 11:33–36

Jesus Christ is a teacher and an educator.

But you, do not be called "Rabbi"; for One is your Teacher, the Christ, and you are all brethren. Do not call anyone on earth your father; for One is your Father, He who is in heaven. And do not be called teachers; for One is your Teacher, the Christ.

—MATTHEW 23:8, 10

You call Me Teacher and Lord, and you say well, for so I am.

—JOHN 13:13

Jesus said to her, "Mary!" She turned and said to Him, "Rabboni!" (which is to say, Teacher).

—JOHN 20:16

Jesus Christ sows truth.

He sowed the words that lead to the kingdom of God. He spread the words of salvation for mankind, of everlasting life, wherever He went: in cities, synagogues, mountains, and deserts.

The sower sows the word.

—MARK 4:14

He answered and said to them: "He who sows the good seed is the Son of Man."

—MATTHEW 13:37

Jesus Christ is called a friend of the sinners.

This is because He didn't come to save the righteous, but to save the sinners.

The Son of Man has come eating and drinking, and you say, "Look, a glutton and a winebibber, a friend of tax collectors and sinners!"

—LUKE 7:34

When Jesus heard that, He said to them, "Those who are well have no need of a physician, but those who are sick. But go and learn what this means: 'I desire mercy and not sacrifice.' For I did not come to call the righteous, but sinners, to repentance."

—MATTHEW 9:12–13

Jesus Christ is a servant.

"For even the Son of Man did not come to be served, but to serve, and to give His life a ransom for many."

—MARK 10:45

But made Himself of no reputation, taking the form of a bondservant, and coming in the likeness of men. And being found in appearance as a man, He humbled Himself and became obedient to the point of death, even the death of the cross.

—PHILIPPIANS 2:7–8

Jesus Christ is a healer and the One who carries our sorrows.

Surely He has borne our griefs And carried our sorrows; Yet we esteemed Him stricken, Smitten by God, and afflicted. But He was wounded for our transgressions, He was bruised for our iniquities; The chastisement for our peace was upon Him, And by His stripes we are healed.

—ISAIAH 53:4–5

When He had come down from the mountain, great multitudes followed Him. And behold, a leper came and worshiped Him, saying, "Lord, if You are willing, You can make me clean." Then Jesus put out His hand and touched him, saying, "I am willing; be cleansed." Immediately his leprosy was cleansed.

—MATTHEW 8:1–3

Now when Jesus had come into Peter's house, He saw his wife's mother lying sick with a fever. So He touched her hand, and the fever left her. And she arose and served them.

—MATTHEW 8:14–15

When they had crossed over, they came to the land of Gennesaret. And when the men of that place recognized Him, they sent out into all that surrounding region, brought to Him all who were sick, and begged Him that they might only touch the hem of His garment. And as many as touched it were made perfectly well.

—MATTHEW 14:34–36

There he found a certain man named Aeneas, who had been bedridden eight years and was paralyzed. And Peter said to him, "Aeneas, Jesus the Christ heals you. Arise and make your bed." Then he arose immediately.

—ACTS 9:33–34

Who Himself bore our sins in His own body on the tree, that we, having died to sin, might live for righteousness—by whose stripes you were healed.

—1 PETER 2:24

Jesus Christ is the Light of the World, the Light for man, the Light for pagans.

The people who walked in darkness Have seen a great light; Those who dwelt in the land of the shadow of death, Upon them a light has shined.

—ISAIAH 9:2

I, the LORD, have called You in righteousness, And will hold Your hand; I will keep You and give You as a covenant to the people, As a light to the Gentiles.

—ISAIAH 42:6

For so the Lord has commanded us: "I have set you as a light to the Gentiles, That you should be for salvation to the ends of the earth."

—ACTS 13:47

Indeed He says, "It is too small a thing that You should be My Servant To raise up the tribes of Jacob, And to restore the preserved ones of Israel; I will also give You as a light to the Gentiles, That You should be My salvation to the ends of the earth."

—ISAIAH 49:6

As long as I am in the world, I am the light of the world.

—JOHN 9:5

Then Jesus spoke to them again, saying, "I am the light of the world. He who follows Me shall not walk in darkness, but have the light of life."

—JOHN 8:12

I have come as a light into the world, that whoever believes in Me should not abide in darkness.

—JOHN 12:46

The city had no need of the sun or of the moon to shine in it, for the glory of God illuminated it. The Lamb is its light. And the nations of those who are saved shall walk in its light, and the kings of the earth bring their glory and honor into it.

—REVELATION 21:23–24

The sun shall no longer be your light by day, Nor for brightness shall the moon give light to you; But the LORD will be to you an everlasting light, And your God your glory. Your sun shall no longer go down, Nor shall your moon withdraw itself; For the LORD will be your everlasting light, And the days of your mourning shall be ended.

—ISAIAH 60:19–20

Jesus Christ is the Bread from heaven, the Living Bread, the Bread of Life.

And Jesus said to them, "I am the bread of life. He who comes to Me shall never hunger, and he who believes in Me shall never thirst....I am the bread of life....This is the bread which comes down from heaven, that one may eat of it and not die. I am the living bread which came down from heaven. If anyone eats of this bread, he will live forever; and the bread that I shall give is My flesh, which I shall give for the life of the world....This is the bread which came down from heaven—not as your fathers ate the manna, and are dead. He who eats this bread will live forever."

—JOHN 6:35, 48, 50–51, 58

Jesus Christ is the Good Shepherd.

He will feed His flock like a shepherd; He will gather the lambs with His arm, And carry them in His bosom, And gently lead those who are with young.

—ISAIAH 40:11

Hear the word of the LORD, O nations, And declare it in the isles afar off, and say, "He who scattered Israel will gather him, And keep him as a shepherd does his flock."

—JEREMIAH 31:10

I am the good shepherd. The good shepherd gives His life for the sheep....I am the good shepherd; and I know My sheep, and am known by My own....My sheep hear My voice, and I know them, and they follow Me. And I give them eternal life, and they shall never perish; neither shall anyone snatch them out of My hand.

—JOHN 10:11, 14, 27–28

Now may the God of peace who brought up our Lord Jesus from the dead, that great Shepherd of the sheep, through the blood of the everlasting covenant, make you complete in every good work to do His will, working in you what is well pleasing in His sight, through Jesus Christ, to whom be glory forever and ever. Amen.

—HEBREWS 13:20–21

Jesus Christ is the only door to everlasting life.

I am the door. If anyone enters by Me, he will be saved, and will go in and out and find pasture....Most assuredly, I say to you, he who does not enter the sheepfold by the door, but climbs up some other way, the same is a thief and a robber."...The Jesus said to them again, "Most assuredly, I say to you, I am the door of the sheep."

—JOHN 10:9, 17

Jesus Christ is the only true vine.

> I am the true vine, and My Father is the vinedresser.... Abide in
> Me, and I in you. As the branch cannot bear fruit of itself, unless
> it abides in the vine, neither can you, unless you abide in Me. I
> am the vine, you are the branches. He who abides in Me, and I in
> him, bears much fruit; for without Me you can do nothing.
>
> —John 15:1, 4–5

Jesus Christ is the Way, the Truth, and the Life.

> Jesus said to him, "I am the way, the truth, and the life. No
> one comes to the Father except through Me."
>
> —John 14:6

Jesus Christ is the resurrection.

> Jesus said to her, "I am the resurrection and the life. He who
> believes in Me, though he may die, he shall live. And whoever
> lives and believes in Me shall never die. Do you believe this?"
>
> —John 11:25–26

Jesus Christ is everlasting life.

> And we know that the Son of God has come and has given us
> an understanding, that we may know Him who is true; and
> we are in Him who is true, in His Son Jesus Christ. This is the
> true God and eternal life.
>
> —1 John 5:20

> The life was manifested, and we have seen, and bear witness,
> and declare to you that eternal life which was with the Father
> and was manifested to us.
>
> —1 John 1:2

And this is the testimony: that God has given us eternal life, and this life is in His Son. He who has the Son has life; he who does not have the Son of God does not have life.

—1 JOHN 5:11–12

By this we know love, because He laid down His life for us. And we also ought to lay down our lives for the brethren.

—1 JOHN 3:16

He who believes in the Son has everlasting life; and he who does not believe the Son shall not see life, but the wrath of God abides on him.

—JOHN 3:36

Jesus Christ is the only Savior and Redeemer of all of mankind.

For I know that my Redeemer lives, And He shall stand at last on the earth.

—JOB 19:25

I, even I, am the LORD, And besides Me there is no savior.

—ISAIAH 43:11

I have made the earth, And created man on it. I—My hands—stretched out the heavens, And all their host I have commanded.... Tell and bring forth your case; Yes, let them take counsel together. Who has declared this from ancient time? Who has told it from that time? Have not I, the LORD? And there is no other God besides Me, A just God and a Savior; There is none besides Me. "Look to Me, and be saved, All you ends of the earth! For I am God, and there is no other.

—ISAIAH 45:12, 21–22

Yet I am the LORD your God Ever since the land of Egypt, And you shall know no God but Me; For there is no savior besides Me.

—Hosea 13:4

For there is born to you this day in the city of David a Savior, who is Christ the Lord.

—LUKE 2:11

Then they said to the woman, "Now we believe, not because of what you said, for we ourselves have heard Him and we know that this is indeed the Christ, the Savior of the world."

—JOHN 4:42

Him God has exalted to His right hand to be Prince and Savior, to give repentance to Israel and forgiveness of sins.

—ACTS 5:31

From this man's seed, according to the promise, God raised up for Israel a Savior—Jesus.

—ACTS 13:23

For our citizenship is in heaven, from which we also eagerly wait for the Savior, the Lord Jesus Christ.

—PHILIPPIANS 3:20

And we have seen and testify that the Father has sent the Son as Savior of the world.

—1 JOHN 4:14

Jesus Christ is the only intercessor between God and man.

For there is one God and one Mediator between God and men, the Man Christ Jesus, who gave Himself a ransom for all, to be testified in due time.

—1 TIMOTHY 2:5–6

Jesus said to him, "I am the way, the truth, and the life. No one comes to the Father except through Me."

—JOHN 14:6

Jesus Christ is the propitiation for the sins of man.

And He Himself is the propitiation for our sins, and not for ours only but also for the whole world.

—1 JOHN 2:2

In this is love, not that we loved God, but that He loved us and sent His Son to be the propitiation for our sins.

—1 JOHN 4:10

For it was fitting for Him, for whom are all things and by whom are all things, in bringing many sons to glory, to make the captain of their salvation perfect through sufferings.

—HEBREWS 2:10

If we confess our sins, He is faithful and just to forgive us our sins and to cleanse us from all unrighteousness.

—1 JOHN 1:9

Jesus Christ is forever the High Priest.

Therefore, holy brethren, partakers of the heavenly calling, consider the Apostle and High Priest of our confession, Christ Jesus.

—HEBREWS 3:1

Seeing then that we have a great High Priest who has passed through the heavens, Jesus the Son of God, let us hold fast our confession. For we do not have a High Priest who cannot sympathize with our weaknesses, but was in all points tempted as we are, yet without sin.

—HEBREWS 4:14–15

Where the forerunner has entered for us, even Jesus, having become High Priest forever according to the order of Melchizedek.

—HEBREWS 6:20

For such a High Priest was fitting for us, who is holy, harmless, undefiled, separate from sinners, and has become higher than the heavens.

—HEBREWS 7:26

Now this is the main point of the things we are saying: We have such a High Priest, who is seated at the right hand of the throne of the Majesty in the heavens, a Minister of the sanctuary and of the true tabernacle which the Lord erected, and not man.

—HEBREWS 8:1–2

Jesus is our intercessor and advocate.

And for this reason He is the Mediator of the new covenant, by means of death, for the redemption of the transgressions under the first covenant, that those who are called may receive the promise of the eternal inheritance.

—Hebrews 9:15

But He, because He continues forever, has an unchangeable priesthood. Therefore He is also able to save to the uttermost those who come to God through Him, since He always lives to make intercession for them.

—Hebrews 7:24–25

But you have come to Mount Zion and to the city of the living God, the heavenly Jerusalem, to an innumerable company of angels, to the general assembly and church of the firstborn who are registered in heaven, to God the Judge of all, to the spirits of just men made perfect, to Jesus the Mediator of the new covenant, and to the blood of sprinkling that speaks better things than that of Abel.

—Hebrews 12:22–24

My little children, these things I write to you, so that you may not sin. And if anyone sins, we have an Advocate with the Father, Jesus Christ the righteous.

—1 John 2:1

Jesus Christ is the Head of the church and of all principalities and powers.

And He is before all things, and in Him all things consist. And He is the head of the body, the church, who is the beginning, the firstborn from the dead, that in all things He may have the preeminence.

—COLOSSIANS 1:17–18

And what is the exceeding greatness of His power toward us who believe, according to the working of His mighty power which He worked in Christ when He raised Him from the dead and seated Him at His right hand in the heavenly places, far above all principality and power and might and dominion, and every name that is named, not only in this age but also in that which is to come. And He put all things under His feet, and gave Him to be head over all things to the church, which is His body, the fullness of Him who fills all in all.

—EPHESIANS 1:19–23

For in Him dwells all the fullness of the Godhead bodily; and you are complete in Him, who is the head of all principality and power.

—COLOSSIANS 2:9–10

Jesus Christ is the judge of the dead and the living. He is a righteous judge.

And He commanded us to preach to the people, and to testify that it is He who was ordained by God to be Judge of the living and the dead.

—ACTS 10:42

When the Son of Man comes in His glory, and all the holy angels with Him, then He will sit on the throne of His glory. All the nations will be gathered before Him, and He will separate them one from another, as a shepherd divides his sheep from the goats. And He will set the sheep on His right hand, but the goats on the left. Then the King will say to those on His right hand, "Come, you blessed of My Father, inherit the kingdom prepared for you from the foundation of the world."...Then He will also say to those on the left hand, "Depart from Me, you cursed, into the everlasting fire prepared for the devil and his angels."...And these will go away into everlasting punishment, but the righteous into eternal life.

—MATTHEW 25:31–34, 41, 46

Finally, there is laid up for me the crown of righteousness, which the Lord, the righteous Judge, will give to me on that Day, and not to me only but also to all who have loved His appearing.

—2 TIMOTHY 4:8

Jesus Christ is the same forever.

Jesus Christ is the same yesterday, today, and forever.

—HEBREWS 13:8

Jesus said to them, "Most assuredly, I say to you, before Abraham was, I AM."

—JOHN 8:58

Jesus Christ is the foundation, the Rock, and the Cornerstone of the Christian faith.

Therefore thus says the Lord GOD: "Behold, I lay in Zion a stone for a foundation, A tried stone, a precious cornerstone, a sure foundation; Whoever believes will not act hastily.

—ISAIAH 28:16

For no other foundation can anyone lay than that which is laid, which is Jesus Christ.

—1 CORINTHIANS 3:11

And all drank the same spiritual drink. For they drank of that spiritual Rock that followed them, and that Rock was Christ.

—1 CORINTHIANS 10:4

Coming to Him as to a living stone, rejected indeed by men, but chosen by God and precious...Therefore it is also contained in the Scripture, "Behold, I lay in Zion A chief cornerstone, elect, precious, And he who believes on Him will by no means be put to shame." Therefore, to you who believe, He is precious; but to those who are disobedient, "The stone which the builders rejected Has become the chief cornerstone," and "A stone of stumbling And a rock of offense." They stumble, being disobedient to the word, to which they also were appointed.

—1 PETER 2:4, 6–8

But Simon Peter answered Him, "Lord, to whom shall we go? You have the words of eternal life. Also we have come to believe and know that You are the Christ, the Son of the living God."

—JOHN 6:68–69

Jesus Christ is the author and finisher of our faith.

Looking unto Jesus, the author and finisher of our faith, who for the joy that was set before Him endured the cross, despising the shame, and has sat down at the right hand of the throne of God.

—HEBREWS 12:2

Jesus Christ is our temple.

But I saw no temple in it, for the Lord God Almighty and the Lamb are its temple.

—REVELATION 21:22

Jesus Christ is the King of kings and Lord of lords.

I watched till thrones were put in place, And the Ancient of Days was seated; His garment was white as snow, And the hair of His head was like pure wool. His throne was a fiery flame, Its wheels a burning fire.... I was watching in the night visions, And behold, One like the Son of Man, Coming with the clouds of heaven! He came to the Ancient of Days, And they brought Him near before Him. Then to Him was given dominion and glory and a kingdom, That all peoples, nations, and languages should serve Him. His dominion is an everlasting dominion, Which shall not pass away, And His kingdom the one Which shall not be destroyed.

—DANIEL 7:9, 13–14

I will cut off the chariot from Ephraim And the horse from Jerusalem; The battle bow shall be cut off. He shall speak peace to the nations; His dominion shall be 'from sea to sea, And from the River to the ends of the earth.

—ZECHARIAH 9:10

These will make war with the Lamb, and the Lamb will overcome them, for He is Lord of lords and King of kings; and those who are with Him are called, chosen, and faithful.

—REVELATION 17:14

And He has on His robe and on His thigh a name written: KING OF KINGS AND LORD OF LORDS.

—REVELATION 19:16

Now to the King eternal, immortal, invisible, to God who alone is wise, be honor and glory forever and ever. Amen.

—1 TIMOTHY 1:17

Which He will manifest in His own time, He who is the blessed and only Potentate, the King of kings and Lord of lords.

—1 TIMOTHY 6:15

Jesus Christ is the Lamb of God.

And looking at Jesus as He walked, he said, "Behold the Lamb of God!"

—JOHN 1:36

Therefore purge out the old leaven, that you may be a new lump, since you truly are unleavened. For indeed Christ, our Passover, was sacrificed for us.

—1 CORINTHIANS 5:7

Jesus Christ is the righteous and true One, who was, and is, and is to come.

John, to the seven churches which are in Asia: Grace to you and peace from Him who is and who was and who is to come, and from the seven Spirits who are before His throne, and from Jesus Christ, the faithful witness, the firstborn from the dead, and the ruler over the kings of the earth. To Him who loved us and washed us from our sins in His own blood.

—REVELATION 1:4–5

Now I saw heaven opened, and behold, a white horse. And He who sat on him was called Faithful and True, and in righteousness He judges and makes war.

—REVELATION 19:11

Jesus Christ is the Lord God Almighty, the omnipotent One.

They sing the song of Moses, the servant of God, and the song of the Lamb, saying: "Great and marvelous are Your works, Lord God Almighty! Just and true are Your ways, O King of the saints! Who shall not fear You, O Lord, and glorify Your name? For You alone are holy. For all nations shall come and worship before You, For Your judgments have been manifested."

—REVELATION 15:3–4

And I heard, as it were, the voice of a great multitude, as the sound of many waters and as the sound of mighty thunderings, saying, "Alleluia! For the Lord God Omnipotent reigns!"

—REVELATION 19:6

Jesus Christ is the conqueror.

These things I have spoken to you, that in Me you may have peace. In the world you will have tribulation; but be of good cheer, I have overcome the world.

—JOHN 16:33

And I looked, and behold, a white horse. He who sat on it had a bow; and a crown was given to him, and he went out conquering and to conquer.

—REVELATION 6:2

Jesus Christ is the living Word of God.

In the beginning was the Word, and the Word was with God, and the Word was God.

—JOHN 1:1

He was clothed with a robe dipped in blood, and His name is called The Word of God.

—Revelation 19:13

Jesus Christ is the Alpha and Omega, the first and last.

Who has performed and done it, Calling the generations from the beginning? 'I, the Lord, am the first; And with the last I am He.'

—Isaiah 41:4

"I am the Alpha and the Omega, the Beginning and the End," says the Lord, "who is and who was and who is to come, the Almighty."...And when I saw Him, I fell at His feet as dead. But He laid His right hand on me, saying to me, "Do not be afraid; I am the First and the Last. I am He who lives, and was dead, and behold, I am alive forevermore. Amen. And I have the keys of Hades and of Death."

—Revelation 1:8, 17–18

And to the angel of the church in Smyrna write, "These things says the First and the Last, who was dead, and came to life."

—Revelation 2:8

"I am the Alpha and the Omega, the Beginning and the End, the First and the Last."

—Revelation 22:13

And to the angel of the church of the Laodiceans write, "These things says the Amen, the Faithful and True Witness, the Beginning of the creation of God."

—Revelation 3:14

Jesus Christ is the Groom and the church is His bride.

> I will betroth you to Me forever; Yes, I will betroth you to Me In righteousness and justice, In lovingkindness and mercy; I will betroth you to Me in faithfulness, And you shall know the LORD.
>
> —HOSEA 2:19–20

> For I am jealous for you with godly jealousy. For I have betrothed you to one husband, that I may present you as a chaste virgin to Christ.
>
> —2 CORINTHIANS 11:2

> Let us be glad and rejoice and give Him glory, for the marriage of the Lamb has come, and His wife has made herself ready.
>
> —REVELATION 19:7

> Then I, John, saw the holy city, New Jerusalem, coming down out of heaven from God, prepared as a bride adorned for her husband.... Then one of the seven angels who had the seven bowls filled with the seven last plagues came to me and talked with me, saying, "Come, I will show you the bride, the Lamb's wife." And he carried me away in the Spirit to a great and high mountain, and showed me the great city, the holy Jerusalem, descending out of heaven from God.
>
> —REVELATION 21:2, 9–10

Jesus Christ's name is higher than any other name.

> Who, being in the form of God, did not consider it robbery to be equal with God, but made Himself of no reputation, taking the form of a bondservant, and coming in the likeness of men. And being found in appearance as a man, He humbled

Himself and became obedient to the point of death, even the death of the cross. Therefore God also has highly exalted Him and given Him the name which is above every name, that at the name of Jesus every knee should bow, of those in heaven, and of those on earth, and of those under the earth, and that every tongue should confess that Jesus Christ is Lord, to the glory of God the Father.

—PHILIPPIANS 2:6–11

All living things, all of creation, will bow before the name of Jesus Christ. Praise and worship the name of God!

Oh, give thanks to the LORD! Call upon His name; Make known His deeds among the peoples! Sing to Him, sing psalms to Him; Talk of all His wondrous works! Glory in His holy name; Let the hearts of those rejoice who seek the LORD! Seek the LORD and His strength; Seek His face evermore! Remember His marvelous works which He has done, His wonders, and the judgments of His mouth.

—1 CHRONICLES 16:8–12

Praise the LORD! Blessed is the man who fears the LORD, Who delights greatly in His commandments. His descendants will be mighty on earth; The generation of the upright will be blessed. Wealth and riches will be in his house, And his righteousness endures forever.

—PSALM 112:1–3

Behold, bless the LORD, All you servants of the LORD, Who by night stand in the house of the LORD! Lift up your hands in the sanctuary, And bless the LORD. The LORD who made heaven and earth Bless you from Zion!

—PSALM 134:1–3

Let them praise the name of the LORD, For His name alone is exalted; His glory is above the earth and heaven.

—PSALM 148:13

And in that day you will say: "Praise the LORD, call upon His name; Declare His deeds among the peoples, Make mention that His name is exalted."

—ISAIAH 12:4

And now, together, lets look at the following words:

Also with the lute I will praise You—And Your faithfulness, O my God! To You I will sing with the harp, O Holy One of Israel. My lips shall greatly rejoice when I sing to You, And my soul, which You have redeemed. My tongue also shall talk of Your righteousness all the day long; For they are confounded, For they are brought to shame Who seek my hurt.

—PSALM 71:22–24

To You, O my Strength, I will sing praises; For God is my defense, My God of mercy.

—PSALM 59:17

The proud have forged a lie against me, But I will keep Your precepts with my whole heart. Their heart is as fat as grease, But I delight in Your law. It is good for me that I have been afflicted, That I may learn Your statutes. The law of Your mouth is better to me Than thousands of coins of gold and silver.... Unless Your law had been my delight, I would then have perished in my affliction. I will never forget Your precepts, For by them You have given me life.

—PSALM 119:69–72, 92–93

I will extol You, my God, O King; And I will bless Your name forever and ever. Every day I will bless You, And I will praise Your name forever and ever. Great is the LORD, and greatly to be praised; And His greatness is unsearchable. One generation shall praise Your works to another, And shall declare Your mighty acts. I will meditate on the glorious splendor of Your majesty, And on Your wondrous works. Men shall speak of the might of Your awesome acts, And I will declare Your greatness. They shall utter the memory of Your great goodness, And shall sing of Your righteousness.

—PSALM 145:1–7

And if it seems evil to you to serve the LORD, choose for yourselves this day whom you will serve, whether the gods which your fathers served that were on the other side of the River, or the gods of the Amorites, in whose land you dwell. But as for me and my house, we will serve the LORD.

—JOSHUA 24:15

Yet I will rejoice in the LORD, I will joy in the God of my salvation.

—HABAKKUK 3:18

26

SALVATION IS ONLY
IN JESUS CHRIST

OUR GREAT AND POWERFUL GOD, CREATOR OF HEAVEN and Earth, established a single path for salvation that unites a sinful people with Himself. The path is through the sacrifice of His one and only Son, Jesus Christ. People who want to be saved and be at peace with God the Father should accept the plan of salvation for their life. They should be submissive to God's will. They must believe in the Son of God; they must trust Him and follow His teachings in their life. They must make Him the Lord of their life. The Creator established so much for His creation. He created everything necessary for His creation to have fellowship with Him. And all He requires in return is for us to be obedient.

God the Father created this plan for all the citizens of this planet.

> After these things I looked, and behold, a great multitude which no one could number, of all nations, tribes, peoples, and tongues, standing before the throne and before the Lamb,

clothed with white robes, with palm branches in their hands, and crying out with a loud voice, saying, "Salvation belongs to our God who sits on the throne, and to the Lamb!"

—REVELATION 7:9–10

God the Father loves all people because each person is His creation, the work of His hands. And He supports His love with reality, with facts.

In this the love of God was manifested toward us, that God has sent His only begotten Son into the world, that we might live through Him. In this is love, not that we loved God, but that He loved us and sent His Son to be the propitiation for our sins.

—1 JOHN 4:9–10

God the Father sent His Son to this planet, our Earth, to save us through Him; to save every citizen of this planet.

For God so loved the world that He gave His only begotten Son, that whoever believes in Him should not perish but have everlasting life. For God did not send His Son into the world to condemn the world, but that the world through Him might be saved. He who believes in Him is not condemned; but he who does not believe is condemned already, because he has not believed in the name of the only begotten Son of God.

—JOHN 3:16–18

Aside from Jesus Christ, God the Father did not appoint any other individual through whom we can be saved—there is no other name that can bring salvation. There is no other plan and no other way under heaven through whom we can be saved. God's Constitution describes the path that Jesus Christ created.

And that repentance and remission of sins should be preached
in His name to all nations, beginning at Jerusalem.

—LUKE 24:47

This is the "stone which was rejected by you builders, which
has become the chief cornerstone." Nor is there salvation in
any other, for there is no other name under heaven given
among men by which we must be saved.

—ACTS 4:11–12

God's plan and will pertain to each person that is in this world.
God the Father commanded that blood was needed for forgiveness—without blood we cannot be forgiven. This law is applicable
and effective today. God the Father required blood to cover Adam's
nakedness, his sins, from the very beginning of Creation. If we
read the Holy Scriptures, we see that blood is a requirement for
forgiveness throughout the entire book. When Adam and Eve broke
God's law with their disobedience, when they sinned in front of
their Creator, they lost fellowship with Him and fear entered their
hearts. They saw their own fall, their sinful nature, their nakedness. To cover them, God made tunics, a process requiring the
shedding of blood.

Also for Adam and his wife the LORD God made tunics of
skin, and clothed them.

—GENESIS 3:21

The lives of animals were taken, their blood was shed, and it
was their blood that covered man's sins. When God sent the last
plague upon Egypt, He ordered His chosen nation to kill a one-
year-old goat or a sheep that was without blemish, and to paint
their doorposts with the blood. The blood would be a sign to the
angel of death that the occupants of that particular house were to

be passed by. In contrast, the firstborn of Pharaoh's family and his servants, the rest of the Egyptians and the animals, were killed because their homes were without the blood. We see that blood was needed to save the nation of Israel.

> For I will pass through the land of Egypt on that night, and will strike all the firstborn in the land of Egypt, both man and beast; and against all the gods of Egypt I will execute judgment: I am the LORD. Now the blood shall be a sign for you on the houses where you are. And when I see the blood, I will pass over you; and the plague shall not be on you to destroy you when I strike the land of Egypt.
>
> —EXODUS 12:12–13

All the firstborn in the land of Egypt were killed, but those who were in homes with blood on the doorposts remained alive. Blood is of great meaning in the eyes of the holy God because He appointed it as the only thing that can cleanse us of sin.

> For when Moses had spoken every precept to all the people according to the law, he took the blood of calves and goats, with water, scarlet wool, and hyssop, and sprinkled both the book itself and all the people, saying, "This is the blood of the covenant which God has commanded you." Then likewise he sprinkled with blood both the tabernacle and all the vessels of the ministry. And according to the law almost all things are purified with blood, and without shedding of blood there is no remission.
>
> —HEBREWS 9:19–22

The New Testament tells of how God the Father sent His only Son, Jesus Christ, to the world. He was the Lamb of God, and He took all the sins of the world upon Himself. Jesus Christ was killed and His holy blood was shed to cleanse us from our sin. The Word of God describes in detail the time when Jesus shed His blood, as well as the significance of His blood.

Each and every citizen of this planet ought to know what the blood of Jesus means for them. The Word of God also teaches us that God established a church for Himself through His own blood:

> For this is My blood of the new covenant, which is shed for many for the remission of sins.
> —MATTHEW 26:28

> Therefore take heed to yourselves and to all the flock, among which the Holy Spirit has made you overseers, to shepherd the church of God which He purchased with His own blood.
> —ACTS 20:28

> Knowing that you were not redeemed with corruptible things, like silver or gold, from your aimless conduct received by tradition from your fathers, but with the precious blood of Christ, as of a lamb without blemish and without spot. He indeed was foreordained before the foundation of the world, but was manifest in these last times for you
> —1 PETER 1:18–20

> For all have sinned and fall short of the glory of God, being justified freely by His grace through the redemption that is in Christ Jesus, whom God set forth as a propitiation by His blood, through faith, to demonstrate His righteousness, because in His forbearance God had passed over the sins that were previously committed,
> —ROMANS 3:23–25

But God demonstrates His own love toward us, in that while we were still sinners, Christ died for us. Much more then, having now been justified by His blood, we shall be saved from wrath through Him.

—Romans 5:8–9

To the praise of the glory of His grace, by which He made us accepted in the Beloved. In Him we have redemption through His blood, the forgiveness of sins, according to the riches of His grace.

—Ephesians 1:6–7

Giving thanks to the Father who has qualified us to be partakers of the inheritance of the saints in the light. He has delivered us from the power of darkness and conveyed us into the kingdom of the Son of His love, in whom we have redemption through His blood, the forgiveness of sins.

—Colossians 1:12–14

And they sang a new song, saying: "You are worthy to take the scroll, And to open its seals; For You were slain, And have redeemed us to God by Your blood Out of every tribe and tongue and people and nation, And have made us kings and priests to our God; And we shall reign on the earth."

—Revelation 5:9–10

Then one of the elders answered, saying to me, "Who are these arrayed in white robes, and where did they come from?" And I said to him, "Sir, you know." So he said to me, "These are the ones who come out of the great tribulation, and washed their robes and made them white in the blood of the Lamb. Therefore they are before the throne of God, and serve Him day and night in His temple. And He who sits on the throne will dwell among them. They shall neither hunger anymore nor thirst anymore; the sun shall not strike them, nor any heat; for the Lamb who is in the midst of the throne will shepherd them and lead them to living fountains of waters. And God will wipe away every tear from their eyes."

—REVELATION 7:13–17

There is no other in the Holy Scriptures, besides Jesus, who is called the Lamb of God. The Bible does not write about another who also shed their blood for our sins, for the sins of all nations, because God the Father appointed only His Son for the task. God prepared one way for salvation. The start of this path is described in the Bible, and the start consists of the Seed of the woman.

And she will bring forth a Son, and you shall call His name JESUS, for He will save His people from their sins.

—MATTHEW 1:21

For there is born to you this day in the city of David a Savior, who is Christ the Lord.

—LUKE 2:11

In the Old Testament, many prophets foretold this single path of salvation:

And He commanded us to preach to the people, and to testify that it is He who was ordained by God to be Judge of the living and the dead. To Him all the prophets witness that, through His name, whoever believes in Him will receive remission of sins.

—ACTS 10:42–43

Many names are recorded on the pages of the Holy Scriptures. The names belong to godly people, to those who had fellowship with the living God and accomplished great work for Him. But not one of these people is called the savior of the human race, of the world. This is because only God, though Jesus Christ, is able to save the world. He is our only Savior.

> And we have seen and testify that the Father has sent the Son as Savior of the world. Whoever confesses that Jesus is the Son of God, God abides in him, and he in God.
>
> —1 JOHN 4:14–15

> Him God has exalted to His right hand to be Prince and Savior, to give repentance to Israel and forgiveness of sins.
>
> —ACTS 5:31

> Then they said to the woman, "Now we believe, not because of what you said, for we ourselves have heard Him and we know that this is indeed the Christ, the Savior of the world."
>
> —JOHN 4:42

> But grow in the grace and knowledge of our Lord and Savior Jesus Christ. To Him be the glory both now and forever. Amen.
>
> —2 PETER 3:18

We all know that the disobedience of the first man, Adam, caused sin to enter the world. From that time on, we all have been sinners. The apostle Paul does not exclude himself:

> This is a faithful saying and worthy of all acceptance, that Christ Jesus came into the world to save sinners, of whom I am chief.
>
> —1 TIMOTHY 1:15

Jesus Christ, without sin, came into this earth to suffer only to take the sins of the world upon Himself.

> For Christ also suffered once for sins, the just for the unjust, that He might bring us to God, being put to death in the flesh but made alive by the Spirit.
>
> —1 PETER 3:18

> And you know that He was manifested to take away our sins, and in Him there is no sin.
>
> —1 JOHN 3:5

> who Himself bore our sins in His own body on the tree, that we, having died to sins, might live for righteousness—by whose stripes you were healed.
>
> —1 PETER 2:24

> The next day John saw Jesus coming toward him, and said, "Behold! The Lamb of God who takes away the sin of the world!"
>
> —JOHN 1:29

> But that you may know that the Son of Man has power on Earth to forgive sins.
>
> —MATTHEW 9:6

> But He whom God raised up saw no corruption. Therefore let it be known to you, brethren, that through this Man is preached to you the forgiveness of sins; and by Him everyone who believes is justified from all things from which you could not be justified by the law of Moses.
>
> —ACTS 13:37–39

God the Father sent His Son into the world with the mission to grant peace, forgiveness, and eternal life to those who believe in Him.

> Then Jesus cried out and said, "He who believes in Me, believes not in Me but in Him who sent Me. And he who sees Me sees Him who sent Me. I have come as a light into the world, that whoever believes in Me should not abide in darkness. And if anyone hears My words and does not believe, I do not judge him; for I did not come to judge the world but to save the world. He who rejects Me, and does not receive My words, has that which judges him—the word that I have spoken will judge him in the last day. For I have not spoken on My own authority; but the Father who sent Me gave Me a command, what I should say and what I should speak. And I know that His command is everlasting life. Therefore, whatever I speak, just as the Father has told Me, so I speak."
>
> —JOHN 12:44–50

God the Father does not want His creation to die. He wants His creation to live with Him forever in His kingdom.

> He who believes in the Son has everlasting life; and he who does not believe the Son shall not see life, but the wrath of God abides on him.
>
> —JOHN 3:36

> And this is the testimony: that God has given us eternal life, and this life is in His Son. He who has the Son has life; he who does not have the Son of God does not have life. These things I have written to you who believe in the name of the Son of God, that you may know that you have eternal life, and that you may continue to believe in the name of the Son of God.
>
> —1 JOHN 5:11–13

What a great difference there is between believers and non-believers! Jesus Himself speaks about eternal life. He wants each of His followers, each person who believes in Him, to have eternal life. Let's read the words that God Himself said and which are written in the Holy Bible:

> And this is the will of Him who sent Me, that everyone who sees the Son and believes in Him may have everlasting life; and I will raise him up at the last day.... Most assuredly, I say to you, he who believes in Me has everlasting life.
>
> —John 6:40, 47

The words of God are alive and active even today in the twenty-first century, and they give each citizen the opportunity for eternal life. What else does Jesus, the Savior of mankind and the only intercessor in the New Testament, say about Himself?

> Then Jesus said to them, "Most assuredly, I say to you, Moses did not give you the bread from heaven, but My Father gives you the true bread from heaven. For the bread of God is He who comes down from heaven and gives life to the world." Then they said to Him, "Lord, give us this bread always." And Jesus said to them, "I am the bread of life. He who comes to Me shall never hunger, and he who believes in Me shall never thirst.... I am the bread of life. Your fathers ate the manna in the wilderness, and are dead. This is the bread which comes down from heaven, that one may eat of it and not die. I am the living bread which came down from heaven. If anyone eats of this bread, he will live forever; and the bread that I shall give is My flesh, which I shall give for the life of the world."
>
> —John 6:32–35, 48–51

For as the Father has life in Himself, so He has granted the
Son to have life in Himself.

—John 5:26

Jesus Christ is the Bread of Life, and life on this planet continues
exclusively through Him. No one else can give life, and no one else
is life. Only Jesus gives life, and Jesus is life.

As long as I am in the world, I am the light of the world.

—John 9:5

No one else but Jesus Christ, the Son of the living God, can be
the Light of the World.

I, the Lord, have called You in righteousness, And will hold
Your hand; I will keep You and give You as a covenant to the
people, As a light to the Gentiles.

—Isaiah 42:6

The prophecy of Isaiah came to pass—Jesus Christ is the Light
for all people:

Then Jesus spoke to them again, saying, "I am the light of the
world. He who follows Me shall not walk in darkness, but
have the light of life."

—John 8:12

Jesus Christ is the Shepherd, a good Shepherd, who loves His
sheep and who gave His own life for them. There is one Shepherd
and one herd. There is no other shepherd for us, nor was there ever
another and neither will there ever be.

I am the good shepherd. The good shepherd gives His life for
the sheep. But a hireling, he who is not the shepherd, one who

does not own the sheep, sees the wolf coming and leaves the sheep and flees; and the wolf catches the sheep and scatters them. The hireling flees because he is a hireling and does not care about the sheep. I am the good shepherd; and I know My sheep, and am known by My own. As the Father knows Me, even so I know the Father; and I lay down My life for the sheep. And other sheep I have which are not of this fold; them also I must bring, and they will hear My voice; and there will be one flock and one shepherd....My sheep hear My voice, and I know them, and they follow Me. And I give them eternal life, and they shall never perish; neither shall anyone snatch them out of My hand.

—JOHN 10:11–16, 27–28

What a great promise for the citizens of this earth, for me and for you too, dear reader. It is worth it to know such a Shepherd, such a good Shepherd.

Jesus said to him, "I am the way, the truth, and the life. No one comes to the Father except through Me."

—JOHN 14:6

Jesus Christ is the truth, the only truth, and there has never been another, nor will there ever be. Jesus Christ is the path to eternal life, and there has never been another, nor will there ever be. Jesus is our only path to heaven, to eternal life, and the kingdom of God. Only through Him can we obtain salvation and be with Him eternally. No one can come to God the Father without Jesus Christ.

Most assuredly, I say to you, he who does not enter the sheepfold by the door, but climbs up some other way, the same is a thief and a robber. But he who enters by the door is the shepherd of the sheep. To him the doorkeeper opens, and the sheep hear his voice; and he calls his own sheep by name and leads them out. And when he brings out his own sheep, he goes before them; and the sheep follow him, for they know his voice. Yet they will by no means follow a stranger, but will flee from him, for they do not know the voice of strangers." Jesus used this illustration, but they did not understand the things which He spoke to them. Then Jesus said to them again, "Most assuredly, I say to you, I am the door of the sheep. All who ever came before Me are thieves and robbers, but the sheep did not hear them. I am the door. If anyone enters by Me, he will be saved, and will go in and out and find pasture. The thief does not come except to steal, and to kill, and to destroy. I have come that they may have life, and that they may have it more abundantly."

—JOHN 10:1–10

Jesus Christ is the doorway, and there is no other. The Son of God made a striking statement: He indeed is the doorway. God describes those who seek other doorways as thieves and robbers. These words, though they are sorrowful, are holy because they are written in God's Constitution and are from the mouth of Jesus, who is the Savior of the world. These words are true and active, even in the twenty-first century.

I will be described as a thief and robber if I seek another path, another truth, another doorway to gain salvation, forgiveness, peace with God, and eternal life in God's kingdom. And you too, my dear and attentive reader, will be called a thief and a robber if you do the same, regardless of who you are on this planet. It will not matter if you are big or small, popular or not. Your appearance will not matter; neither will your profession, your financial status, or your wardrobe. God said that there is one path to the doorway and one doorway to the kingdom. It doesn't matter if the path suits some and is unpleasant for others—God will not change and His laws will remain the same. Man is God's creation, and the created being must always be submissive to the Creator. The creation should accept the plan of salvation provided by the Creator and not vice versa. Man should never forget that he is a creation. He should always see himself from the point of view of the Creator. Man should ask himself: Do I fulfill God's will, or do I break God's will? Have I accepted God's plan of salvation, and have I dedicated my life to His will, or do I seek other paths?

We all know that everyone who is born must die. This is a fact; we all are witnesses to this. The Word teaches that we will stand in front of our Creator and give an account of our life on this earth. Do you know who will be the judge?

> And if anyone hears My words and does not believe, I do not judge him; for I did not come to judge the world but to save the world. He who rejects Me, and does not receive My words, has that which judges him—the word that I have spoken will judge him in the last day.
>
> —JOHN 12:47–48

God the Father has done everything possible since our creation so that we would be saved, have fellowship with Him, and receive eternal life in the kingdom of heaven. All He requires in exchange is obedience and acceptance of His plan of salvation.

The kingdom of God is a place like no other; in fact, there isn't any other. There is only one entrance to it, only one way that leads into it, and the way is Jesus Christ.

Jesus Christ, the Son of the living God, came to this earth and prepared a way. He then went to heaven to prepare an eternal place for His chosen ones, for His followers—for us.

"Let not your heart be troubled; you believe in God, believe also in Me. In My Father's house are many mansions; if it were not so, I would have told you. I go to prepare a place for you. And if I go and prepare a place for you, I will come again and receive you to Myself; that where I am, there you may be also.

—JOHN 14:1–3

What a great promise. Is it even possible to desire something better? There is nothing better for man on this earth than to know God's truth and to receive salvation. It is worth trusting God and giving your life into His hands. It is to our advantage to serve Him and to live for Him only.

He alone established a plan for salvation for the human race.

27

WHAT TO DO TO BE SAVED

W E HAVE READ A LOT ABOUT JESUS CHRIST, HIS DEEDS, His mission, His purpose of coming to Earth, His strength, and power. We know that Jesus is the only Savior and that He is the only path to truth and life. We know that He left His heavenly glory and came down to Earth to save those who are lost. He came here to unite a sinful people with God the Father. Now a few questions arise: how can you get salvation and forgiveness, and what must one do to be reconciled with their Maker?

Not only are these questions important today, but they were important in the time of the apostles. Let's read a few verses from the book of the apostles, when Paul and Silas were preaching the Word of God and encountered great obstacles in their own spiritual path:

> And they brought them to the magistrates, and said, "These men, being Jews, exceedingly trouble our city; and they teach customs which are not lawful for us, being Romans, to receive or observe." Then the multitude rose up together against them; and the magistrates tore off their clothes and

commanded them to be beaten with rods. And when they had laid many stripes on them, they threw them into prison, commanding the jailer to keep them securely. Having received such a charge, he put them into the inner prison and fastened their feet in the stocks. But at midnight Paul and Silas were praying and singing hymns to God, and the prisoners were listening to them. Suddenly there was a great earthquake, so that the foundations of the prison were shaken; and immediately all the doors were opened and everyone's chains were loosed. And the keeper of the prison, awaking from sleep and seeing the prison doors open, supposing the prisoners had fled, drew his sword and was about to kill himself. But Paul called with a loud voice, saying, "Do yourself no harm, for we are all here." Then he called for a light, ran in, and fell down trembling before Paul and Silas. And he brought them out and said, "Sirs, what must I do to be saved?" So they said, "Believe on the Lord Jesus Christ, and you will be saved, you and your household." Then they spoke the word of the Lord to him and to all who were in his house. And he took them the same hour of the night and washed their stripes. And immediately he and all his family were baptized. Now when he had brought them into his house, he set food before them; and he rejoiced, having believed in God with all his household.

—Acts 16:20–34

After this event in prison, the guard saw that Paul and Silas were not usual people. He saw that these people had fellowship with a living God and that they were saved. The guard also had the desire for salvation in his heart.

What does one have to do to be saved? The jailer also asked this, and the answer is very simple: believe in Jesus Christ. What a simple task! Each person can accomplish this task. God the Father teaches us that without faith it is impossible to please God. Let's read from the book of Hebrews.

> But without faith it is impossible to please Him, for he who comes to God must believe that He is, and that He is a rewarder of those who diligently seek Him.
>
> —Hebrews 11:6

The first step to salvation is to believe that Jesus Christ is the Son of the living God. We must believe that He came to this Earth in human flesh—became the Son of Man—with the mission to unite us, sinners, with God. In other words, that He came to find and save the lost and to establish the kingdom of God.

God the Father prepared a very simple path for salvation. All we must do is accept this plan, believe in the truth of God's law, and fulfill His commands in your life. Listen now to what God the Father is speaking to you, especially to you, about your great sins:

> So the daughter of Zion is left as a booth in a vineyard, As a hut in a garden of cucumbers, As a besieged city.
>
> —Isaiah 1:18

These words are true and alive because each Word of God has gone through fire. There is no sin that God cannot forgive. And when you come to God and confess your sins, He will not push you away.

> All that the Father gives Me will come to Me, and the one who comes to Me I will by no means cast out.
>
> —John 6:37

These are very interesting words that God has spoken to everyone who feels to be lost, hopeless, and in great sin.

> Jesus answered and said to them, "Those who are well have no need of a physician, but those who are sick. I have not come to call the righteous, but sinners, to repentance."
>
> —LUKE 5:31–32

Let's go now to when Jesus Christ hung on the cross between the two thieves.

> Then one of the criminals who were hanged blasphemed Him, saying, "If You are the Christ, save Yourself and us." But the other, answering, rebuked him, saying, "Do you not even fear God, seeing you are under the same condemnation? And we indeed justly, for we receive the due reward of our deeds; but this Man has done nothing wrong." Then he said to Jesus, "Lord, remember me when You come into Your kingdom." And Jesus said to him, "Assuredly, I say to you, today you will be with Me in Paradise."
>
> —LUKE 23:39–43

From the above, we see that one of the thieves believed in Jesus Christ. This person evidently had learned about Jesus and knew a bit of His actions, wonders, work, and teachings. And we know this because the thief even said that Jesus had done nothing wrong, that He didn't sin in any way. Maybe this man had a chance to listen to Jesus as He taught, and maybe the thief even witnessed some of Jesus' deeds and miracles. In his heart the thief believed that the person in the middle cross was the Son of God. And even though Jesus Christ was beaten, wounded, and bloody as he hung on the cross, this thief believed in Him. He saw the King in Him, as well as His kingdom. We must admit that believing something like this was not easy. The scene is tragically sad and filled with laughter and curses from the surrounding witnesses—all of which contradicts the belief that Jesus is the Son of God. In spite of this, the one thief saw authority and strength in Him; he saw a Savior in Him. And when the thief began to believe, he took the first step to salvation.

Many people gathered to witness the crucifixion of Jesus Christ. Roman soldiers, the mother of Jesus, and many other women who had served Him were present. There were also authority figures, such as the chief priests. But the simple people made up the mass of those congregated. And this one thief, in front of them all, and most importantly, in front of God, admitted that he was a sinner. He publicly announced that he deserved death for his own actions and that his crucifixion was indeed the punishment he deserved.

Admitting that you are a sinner is the second step to salvation. Each person who wants to be saved must admit that he or she is a sinner and needs salvation. This thief also believed in eternal life. He believed that the kingdom of God exists and that God exists. But this thief did not have any fellowship with Him. He did not respect or seek God's will and did not pay any attention to our living God during his life. He instead lived a sinful life and did not bother himself with eternity. But in the last minutes of his life he realized his situation, admitted his lawless path, admitted that he was a sinner, and most importantly, he repented. He turned to our Savior and said, "Lord, remember me when You come into Your kingdom." Repenting and turning to God is the next step to salvation. Consider the following words of God:

> Repent therefore and be converted, that your sins may be blotted out, so that times of refreshing may come from the presence of the Lord.
>
> —ACTS 3:19

When we repent, we first admit that we are sinners, and secondly, we turn from our sin. Repenting is changing your life.

313

Prior to repentance, people do not interact with God. They live their own life and grow increasingly further from God. But after a person repents, they grow closer to God. They want to hear His voice, know His will for their life, and have fellowship with God:

> And Jesus said to him, "Assuredly, I say to you, today you will be with Me in Paradise."
> —LUKE 23:43

Jesus Christ knew who this man was. In fact, He knew very well. Jesus Christ knew that this man was a criminal. But Jesus Christ forgave him when he repented. Jesus Christ did not remember his past sins, his dark days, and He did not hold his sins against him. Jesus no longer saw the man's sin. And then, in a quiet and gentle, yet decisive voice, Jesus said, "Assuredly, I say to you, today you will be with Me in Paradise" (Luke 23:43). Jesus said that when people repent, "Their sins and their lawless deeds I will remember no more" (Heb. 10:17).

The prophecy of the Old Testament was fulfilled. Jesus Christ did not change. He is the same today, yesterday, and forever. Today His words are like they were two thousand years ago.

> For "whoever calls on the name of the Lord shall be saved."
> —ROMANS 10:13

The Word of God teaches us that we need to share our faith with people. We must share with our friends, family, and strangers. We need to announce that Jesus Christ is the Son of God, that He is the one and only Savior and Redeemer of the entire human race, for all the sons of man. He is my Savior, and yours, too.

> Therefore whoever confesses Me before men, him I will also confess before My Father who is in heaven. But whoever

denies Me before men, him I will also deny before My Father who is in heaven.

—MATTHEW 10:32–33

That if you confess with your mouth the Lord Jesus and believe in your heart that God has raised Him from the dead, you will be saved. For with the heart one believes unto righteousness, and with the mouth confession is made unto salvation.

—ROMANS 10:9–10

We must partake in water baptism to profess our faith. It is the fist step of obedience to your Creator and Savior.

And He said to them, "Go into all the world and preach the gospel to every creature. He who believes and is baptized will be saved; but he who does not belicve will be condemned."

—MARK 16:15–16

What a great plan of salvation the Creator prepared for His creation, man.

For the Scripture says, "whoever believes on Him will not be put to shame."

—ROMANS 10:11

God prepared a way of reconciliation that is easy and available to everyone. We must only believe and accept His plan.

28

WHAT IT MEANS
TO BELIEVE IN GOD
AND TO BELIEVE GOD

I NITIALLY, I THINK IT IS IMPORTANT TO STOP AND CONSIDER what faith is by seeking a definition from the Word of God:

> Now faith is the substance of things hoped for, the evidence of things not seen. For by it the elders obtained a good testimony. By faith we understand that the worlds were framed by the word of God, so that the things which are seen were not made of things which are visible.
> —HEBREWS 11:1–3

Faith is a deep conviction that God reigns. It is also the belief that He created the earth and all of mankind, that He loves His creation, remembers His creation, wants to have fellowship with it, and has a great and unique plan for each person. Faith is also believing that the Bible is a holy Book and God's Constitution. By faith we believe that the words in the Book are God's and are alive and active. By faith we believe in God's plan of salvation, which He prepared for the human race.

What does it mean to believe in God and to believe God? There is a great similarity and difference in the answer to this question.

To believe in God means to believe that God exists somewhere there, far away. It also means believing that He created everything, that He loves His creation, remembers it, looks after it, and that He blesses and punishes also. In other words, it means that while God does His work, we do ours. We are independent of each other. I do what I want, what pleases me, what suits my imagination, and/ or what my grandparents and parents taught me. God, with His loving mercy, proposes salvation, forgiveness of sin, and closeness with our Creator. In response, sometimes people say, "I have my faith, which my elders taught me. I have my own religion, which I was born into and raised in, and I treasure it highly and am proud of myself for being a believer." Will such faith save a person? I think that each reader will say that this faith will not help a man. A person with this kind of faith believes that God exists, but he does not have any fellowship with Him. He does not have a relationship with his very own Creator.

What does it mean to believe God? When we believe God, we listen to His voice and do as He commands. We fulfill His laws. But in order to fulfill His commands, we must first know what they are. We must know what He has taught, and we must apply His teachings to our daily life. We must live by His words. When a person is ignorant of God's will and the teachings of Jesus Christ, how then can he or she use them for the benefit of their lives? A question now arises: what must we do to know God's laws and His will? The answer is very simple. We must read the Word of God, His Constitution, the Holy Bible. When we read the Word of God, we learn of His will, laws, commands, and what He requires from us.

Now my dear reader can ask the following: Why does God establish laws for man? What purpose do they serve? God is the Creator and we are His creation. The Creator requires obedience from His creation. When we, God's creation, know His will and laws and are obedient to them by fulfilling them to the fullest, we provide proof of our obedience and faithfulness to our Creator.

When we carry out God's will to the letter, we profess our faith in Him and we confess our respect and honor for His laws and commands, and therefore, our respect and honor for God—the Creator of the law. By doing this, we have fellowship with the living God and are able to hear Him when He speaks to us. Our connection with Him is closer when we do as the Word of God teaches us.

> And whatever we ask we receive from Him, because we keep His commandments and do those things that are pleasing in His sight. And this is His commandment: that we should believe on the name of His Son Jesus Christ and love one another, as He gave us commandment. Now he who keeps His commandments abides in Him, and He in him. And by this we know that He abides in us, by the Spirit whom He has given us.
>
> —1 John 3:22-24

When we do not completely fulfill God's laws or when we subtract, add, or alter something, then we do not believe in their truthfulness. When we disregard God's laws and do not fully believe in them, by default we disregard the Giver of the law. And when we are disobedient to His Word, we tell Him that we do not love Him and that we lack faith both in His Words and in Him. God's Constitution speaks of this:

He who does not love Me does not keep My words; and the word which you hear is not Mine but the Father's who sent Me.

—JOHN 14:24

A very interesting fact regarding faith is written on the pages of the Holy Word, and it will serve each citizen well to know of it. Let's read these words together:

You believe that there is one God. You do well. Even the demons believe—and tremble!

—JAMES 2:19

The Word of God writes that even demons believe in God's existence, and, in fact, they tremble knowing this. Still, they do not do His will. They do not yield to His laws, nor do they listen to His voice and have fellowship with Him. What are demons? Demons are evil spirits, fallen angels. When Satan was cast to Earth, he took one-third of the angels with him, and these fallen angels are unclean spirits, also known as demons. They know very well that God exists, but they do not bow down to Him. In fact, they work against their Creator. They break His commands and they lead everyone they can into the darkness, which they inhabit.

Now there was a man in their synagogue with an unclean spirit. And he cried out, saying, "Let us alone! What have we to do with You, Jesus of Nazareth? Did You come to destroy us? I know who You are—the Holy One of God!" But Jesus rebuked him, saying, "Be quiet, and come out of him!"

—MARK 1:23–25

Demons know very well who Jesus Christ is. They know that the Son of God is holy. They know why Jesus came to this earth. They know that the Son of God came to save the lost, to establish the kingdom of God, and to break the work of Satan. For this reason, they tremble in front of God. When they see their imminent destruction, they shake and yell and work against Him.

> Now it happened, as we went to prayer, that a certain slave girl possessed with a spirit of divination met us, who brought her masters much profit by fortune-telling. This girl followed Paul and us, and cried out, saying, "These men are the servants of the Most High God, who proclaim to us the way of salvation." And this she did for many days. But Paul, greatly annoyed, turned and said to the spirit, "I command you in the name of Jesus Christ to come out of her." And he came out that very hour.
>
> —Acts 16:16–18

We see from these words that even unclean spirits can identify who is working for the kingdom of God. They know that there is a path of salvation that God Himself prepared for the sons of God. Demons know everyone who walks in the path of salvation. And today they create all kinds of obstacles for the people in this path.

Believing in God's existence is good; it is the first step to salvation and fellowship with God the Father. The second step is believing God and in His will and believing in His plan of salvation. In essence, the second step is walking according to this plan. It is using His will for our life and fulfilling His commands daily. We must adjust our life to God's requirements, and when we do, we confirm our belief, respect, and obedience to our Creator. This is when we can have complete fellowship with God.

> Jesus answered and said to him, "If anyone loves Me, he will keep My word; and My Father will love him, and We will come to him and make Our home with him."
>
> —John 14:23

Our faith in God opens the door of our heart to Jesus. God knocks on our hearts and we are the ones who must open the door.

> Behold, I stand at the door and knock. If anyone hears My voice and opens the door, I will come in to him and dine with him, and he with Me.
>
> —REVELATION 3:20

What a great plan God has prepared for His creation, for each citizen of this planet—for me and especially for you, dear reader. God is love, and He extends His love to all of His creation.

29

SALVATION IS A GIFT FROM GOD

THE WORD OF GOD TEACHES US THAT SALVATION IS impossible to earn with our own personal deeds, with our works. Salvation is a gift from God. It is God's grace for His creation. And we can only receive this gift by faith in Jesus. The Creator has made this gift available to each citizen, for me and for you too, dear reader. There are many verses on the pages of the Holy Word that speak of this blessing, of this precious gift:

> For the law was given through Moses, but grace and truth came through Jesus Christ.
>
> —JOHN 1:17

> But God, who is rich in mercy, because of His great love with which He loved us, even when we were dead in trespasses, made us alive together with Christ (by grace you have been saved), and raised us up together, and made us sit together in the heavenly places in Christ Jesus, that in the ages to come He might show the exceeding riches of His grace in His kind-

ness toward us in Christ Jesus. For by grace you have been saved through faith, and that not of yourselves; it is the gift of God, not of works, lest anyone should boast. For we are His workmanship, created in Christ Jesus for good works, which God prepared beforehand that we should walk in them.

—EPHESIANS 2:4–10

Therefore by the deeds of the law no flesh will be justified in His sight, for by the law is the knowledge of sin. But now the righteousness of God apart from the law is revealed, being witnessed by the Law and the Prophets, even the righteousness of God, through faith in Jesus Christ, to all and on all who believe. For there is no difference; for all have sinned and fall short of the glory of God, being justified freely by His grace through the redemption that is in Christ Jesus, whom God set forth as a propitiation by His blood, through faith, to demonstrate His righteousness, because in His forbearance God had passed over the sins that were previously committed, to demonstrate at the present time His righteousness, that He might be just and the justifier of the one who has faith in Jesus. Where is boasting then? It is excluded. By what law? Of works? No, but by the law of faith. Therefore we conclude that a man is justified by faith apart from the deeds of the law.

—ROMANS 3:20–28

Knowing that a man is not justified by the works of the law but by faith in Jesus Christ, even we have believed in Christ Jesus, that we might be justified by faith in Christ and not by the works of the law; for by the works of the law no flesh shall be justified.

—GALATIANS 2:16

But we believe that through the grace of the Lord Jesus Christ we shall be saved in the same manner as they.

—ACTS 15:11

Who has saved us and called us with a holy calling, not according to our works, but according to His own purpose and grace which was given to us in Christ Jesus before time began.

—2 TIMOTHY 1:9

But when the kindness and the love of God our Savior toward man appeared, not by works of righteousness which we have done, but according to His mercy He saved us, through the washing of regeneration and renewing of the Holy Spirit, whom He poured out on us abundantly through Jesus Christ our Savior, that having been justified by His grace we should become heirs according to the hope of eternal life.

—TITUS 3:4–7

Even so then, at this present time there is a remnant according to the election of grace. And if by grace, then it is no longer of works; otherwise grace is no longer grace. But if it is of works, it is no longer grace; otherwise work is no longer work.

—ROMANS 11:5–6

Therefore, having been justified by faith, we have peace with God through our Lord Jesus Christ, through whom also we have access by faith into this grace in which we stand, and rejoice in hope of the glory of God.

—ROMANS 5:1–2

We see that salvation is possible because of God's mercy. It is His gift to mankind, and all we have to do to receive it is simply believe in Jesus Christ, who was the sacrifice of mercy. The Word of God teaches us that the basis for salvation is the forgiveness of our sins, which we cannot earn by our good behavior, buy with money, or exchange for some highly valued material thing. This gift is given for free to all who believe in Jesus Christ.

No one can say, "I am earning salvation because I take an active role in social work. I visit the sick in the hospital, I visit the elderly, I feed and clothe the fatherless, and do many other good deeds. And therefore all of my good works will save me. All of my sins are forgiven, and because of this, I am proud of myself and have the right to boast."

Also, not a single person can say, "I am saved because my parents are saved. They are strong believers and do great work for the kingdom of heaven. My father is the pastor in a sizeable church; my mother is an evangelist and travels to poor countries to preach the Holy Word. I received salvation via an inheritance because I was born into a family of believers."

No one can say, "I am saved because each Sunday, both in the morning and in the evening, I go to church. I have a great voice, and I sing in the choir. I also try to attend as many prayer meetings as possible. All of my effort and work in the church causes God to forgive me; my hard work has earned salvation. I am a saved man because of what I do."

No one can say, "I have donated a lot of money, almost all of my savings, to the church, which does a lot of work in the world. God has seen my donations, and because of them He forgives me of my sins. I am also proud of myself and salvation is my right because of my financial contributions."

Neither can anyone say, "I am saved because I have led and continue to lead a moral, righteous life. I do not murder, I do not steal, and I do not lust after people or things. I lead an orderly life, and generally speaking, I do not need forgiveness because I am not a sinner. My proper and honest actions have paved the way for salvation."

All the actions I have mentioned above are good, and we should strive to lead honest and moral lives. But if salvation could be attained by our actions and our personal morals, then God the Father would not have had to send His one and only Son, Jesus Christ, to Earth to suffer, be crucified, and shed His holy and precious blood on the cross. The Word of God writes that no person can use their deeds as a means to salvation. The Word of God teaches that we receive salvation only when we believe in Jesus Christ; this is the only way. Our mighty God forgives us and washes us with His blood when we confess with our mouth that Jesus Christ is the Son of God and that He is the one and only Savior. When we confess this, the evil that stands between Him and us is removed. We draw closer to God when we open our hearts to Him and admit our sins. He is sure to forgive us and remove the evil barrier that stands between us. We are united with Him when we place our life into His hands and profess our faith in Him. We become part of God's family when we receive His mercy. We become a new creation in Christ—we are born again—when we believe in Him. We become a new people, a saved people, a reconciled people with God the Father when we receive His mercy. We become part of God's kingdom! This rebirth is a meeting between God the Creator and us, and we are united with Him from that moment.

Let's read what was said between Jesus and Nicodemus, a ruler and teacher of the Jews:

> There was a man of the Pharisees named Nicodemus, a ruler of the Jews. 2 This man came to Jesus by night and said to Him, "Rabbi, we know that You are a teacher come from God; for no one can do these signs that You do unless God is with him." Jesus answered and said to him, "Most assuredly, I say

to you, unless one is born again, he cannot see the kingdom of God." Nicodemus said to Him, "How can a man be born when he is old? Can he enter a second time into his mother's womb and be born?" Jesus answered, "Most assuredly, I say to you, unless one is born of water and the Spirit, he cannot enter the kingdom of God. That which is born of the flesh is flesh, and that which is born of the Spirit is spirit. Do not marvel that I said to you, 'You must be born again.' The wind blows where it wishes, and you hear the sound of it, but cannot tell where it comes from and where it goes. So is everyone who is born of the Spirit."

—JOHN 3:1–8

Many of my readers might be asking themselves the following: what kind of faith can a person have, and how can I know that God the Father has heard my confession and has forgiven me my sins? Dear and most attentive reader, when you turn to Jesus and with all your heart believe that He is the Son of God, when you confess your sins and ask for forgiveness, in that very moment you will feel relief. You will experience great happiness—happiness like you have never felt before in your entire life. You will feel God's great love, which is like no other. You will feel God's presence; you will feel Him residing in you and you in Him. I know this because I have experienced it. I am saved. I am a new creation in Jesus Christ. I was reborn in Him. The whole world may try to contradict your experience, but you will never forget that you are saved by Jesus. You will always remember and repeat the following: "I am saved by Jesus Christ. Jesus has saved me. I know this because I know that Jesus is in me and I in Him." This will be happiness for you, and this kind of joy cannot be described by human words. You can only experience it for yourself. God the Father has blessed all of mankind with the gift of His only begotten Son. Through His

Son, God gave each citizen the opportunity to accept salvation and to be reconciled with his or her Creator—all of which is free to us.

> For by grace you have been saved through faith, and that not of yourselves; it is the gift of God, not of works, lest anyone should boast. For we are His workmanship, created in Christ Jesus for good works, which God prepared beforehand that we should walk in them.... But now in Christ Jesus you who once were far off have been brought near by the blood of Christ.... For through Him we both have access by one Spirit to the Father. Now, therefore, you are no longer strangers and foreigners, but fellow citizens with the saints and members of the household of God, having been built on the foundation of the apostles and prophets, Jesus Christ Himself being the chief cornerstone
>
> —EPHESIANS 2:8–10, 13, 18–20

What a great plan God prepared for His creation. By this plan God shows His great and boundless love toward His creation.

30

NEW LIFE IN CHRIST
AND THE NARROW WAY

THE WORD OF GOD TEACHES US THAT WE ARE FORGIVEN, reconciled, and saved when we believe in Jesus Christ. Forgiveness, reconciliation, and salvation do not depend on our actions. We receive salvation at no cost to us; there is nothing we can give to pay for it. No material thing can be exchanged for it. Salvation can only be received through faith in Jesus Christ after we admit our sins, ask for forgiveness, and turn from our old ways. This is not to say that life after salvation is easy—it may be hard.

When people turn to God in their youth as young men or women, they need to work hard for the rest of their lives as children of God. The old life of the born-again person begins to change and a new life begins—a life with Christ. In fact, a new era begins—the Christian era, the era of the person born from above, the era of the saved person who is reconciled with God. It is the era of a person who is a new creation in Jesus Christ. The born-again person has faith in salvation and experiences great joy, which they never experienced in their previous life. Simultaneously, this person also encounters great problems and hardships that were not encountered before. The born-again Christian will witness to others about their turn to the living God and with faith will tell their relatives, immediate family, and friends of their salvation. But he or she may be attacked with criticism for their faith, while other people that participate in mainstream or even fad religious practices will not be questioned or criticized. The godless or atheists also receive little opposition, contradiction, persecution, or hurt for their beliefs.

But critics will rise against the born-again believer who says, "Jesus Christ is the Son of the living God and He came to Earth to save sinners such as myself. I believe in Him and I believe Him. I confessed all my sins to Him, and He forgave me and reconciled me with God the Father. I admit that He is my personal Savior and Redeemer and that He is the only way that leads to truth and life. And no one can come to God without first coming to Jesus, who is the only One who can save and give eternal life. And I, a sinner whom Jesus saved, will serve Him to the end of my life. I will submit my life to His will, I will live by His teachings, and I will walk in His path. He will be my leader, my guidance, and the Lord of my existence." Before this testimony will even be finished, the critics will contradict and try to invalidate the testimony. People may begin to dislike and even hate the born-again Christian; they may become upset and exclude him or her. The Christian path isn't easy on this earth, and Jesus Christ did not try to remove the thorns from the path. In fact, He warned about the hardships that are involved in following Him. He warned me, and He warns you, dear reader. Let's read the warnings as they are written on the pages of God's Constitution:

> "If the world hates you, you know that it hated Me before it hated you. If you were of the world, the world would love its own. Yet because you are not of the world, but I chose you

out of the world, therefore the world hates you. Remember the word that I said to you, 'A servant is not greater than his master.' If they persecuted Me, they will also persecute you. If they kept My word, they will keep yours also. But all these things they will do to you for My name's sake, because they do not know Him who sent Me. If I had not come and spoken to them, they would have no sin, but now they have no excuse for their sin. He who hates Me hates My Father also.

—John 15:18–23

And you will be hated by all for My name's sake. But he who endures to the end will be saved.

—Matthew 10:22

Then they will deliver you up to tribulation and kill you, and you will be hated by all nations for My name's sake. And then many will be offended, will betray one another, and will hate one another.

—Matthew 24:9–10

But watch out for yourselves, for they will deliver you up to councils, and you will be beaten in the synagogues. You will be brought before rulers and kings for My sake, for a testimony to them. And the gospel must first be preached to all the nations. But when they arrest you and deliver you up, do not worry beforehand, or premeditate what you will speak. But whatever is given you in that hour, speak that; for it is not you who speak, but the Holy Spirit. Now brother will betray brother to death, and a father his child; and children will rise up against parents and cause them to be put to death. And you will be hated by all for My name's sake. But he who endures to the end shall be saved.

—Mark 13:9–13

But before all these things, they will lay their hands on you and persecute you, delivering you up to the synagogues and prisons. You will be brought before kings and rulers for My name's sake. But it will turn out for you as an occasion for testimony. Therefore settle it in your hearts not to meditate beforehand on what you will answer; for I will give you a mouth and wisdom which all your adversaries will not be able to contradict or resist. You will be betrayed even by parents and brothers, relatives and friends; and they will put some of you to death. And you will be hated by all for My name's sake. But not a hair of your head shall be lost. By your patience possess your souls.

—LUKE 21:12–19

Yes, and all who desire to live godly in Christ Jesus will suffer persecution.

—2 TIMOTHY 3:12

Imagine with me the following scenario. An entire family is religious. They all go to church, fulfill their obligations there, and lead normal lives. Imagine another family, one who does not observe any religion; not one member of this family has been in church. At home they do not discuss God, Jesus Christ, salvation, or eternal life. Still, their life is normal, too. And then someone from this family learns of the gospel and that Jesus Christ is the Savior. They learn that by believing in Him they can be forgiven, reconciled, and saved. They learn that they can be born again and receive eternal life after death. When this member of the family believes in God's truth, they begin to share it with their family. Who wants to know what will begin in this family? Let's read the following:

Now brother will deliver up brother to death, and a father his child; and children will rise up against parents and cause them to be put to death. And you will be hated by all for My name's sake. But he who endures to the end will be saved....Do not think that I came to bring peace on earth. I did not come to bring peace but a sword. For I have come to "set a man against his father, a daughter against her mother, and a daughter-in-law against her mother-in-law"; and "a man's enemies will be those of his own household." He who loves father or mother more than Me is not worthy of Me. And he who loves son or daughter more than Me is not worthy of Me. And he who does not take his cross and follow after Me is not worthy of Me.

—MATTHEW 10:21–22, 34–38

As we see from the reading, the life of the newborn is not easy. Now a question arises: How should a believer act in such terrible circumstances? What must he do? How must he act in this environment? Jesus answers these questions:

Blessed are those who are persecuted for righteousness' sake, For theirs is the kingdom of heaven. Blessed are you when they revile and persecute you, and say all kinds of evil against you falsely for My sake. Rejoice and be exceedingly glad, for great is your reward in heaven, for so they persecuted the prophets who were before you....But I say to you, love your enemies, bless those who curse you, do good to those who hate you, and pray for those who spitefully use you and persecute you.

—MATTHEW 5:10–12, 44

Blessed are you when men hate you, And when they exclude you, And revile you, and cast out your name as evil, For the Son of Man's sake. Rejoice in that day and leap for joy! For indeed your reward is great in heaven, For in like manner their fathers did to the prophets.

—LUKE 6:22–23

Beloved, do not think it strange concerning the fiery trial which is to try you, as though some strange thing happened to you; but rejoice to the extent that you partake of Christ's sufferings, that when His glory is revealed, you may also be glad with exceeding joy. If you are reproached for the name of Christ, blessed are you, for the Spirit of glory and of God rests upon you. On their part He is blasphemed, but on your part He is glorified. But let none of you suffer as a murderer, a thief, an evildoer, or as a busybody in other people's matters. Yet if anyone suffers as a Christian, let him not be ashamed, but let him glorify God in this matter.

—1 Peter 4:12–16

Rejoicing in hope, patient in tribulation, continuing steadfastly in prayer; distributing to the needs of the saints, given to hospitality. Bless those who persecute you; bless and do not curse. Rejoice with those who rejoice, and weep with those who weep.

—Romans 12:12–15

"And I say to you, My friends, do not be afraid of those who kill the body, and after that have no more that they can do. But I will show you whom you should fear: Fear Him who, after He has killed, has power to cast into hell; yes, I say to you, fear Him! Are not five sparrows sold for two copper coins? And not one of them is forgotten before God. But the very hairs of your head are all numbered. Do not fear therefore; you are of more value than many sparrows. Also I say to you, whoever confesses Me before men, him the Son of Man also will confess before the angels of God. But he who denies Me before men will be denied before the angels of God.

—Luke 12:4–9

> But he who endures to the end shall be saved. And this gospel
> of the kingdom will be preached in all the world as a witness
> to all the nations, and then the end will come.
>
> —MATTHEW 24:13–14

Some of you reading this book may be thinking to yourself, "I will not believe in Jesus Christ. I will not fulfill His will, nor will I speak His name to others because that simply isn't me. And besides, it's too hard; it's impossible to please Him. I have my own religion, which happens to be the religion of my parents and grandparents. I was born into this religion, and no one persecutes or attacks me because of it. It doesn't draw attention to me. And I'm a good person. I go to church and I bow before the icons, which are made holy. I give a tenth of my finances. I lead an ordinary life. I even take an active part in church. I light the candles, I wipe the dust off the icons sometimes, and I stand on my knees before these icons as I ask their blessing for my life. I must admit that everyone likes and respects me. People see me as a highly religious person, and everything I have just said is good for me. I will continue to live my life in this way."

Dear reader, you have a choice right now about what to do, how to act, and who to serve. From the start of Creation, God gave each person the right of choice, which remains to this day. But listen to what Jesus Christ says especially to you:

> Therefore whoever confesses Me before men, him I will also
> confess before My Father who is in heaven. But whoever
> denies Me before men, him I will also deny before My Father
> who is in heaven.
>
> —MATTHEW 10:32–33

He who believes in Him is not condemned; but he who does not believe is condemned already, because he has not believed in the name of the only begotten Son of God.

—John 3:18

It is true that the Christian path on this planet is not easy, but it is a blessed path. Let's read the testimony of those who walked in this narrow, hard path:

We are hard-pressed on every side, yet not crushed; we are perplexed, but not in despair; persecuted, but not forsaken; struck down, but not destroyed... For we who live are always delivered to death for Jesus' sake, that the life of Jesus also may be manifested in our mortal flesh. So then death is working in us, but life in you.... Therefore we do not lose heart. Even though our outward man is perishing, yet the inward man is being renewed day by day. For our light affliction, which is but for a moment, is working for us a far more exceeding and eternal weight of glory, while we do not look at the things which are seen, but at the things which are not seen. For the things which are seen are temporary, but the things which are not seen are eternal.

—2 Corinthians 4:8–9, 11–12, 16–18

We give no offense in anything, that our ministry may not be blamed. But in all things we commend ourselves as ministers of God: in much patience, in tribulations, in needs, in distresses, in stripes, in imprisonments, in tumults, in labors, in sleeplessness, in fastings; by purity, by knowledge, by long-suffering, by kindness, by the Holy Spirit, by sincere love, by the word of truth, by the power of God, by the armor of righteousness on the right hand and on the left, by honor and dishonor, by evil report and good report; as deceivers, and yet true; as unknown, and yet well known; as dying, and behold we live; as chastened, and yet not killed; as sorrowful, yet always rejoicing; as poor, yet making many rich; as having nothing, and yet possessing all things.

—2 Corinthians 6:3–10

For I consider that the sufferings of this present time are not worthy to be compared with the glory which shall be revealed in us.

—Romans 8:18

As we have read, Christians who have gone through hardships did not cry or complain. In fact, they felt victorious and accomplished. Now we will read the testimony of a great man of God, the apostle Paul, who was chosen by God Himself to preach the holy gospel:

Are they Hebrews? So am I. Are they Israelites? So am I. Are they the seed of Abraham? So am I. Are they ministers of Christ?—I speak as a fool—I am more: in labors more abundant, in stripes above measure, in prisons more frequently, in deaths often. From the Jews five times I received forty stripes minus one. Three times I was beaten with rods; once I was stoned; three times I was shipwrecked; a night and a day I have been in the deep; in journeys often, in perils of waters, in perils of robbers, in perils of my own countrymen, in perils of the Gentiles, in perils in the city, in perils in the wilderness, in perils in the sea, in perils among false brethren; in weariness and toil, in sleeplessness often, in hunger and thirst, in fastings often, in cold and nakedness—besides the other things, what comes upon me daily: my deep concern for all the churches. Who is weak, and I am not weak? Who is made to stumble, and I do not burn with indignation? If I must boast, I will boast in the things which concern my infirmity.

—2 CORINTHIANS 11:22–30

Therefore I take pleasure in infirmities, in reproaches, in needs, in persecutions, in distresses, for Christ's sake. For when I am weak, then I am strong.

—2 CORINTHIANS 12:10

I have been crucified with Christ; it is no longer I who live, but Christ lives in me; and the life which I now live in the flesh I live by faith in the Son of God, who loved me and gave Himself for me.

—GALATIANS 2:20

For to me, to live is Christ, and to die is gain.

—PHILIPPIANS 1:21

The apostle Paul went through great trials and suffering, but he did not break. The Word of God teaches each of us to walk straight with our eye on God and not our circumstances. I believe that God will not test us beyond our abilities. The Word of God teaches us to work hard for Him and to be faithful to our Savior till the end of our life:

And from the days of John the Baptist until now the kingdom of heaven suffers violence, and the violent take it by force.

—MATTHEW 11:12

The law and the prophets were until John. Since that time the kingdom of God has been preached, and everyone is pressing into it.

—LUKE 16:16

Enter by the narrow gate; for wide is the gate and broad is the way that leads to destruction, and there are many who go in by it. Because narrow is the gate and difficult is the way which leads to life, and there are few who find it.

—MATTHEW 7:13–14

By your patience possess your souls.

—LUKE 21:19

Then Jesus said to His disciples, "If anyone desires to come after Me, let him deny himself, and take up his cross, and follow Me. For whoever desires to save his life will lose it, but whoever loses his life for My sake will find it. For what profit is it to a man if he gains the whole world, and loses his own soul? Or what will a man give in exchange for his soul? For the Son of Man will come in the glory of His Father with His angels, and then He will reward each according to his works.

—MATTHEW 16:24–27

He who loves father or mother more than Me is not worthy of Me. And he who loves son or daughter more than Me is not worthy of Me. And he who does not take his cross and follow after Me is not worthy of Me.

—MATTHEW 10:37–38

Strengthening the souls of the disciples, exhorting them to continue in the faith, and saying, "We must through many tribulations enter the kingdom of God."

—ACTS 14:22

Jesus Christ did not promise His followers an earthly path filled with roses. In fact, He warns us that following Him is difficult. Jesus told His disciples to follow all that He commanded, and

He promised to remain among them through the Holy Spirit, who would give us strength and peace during all the hard times of life:

> These things I have spoken to you, that in Me you may have peace. In the world you will have tribulation; but be of good cheer, I have overcome the world.
>
> —John 16:33

Jesus Christ overcame the world, and He continues to give strength to His followers. He gives us strength to conquer all hardships and trials, which no doubt will meet us. You will be victorious over all the trials that you cross when you have fellowship with God and when you are born again.

> For whatever is born of God overcomes the world. And this is the victory that has overcome the world—our faith. Who is he who overcomes the world, but he who believes that Jesus is the Son of God?
>
> —1 John 5:4–5

> I write to you, little children, Because your sins are forgiven you for His name's sake. I write to you, fathers, Because you have known Him who is from the beginning. I write to you, young men, Because you have overcome the wicked one. I write to you, little children, Because you have known the Father. I have written to you, fathers, Because you have known Him who is from the beginning. I have written to you, young men, Because you are strong, and the word of God abides in you, And you have overcome the wicked one.
>
> —1 John 2:12–14

340

> You are of God, little children, and have overcome them, because He who is in you is greater than he who is in the world.
>
> —1 JOHN 4:4

When a newborn man is in Christ and Christ in him, then his life on the narrow path will be blessed. He will go through all trials with a smile on his face, and they will not hurt him because of his belief in God's Word.

> Fear not, for I am with you; Be not dismayed, for I am your God. I will strengthen you, Yes, I will help you, I will uphold you with My righteous right hand.'
>
> —ISAIAH 41:10

> When you pass through the waters, I will be with you; And through the rivers, they shall not overflow you. When you walk through the fire, you shall not be burned, Nor shall the flame scorch you.
>
> —ISAIAH 43:2

It might happen that some of my dear readers will ask if it is worth the trouble being a believer—being persecuted, upset, or hurt for the name of Jesus; walking in the narrow path, battling the enemy. What do we gain by all the trouble? What reward is there for all the suffering? I have found that in my own life, the trouble of walking in God's path is definitely worth it. It is to my advantage, as to yours, to receive God's plan of salvation and to do His will. It is worth having fellowship with our Creator. From my personal experience, there is no greater happiness in this world than knowing God's truth and having fellowship with the Creator, God the Father.

There are children in this world who have been born into

privilege because their parents have been financially successful. These kids have opportunity no matter what direction they chose in life. They are considered blessed from the beginning, and the respect people have for their parents surely rests upon them at times, too. These kids have faith that their future will lack nothing. But the Father of the born-again believer is God, the Creator, who is greater than any earthly father.

> I will be a Father to you, And you shall be My sons and daughters, Says the LORD Almighty.
> —2 CORINTHIANS 6:18

> For you are all sons of God through faith in Christ Jesus.
> —GALATIANS 3:26

> For where two or three are gathered together in My name, I am there in the midst of them.
> —MATTHEW 18:20

> No man shall be able to stand before you all the days of your life; as I was with Moses, so I will be with you. I will not leave you nor forsake you.
> —JOSHUA 1:5

> But as many as received Him, to them He gave the right to become children of God, to those who believe in His name: who were born, not of blood, nor of the will of the flesh, nor of the will of man, but of God.
> —JOHN 1:12–13

> For through Him we both have access by one Spirit to the Father.
> —EPHESIANS 2:18

According to the eternal purpose which He accomplished in Christ Jesus our Lord, in whom we have boldness and access with confidence through faith in Him.

—EPHESIANS 3:11–12

Can a woman forget her nursing child, And not have compassion on the son of her womb? Surely they may forget, Yet I will not forget you. See, I have inscribed you on the palms of My hands; Your walls are continually before Me.

—ISAIAH 49:15–16

If you love Me, keep My commandments....I will not leave you orphans; I will come to you. A little while longer and the world will see Me no more, but you will see Me. Because I live, you will live also. At that day you will know that I am in My Father, and you in Me, and I in you.

—JOHN 14:15, 18–20

We all know and have witnessed the fact that life for us on this planet is very short. The days, weeks, months, and years go by too fast. People do not even have the time to notice that they are already forty, fifty, sixty, and seventy years old. And then what? You must leave this planet. But leave to where? The Word of God teaches us that all who are born must also die and that they will be judged at the end of time. Our bodies are made from dust and will return to dust. But our souls will face our Creator. Each soul will be told by God where he or she will be spending eternity. The saved will go with God into the kingdom of God, but those who have not believed and are not saved will go into the kingdom of darkness. If a person lives their life in Christ here on Earth, then he or she will remain with God in eternity. But if a person does not have fellowship with God here on Earth, then that person will not have fellowship with Him in eternity. If a person is distanced from the

Savior while on Earth, then that person will be even farther from Him in eternity.

I have lived in America for thirty-five years. I have worked in great places and have been an accountant for some of the millionaires of America. I must admit that these millionaires have been great people. They were unusual, honored citizens of this planet, and to top it off, they were rich. They had everything anyone could desire here on Earth. I was in their homes, which seemed to me more like castles surrounded by lush green gardens, trees, and flowers. It appeared to me that their homes were like bits of heaven on Earth. But time came when these people had to leave their earthly life. I attended some funerals, and I noticed that when a man leaves this earth, he takes only that which he brought with him at his birth—nothing but nakedness. He does not take any material thing with him. Only his deeds will follow.

> Then I heard a voice from heaven saying to me, "Write: 'Blessed are the dead who die in the Lord from now on.'" "Yes," says the Spirit, "that they may rest from their labors, and their works follow them."
> —Revelation 14:13

The Word of God says that those who die in Christ are blessed. In other words, those who had fellowship with God here on Earth are blessed at their death. Those who believed in Jesus, who proclaimed Him in front of other people, and who walked in the narrow path are blessed when they enter eternity. They are also the ones who suffer persecution, pain, and trials but remain faithful to their Creator during their life and at their death. And at their death, they leave this earth victoriously. Maybe one of my attentive readers will ask what believers expect in eternity. The Word of God answers this question:

He who overcomes shall be clothed in white garments, and I will not blot out his name from the Book of Life; but I will confess his name before My Father and before His angels.... He who overcomes, I will make him a pillar in the temple of My God, and he shall go out no more. I will write on him the name of My God and the name of the city of My God, the New Jerusalem, which comes down out of heaven from My God. And I will write on him My new name.... To him who overcomes I will grant to sit with Me on My throne, as I also overcame and sat down with My Father on His throne.

—REVELATION 3:5, 12, 21

He who has an ear, let him hear what the Spirit says to the churches. To him who overcomes I will give to eat from the tree of life, which is in the midst of the Paradise of God.... He who has an ear, let him hear what the Spirit says to the churches. To him who overcomes I will give some of the hidden manna to eat. And I will give him a white stone, and on the stone a new name written which no one knows except him who receives it.

—REVELATION 2:7, 17

He who overcomes shall inherit all things, and I will be his God and he shall My son.

—REVELATION 21:7

But as it is written: "Eye has not seen, nor ear heard, Nor have entered into the heart of man The things which God has prepared for those who love Him."

—1 CORINTHIANS 2:9

What a great future awaits those who die with Christ. After reading these promises, we can say with faith that it is worth believing in God; it is worth suffering for Him in our short Earthly lives; it is worth battling and walking in the narrow path; it is worth living your entire life for Him.

The Word of God writes much about those who follow God on Earth by walking in the narrow path. It also writes much of the great future that awaits these people in eternity, a future that God prepared personally for his disciples.

After reading these verses, one of the atheists thought and said, "What will happen to me? Where will I spend eternity? Where will my place be in the afterlife?" These are very important questions, and they pertain to many people in the twenty-first century. And what will happen to those who neglect God and His gift of salvation? Where will those who walk in the wide path end up? What about the ones who cherished their work so highly and acted according to their desires and not God's? There are many people today who rely on themselves. What will happen to them? What awaits them? Where will their eternity be? What does God's Constitution say about these people? The Word of God is very thorough, and it answers a lot of these questions. Let's travel through the Word of God and find the answers to these very important questions:

> Now the works of the flesh are evident, which are: adultery, fornication, uncleanness, lewdness, idolatry, sorcery, hatred, contentions, jealousies, outbursts of wrath, selfish ambitions, dissensions, heresies, envy, murders, drunkenness, revelries, and the like; of which I tell you beforehand, just as I also told you in time past, that those who practice such things will not inherit the kingdom of God.
>
> —GALATIANS 5:19–21

Do you not know that the unrighteous will not inherit the kingdom of God? Do not be deceived. Neither fornicators, nor idolaters, nor adulterers, nor homosexuals, nor sodomites, nor thieves, nor covetous, nor drunkards, nor revilers, nor extortioners will inherit the kingdom of God.

—1 CORINTHIANS 6:9–10

For this you know, that no fornicator, unclean person, nor covetous man, who is an idolater, has any inheritance in the kingdom of Christ and God.

—EPHESIANS 5:5

Since the people mentioned above will not be in the kingdom of God after the great judgment day, then where will they be? Let's read the words of the judge:

Then He will also say to those on the left hand, "Depart from Me, you cursed, into the everlasting fire prepared for the devil and his angels."

—MATTHEW 25:41

There will be weeping and gnashing of teeth, when you see Abraham and Isaac and Jacob and all the prophets in the kingdom of God, and yourselves thrust out.

—LUKE 13:28

But the cowardly, unbelieving, abominable, murderers, sexually immoral, sorcerers, idolaters, and all liars shall have their part in the lake which burns with fire and brimstone.

—REVELATION 21:8

God the Father did not prepare this place for people. He prepared this place for the devil and his angels. But people find their way to it when they deny God's grace and gift of salvation and chose to lead a sinful life.

Possibly more than one reader of this book will say, "I am not part of the category of people mentioned above. I am an honest, decent person, and I lead a moral life. I simply do not do business with God and Jesus. I have never believed in God, nor have I believed God. I have never turned to Him to confess my sins, and I have never asked for forgiveness because I do not think I am a sinner. I have never had to accept Jesus as my Savior, and I have not witnessed for Him, nor have I had fellowship with Him." Dear reader, Jesus Christ has an answer for you. Read the following words with great attention:

> Therefore whoever confesses Me before men, him I will also confess before My Father who is in heaven. But whoever denies Me before men, him I will also deny before My Father who is in heaven.
>
> —MATTHEW 10:32–33

> For whoever is ashamed of Me and My words in this adulterous and sinful generation, of him the Son of Man also will be ashamed when He comes in the glory of His Father with the holy angels.
>
> —MARK 8:38

> Also I say to you, whoever confesses Me before men, him the Son of Man also will confess before the angels of God. But he who denies Me before men will be denied before the angels of God.
>
> —LUKE 12:8–9

> This is a faithful saying: For if we died with Him, We shall also live with Him. If we endure, We shall also reign with Him. If we deny Him, He also will deny us. If we are faithless, He remains faithful; He cannot deny Himself.
>
> —2 TIMOTHY 2:11–13

Can a person receive salvation after their death if they did not have fellowship with God the Father, believe in Jesus Christ, or accept His teachings while they lived on Earth? Many of us have heard that it is necessary to pray for the dead so that their souls will go to the kingdom of God and not to hell. As I have read and studied the Bible, I did not find any passage indicating that we should pray for the dead. All of God's teachings are directed toward living people. All of His commands, wills, and laws apply only to the living. Jesus Christ spoke a lot about prayer and the meaning of prayer. He prayed Himself and told us to pray for each other. But not once did He tell us to pray for the dead. The apostles prayed and told us to pray also, and not only for ourselves but for others too. And they also did not teach us to pray for the dead. Nowhere in the Bible does it say to pray for the dead. Everything Jesus teaches, all His sermons, are directed at prayer for the living.

> Come to Me, all you who labor and are heavy laden, and I will give you rest. Take My yoke upon you and learn from Me, for I am gentle and lowly in heart, and you will find rest for your souls. For My yoke is easy and My burden is light.
> —MATTHEW 11:28–30

The Words of Jesus Christ apply only and exclusively to living people, to those who can hear, judge, and decide for themselves. And some will chose to accept His teachings and to use them in their daily life, and others will chose to reject them.

> Also I say to you, whoever confesses Me before men, him the Son of Man also will confess before the angels of God. But he who denies Me before men will be denied before the angels of God.
> —LUKE 12:8–9

Therefore whoever confesses Me before men, him I will also confess before My Father who is in heaven. But whoever denies Me before men, him I will also deny before My Father who is in heaven.

—MATTHEW 10:32–33

From these words, we distinctly see that God the Father will accept a person into heaven only if they accept Jesus Christ and profess Him in their life. But if a person does not take the first step, then he will be judged come Judgment Day. The apostle Paul taught as Jesus did:

That if you confess with your mouth the Lord Jesus and believe in your heart that God has raised Him from the dead, you will be saved. For with the heart one believes unto righteousness, and with the mouth confession is made unto salvation.

—ROMANS 10:9–10

The Bible describes those who died in Christ, who had fellowship with Him on earth, and who followed His teachings, lived by His Word, and walked in the narrow path:

Then I heard a voice from heaven saying to me, "Write: 'Blessed are the dead who die in the Lord from now on.'" "Yes," says the Spirit, "that they may rest from their labors, and their works follow them."

—REVELATION 14:13

But I do not want you to be ignorant, brethren, concerning those who have fallen asleep, lest you sorrow as others who have no hope. For if we believe that Jesus died and rose again, even so God will bring with Him those who sleep in Jesus. For this we say to you by the word of the Lord, that we who are alive and remain until the coming of the Lord will by no means precede those who are asleep. For the Lord Himself will descend from heaven with a shout, with the voice of an archangel, and with the trumpet of God. And the dead in Christ will rise first. Then we who are alive and remain shall be caught up together with them in the clouds to meet the Lord in the air. And thus we shall always be with the Lord. Therefore comfort one another with these words.

—1 Thessalonians 4:13–18

For none of us lives to himself, and no one dies to himself. For if we live, we live to the Lord; and if we die, we die to the Lord. Therefore, whether we live or die, we are the Lord's. For to this end Christ died and rose and lived again, that He might be Lord of both the dead and the living.

—Romans 14:7–9

How blessed are those who choose God's plan of salvation and accept it for their lives! They live and die, too, but they always will remain with their Creator. A plan such as this could only be created by our Creator, and we owe Him our praise and thanksgiving.

And as it is appointed for men to die once, but after this the judgment.

—Hebrews 9:27

The Word of God does not write that there is an opportunity between death and judgment day to receive salvation and peace with God the Father through Jesus Christ. An opportunity such as this is not mentioned in God's Holy Word. In other words, an opportunity such as this does not exist. If it is not mentioned in the Holy Word, then it will not come about to be fulfilled. People who do not have fellowship with God while they are alive here on Earth will not have fellowship with Him in heaven and in eternity.

31

FAITH WITHOUT DEEDS IS DEAD

O UR GREAT AND MIGHTY GOD, THE CREATOR OF HEAVEN and Earth, the human race, the animals and plants—the Creator of all life—treasures His words highly. His words brought everything into being, and everything exists because of them. In the Holy Book, there are many passages that describe how God spoke and how what He spoke came to pass. This means that God spoke and created that which is seen:

> Then God said, "Let there be light"; and there was light.
> —GENESIS 1:3

> For He spoke, and it was done; He commanded, and it stood fast.
> —Psalm 33:9

Then God said, "Let the waters under the heavens be gathered together into one place, and let the dry land appear"; and it was so.

—GENESIS 1:9

The Holy Bible writes that His Word created everything.

In the beginning was the Word, and the Word was with God, and the Word was God. He was in the beginning with God. All things were made through Him, and without Him nothing was made that was made. In Him was life, and the life was the light of men.

—JOHN 1:1–4

By the word of the LORD the heavens were made, And all the host of them by the breath of His mouth

—PSALM 33:6

By faith we understand that the worlds were framed by the word of God, so that the things which are seen were not made of things which are visible.

—HEBREWS 11:3

The Word of God holds life in itself, and it is active.

And the Word became flesh and dwelt among us, and we beheld His glory, the glory as of the only begotten of the Father, full of grace and truth.

—JOHN 1:14

The Son of the living God is called the Word of God.

He was clothed with a robe dipped in blood, and His name is called The Word of God.

—REVELATION 19:13

The Word of God is everlasting and unchanging.

The grass withers, the flower fades, but the word of our God stands forever.

—ISAIAH 40:8

Forever, O LORD, Your word is settled in heaven.

—PSALM 119:89

Heaven and earth will pass away, but My words will by no means pass away.

—MATTHEW 24:35

Having been born again, not of corruptible seed but incorruptible, through the word of God which lives and abides forever, because All flesh is as grass, And all the glory of man as the flower of the grass. The grass withers, And its flower falls away, But the word of the LORD endures forever.

—1 PETER 1:23–25

Each word that comes from the mouth of the living God is clean, holy, and refined by fire.

Every word of God is pure; He is a shield to those who put their trust in Him. Do not add to His words, Lest He rebuke you, and you be found a liar.

—PROVERBS 30:5–6

As for God, His way is perfect; The word of the LORD is proven; He is a shield to all who trust in Him.

—2 SAMUEL 22:31

The Holy Word says that God Himself preserves His own words and requires His creation to do also.

> The words of the LORD are pure words, Like silver tried in a furnace of earth, Purified seven times. You shall keep them, O LORD, You shall preserve them from this generation forever.
> —PSALM 12:6–7

Everything that God created is for our enjoyment. All that is required of us in return is obedience. For this reason, God established laws from the beginning of time. Throughout the scriptures, both in the Old and New Testaments, God reminds us to keep His commands. It is very important to the Creator that we listen to His voice and be obedient by fulfilling His commands. God the Creator is holy, and therefore His laws are holy also. We, being the creation, cannot change God's laws; we cannot add or delete anything from them. Our great and mighty God highly regards His laws and warns us against changing them. Let's take a look in the Old Testament to see what God told His people about His laws:

> You shall not add to the word which I command you, nor take from it, that you may keep the commandments of the LORD your God which I command you.
> —DEUTERONOMY 4:2

> That you may fear the LORD your God, to keep all His statutes and His commandments which I command you, you and your son, and your grandson, all the days of your life, and that your days may be prolonged....You shall diligently keep the commandments of the LORD your God, His testimonies, and His statutes which He has commanded you....Then it will be righteousness for us, if we are careful to observe all

theses commandments before the LORD our God, as He has commanded us.

—DEUTERONOMY 6:2, 17, 25

Therefore you shall keep the commandments of the LORD your God, to walk in His ways and to fear Him....Beware that you do not forget the LORD your God by not keeping His commandments, His judgments, and His statutes which I command you today.

—DEUTERONOMY 8:6, 11

Whatever I command you, be careful to observe it; you shall not add to it or take away from it.

—DEUTERONOMY 12:32

God treasures His Word and laws highly and wants us, His creation, to be obedient so that He may bless us. Let's see what blessings God sends when we fulfill His commands:

If you walk in My statutes and keep My commandments, and perform them, then I will give you rain in its season, the land shall yield its produce, and the trees of the field shall yield their fruit. Your threshing shall last till the time of vintage, and the vintage shall last till the time of sowing; you shall eat your bread to the full, and dwell in your land safely. I will give peace in the land, and you shall lie down, and none will make you afraid; I will rid the land of evil beasts, and the sword will not go through your land. You will chase your enemies, and they shall fall by the sword before you. Five of you shall chase a hundred, and a hundred of you shall put ten thousand to flight; your enemies shall fall by the sword before you. "For I will look on you favorably and make you fruitful, multiply you and confirm My covenant with you.

You shall eat the old harvest, and clear out the old because of the new. I will set My tabernacle among you, and My soul shall not abhor you. I will walk among you and be your God, and you shall be My people."

—Leviticus 26:3–12

But if we neglect His commands, these are the punishments He will send:

But if you do not obey Me, and do not observe all these commandments, and if you despise My statutes, or if your soul abhors My judgments, so that you do not perform all My commandments, but break My covenant, I also will do this to you: I will even appoint terror over you, wasting disease and fever which shall consume the eyes and cause sorrow of heart. And you shall sow your seed in vain, for your enemies shall eat it. I will set My face against you, and you shall be defeated by your enemies. Those who hate you shall reign over you, and you shall flee when no one pursues you. And after all this, if you do not obey Me, then I will punish you seven times more for your sins. I will break the pride of your power; I will make your heavens like iron and your earth like bronze. And your strength shall be spent in vain; for your land shall not yield its produce, nor shall the trees of the land yield their fruit. Then, if you walk contrary to Me, and are not willing to obey Me, I will bring on you seven times more plagues, according to your sins.

—Leviticus 26:14–21

When we fulfill God's will, we express great faith in God, as well as deep regard for our Creator. God offers us the chance to obey His will; He does not force us. And when we do fulfill His will, He rewards us with abundant life.

See, I have set before you today life and good, death and evil, in that I command you today to love the LORD your God, to walk in His ways, and to keep His commandments, His statutes, and His judgments, that you may live and multiply; and the LORD your God will bless you in the land which you go to possess. But if your heart turns away so that you do not hear, and are drawn away, and worship other gods and serve them, I announce to you today that you shall surely perish; you shall not prolong your days in the land which you cross over the Jordan to go in and possess. I call heaven and earth as witnesses today against you, that I have set before you life and death, blessing and cursing; therefore choose life, that both you and your descendants may live; that you may love the LORD your God, that you may obey His voice, and that you may cling to Him, for He is your life and the length of your days; and that you may dwell in the land which the LORD swore to your fathers, to Abraham, Isaac, and Jacob, to give them.

—DEUTERONOMY 30:15–20

Let's now travel through the pages of the New Testament and read the words that Jesus Christ spoke while on Earth:

As He spoke these words, many believed in Him. Then Jesus said to those Jews who believed Him, "If you abide in My word, you are My disciples indeed. And you shall know the truth, and the truth shall make you free.... Most assuredly, I say to you, if anyone keeps My word he shall never see death."

—JOHN 8:30–32, 51

"If you love Me, keep My commandments.... He who has My commandments and keeps them, it is he who loves Me. And he who loves Me will be loved by My Father, and I will love him and manifest Myself to him."...Jesus answered and said to him, "If anyone loves Me, he will keep My word; and My Father will love him, and We will come to him and make Our home with him."

—JOHN 14:15, 21, 23

You are My friends if you do whatever I command you. No longer do I call you servants, for a servant does not know what his master is doing; but I have called you friends, for all things that I heard from My Father I have made known to you.

—JOHN 15:14–15

Whoever believes that Jesus is the Christ is born of God, and everyone who loves Him who begot also loves him who is begotten of Him. By this we know that we love the children of God, when we love God and keep His commandments. For this is the love of God, that we keep His commandments. And His commandments are not burdensome.

—1 JOHN 5:1–3

Now by this we know that we know Him, if we keep His commandments...But whoever keeps His word, truly the love of God is perfected in him. By this we know that we are in Him. He who says he abides in Him ought himself also to walk just as He walked.

—1 JOHN 2:3, 5–6

And whatever we ask we receive from Him, because we keep His commandments and do those things that are pleasing in His sight. And this is His commandment: that we should believe on the name of His Son Jesus Christ and love one another, as He gave us commandment. Now he who keeps His commandments abides in Him, and He in him. And by this we know that He abides in us, by the Spirit whom He has given us

—1 JOHN 3:22–24

And the world is passing away, and the lust of it; but he who does the will of God abides forever.

—1 JOHN 2:17

But He said, "More than that, blessed are those who hear the word of God and keep it!"

—LUKE 11:28

Blessed are those who do His commandments, that they may have the right to the tree of life, and may enter through the gates into the city.

—REVELATION 22:14

After reading from the Old and New Testament about the laws of God, it is evident that He treasures His Word and does not want us to change it in any way.

For You have magnified Your word above all Your name.

—PSALM 138:2

When we carry out God's will exactly, we profess our belief, respect, and love to God, the author of the words. And when we are obedient, we feel His love toward us immediately. Jesus Christ calls His followers His students, but more importantly, His friends. And to His followers He gives eternal life. When we fulfill God's laws, we then reside in Him and He resides in us. At this point, we have the privilege to ask God for anything that we need, and we also have the privilege to receive all that God has promised His disciples. The Word of God says that people who obey God are blessed, and this is indeed true. And today, in the twenty-first century, Jesus calls everyone to Him, each citizen of this planet. When we live in Him and He in us, we receive His strength and become spiritually strong.

> Abide in Me, and I in you. As the branch cannot bear fruit of itself, unless it abides in the vine, neither can you, unless you abide in Me. I am the vine, you are the branches. He who abides in Me, and I in him, bears much fruit; for without Me you can do nothing. If anyone does not abide in Me, he is cast out as a branch and is withered; and they gather them and throw them into the fire, and they are burned. If you abide in Me, and My words abide in you, you will ask what you desire, and it shall be done for you.
>
> —JOHN 15:4–7

When Jesus Christ rose from the dead, He appeared to the eleven apostles, and when they sat together around a table, He told them the following:

> And He said to them, "Go into all the world and preach the gospel to every creature. He who believes and is baptized will be saved; but he who does not believe will be condemned."
>
> —MARK 16:15–16

This was Jesus' last command, and it remains alive and effective today in the twenty-first century. This command applies to the entire human race. It applies to me and to you too, dear reader. Jesus Christ commanded us to preach the gospel and to baptize new believers in water. The person who simply listens to the Word of God is not a candidate—only the person who believes God's Word can receive water baptism. This was decided by Jesus, the Son of God, the King of kings, the Savior of mankind. We must

361

read, treasure, and fulfill this command without error because the Creator requires this of us.

> So Samuel said: "Has the LORD as great delight in burnt offerings and sacrifices, As in obeying the voice of the LORD? Behold, to obey is better than sacrifice, And to heed than the fat of rams. For rebellion is as the sin of witchcraft, And stubbornness is as iniquity and idolatry. Because you have rejected the word of the LORD, He also has rejected you from being king."
>
> —1 SAMUEL 15:22–23

Our faith is dead when we are aware of God's laws but do not do what He tells us to. We lose fellowship with Him and we no longer remain in Him when we fail to fulfill His will. And when we do not have fellowship with God, we depart from Him spiritually. We do not love Him, nor His commands—we lose love for our own Creator—when we lack fellowship with Him, and our spiritual life becomes progressively worse to the point that it becomes dead.

> He who does not love Me does not keep My words; and the word which you hear is not Mine but the Father's who sent Me.
>
> —JOHN 14:24

> What does it profit, my brethren, if someone says he has faith but does not have works? Can faith save him?...Thus also faith by itself, if it does not have works, is dead...You believe that there is one God. You do well. Even the demons believe—and tremble! But do you want to know, O foolish man, that faith without works is dead?....For as the body without the spirit is dead, so faith without works is dead also.
>
> —JAMES 2:14, 17, 19–20, 26

When a born-again Christian does not follow God's teachings, he will soon fail to remain in contact with God and follow His example. If the disobedience continues without repentance, he will be at risk of leaving the faith and losing his salvation. The Word of God warns about this:

> For if, after they have escaped the pollutions of the world through the knowledge of the Lord and Savior Jesus Christ, they are again entangled in them and overcome, the latter end is worse for them than the beginning. For it would have been better for them not to have known the way of righteousness, than having known it, to turn from the holy commandment delivered to them.
>
> —2 PETER 2:20–21

> He who is not with Me is against Me, and he who does not gather with Me scatters. When an unclean spirit goes out of a man, he goes through dry places, seeking rest; and finding none, he says, "I will return to my house from which I came. And when he comes, he finds it swept and put in order. Then he goes and takes with him seven other spirits more wicked than himself, and they enter and dwell there; and the last state of that man is worse than the first."
>
> —LUKE 11:23–26

> For it is impossible for those who were once enlightened, and have tasted the heavenly gift, and have become partakers of the Holy Spirit, and have tasted the good word of God and the powers of the age to come, if they fall away, to renew them again to repentance, since they crucify again for themselves the Son of God, and put Him to an open shame.
>
> —HEBREWS 6:4–6

> For if we sin willfully after we have received the knowledge
> of the truth, there no longer remains a sacrifice for sins, but
> a certain fearful expectation of judgment, and fiery indig-
> nation which will devour the adversaries. Anyone who has
> rejected Moses' law dies without mercy on the testimony of
> two or three witnesses. Of how much worse punishment, do
> you suppose, will he be thought worthy who has trampled the
> Son of God underfoot, counted the blood of the covenant by
> which he was sanctified a common thing, and insulted the
> Spirit of grace?
>
> —HEBREWS 10:26–29

The life of a Christian is a constant battle with evil. To become
a born-again Christian and to maintain fellowship with the Creator
requires a lot of effort. You must battle with the godless environment that is present today and surrounds you. You will be enticed
by the world to act out of God's laws and to break His commands.
But mostly, you must battle with yourself, with your desires. You
must not look to the path that leads to sin. And most importantly,
you must battle with your own tongue.

> Even so the tongue is a little member and boasts great things.
> See how great a forest a little fire kindles! And the tongue
> is a fire, a world of iniquity. The tongue is so set among our
> members that it defiles the whole body, and sets on fire the
> course of nature; and it is set on fire by hell. For every kind
> of beast and bird, of reptile and creature of the sea, is tamed
> and has been tamed by mankind. But no man can tame the
> tongue. It is an unruly evil, full of deadly poison. With it we
> bless our God and Father, and with it we curse men, who have
> been made in the similitude of God. Out of the same mouth

proceed blessing and cursing. My brethren, these things ought not to be so.

—JAMES 3:5–10

New Christians must control their tongues because the words that come from the soul of man have great meaning, both to man and to God. Let's read what God's Constitution says about our tongue, our conversations, and the words that come from our innermost being:

But I say to you that for every idle word men may speak, they will give account of it in the day of judgment. For by your words you will be justified, and by your words you will be condemned.

—MATTHEW 12:36–37

Not what goes into the mouth defiles a man; but what comes out of the mouth, this defiles a man.

—MATTHEW 15:11

Keep your tongue from evil, And your lips from speaking deceit. Depart from evil and do good; Seek peace and pursue it.

—PSALM 34:13–14

Let's examine Jesus' conversation with His followers, which proves that the words that come from a person's soul are meaningful:

When Jesus came into the region of Caesarea Philippi, He asked His disciples, saying, "Who do men say that I, the Son of Man, am?" So they said, "Some say John the Baptist, some Elijah, and others Jeremiah or one of the prophets." He said to them, "But who do you say that I am?" Simon Peter answered and said, "You are the Christ, the Son of the living God." Jesus answered and said to him, "Blessed are you, Simon Bar-Jonah, for flesh and blood has not revealed this to you, but My Father who is in heaven. And I also say to you that you are Peter, and on this rock I will build My church, and the gates of Hades shall not prevail against it. And I will give you the keys of the kingdom of heaven, and whatever you bind on earth will be bound in heaven, and whatever you loose on earth will be loosed in heaven." Then He commanded His disciples that they should tell no one that He was Jesus the Christ.

—MATTHEW 16:13–20

After hearing Simon Peter's answer, Jesus changed his name to Peter, which means "stone, or foundation." And on this foundation—on words such as Peter's, "You are the Christ, the son of the living God,"—God the Father will establish His church, which the powers of hell cannot destroy. And what happened later in their conversation?

From that time Jesus began to show to His disciples that He must go to Jerusalem, and suffer many things from the elders and chief priests and scribes, and be killed, and be raised the third day. Then Peter took Him aside and began to rebuke Him, saying, "Far be it from You, Lord; this shall not happen to You!" But He turned and said to Peter, "Get behind Me, Satan! You are an offense to Me, for you are not mindful of the things of God, but the things of men."

—MATTHEW 16:21–23

Jesus knew His mission on Earth from the beginning. He knew that He must suffer, shed His holy blood, and be crucified for our sins. And eventually He was able to share this with His apostles. But Peter, when he heard Jesus talk about what He would endure on the cross, tried to tell Jesus otherwise. Jesus, when He heard Peter's reaction, exclaimed, "Get behind me, Satan" (Matt. 16:23).

After Peter said that Jesus was the Christ, Jesus called him a stone, but after Peter told Jesus that He shouldn't have to suffer, He rebuked Peter's words.

It is obvious that our words have great meaning. We are condemned and saved by our words. Our Christian actions and deeds must be good, fully thought-out, and in agreement with God's will and commands. Our words will be judged and be like Paul described:

> Let your speech always be with grace, seasoned with salt, that you may know how you ought to answer each one.
> —COLOSSIANS 4:6

> Depart from evil and do good; Seek peace and pursue it. The eyes of the LORD are on the righteous, And His ears are open to their cry.
> —PSALM 34:14–15

The born-again Christian must control each step in their life. Our Christian faith must be backed by correct moral actions and we must always remember that faith without works is dead. The Christian path is not easy—but it is blessed because Christians have been given the armor to battle with evil and dark spirits. God the Father, on the pages of His Constitution, describes the armor:

> Finally, my brethren, be strong in the Lord and in the power of His might. Put on the whole armor of God, that you may be able to stand against the wiles of the devil. For we do not wrestle against flesh and blood, but against principalities, against powers, against the rulers of the darkness of this age, against spiritual hosts of wickedness in the heavenly places.

Therefore take up the whole armor of God, that you may be able to withstand in the evil day, and having done all, to stand. Stand therefore, having girded your waist with truth, having put on the breastplate of righteousness, and having shod your feet with the preparation of the gospel of peace; above all, taking the shield of faith with which you will be able to quench all the fiery darts of the wicked one. And take the helmet of salvation, and the sword of the Spirit, which is the word of God; praying always with all prayer and supplication in the Spirit, being watchful to this end with all perseverance and supplication for all the saints.

—EPHESIANS 6:10–18

The Word of God, the armor that we have, will help us be victorious in all circumstances. With His Words you can overcome all the arrows of evil, but to use this armor you must know the Word of God. For the Christian person to be victorious, they must always—daily—read the Word of God. We must read the Bible because this is the bread for our spirit and the sword for our battle. We must also learn to speak with God using the name of Jesus—we must learn to pray. Prayer is conversation with our Creator. Prayer is very important to the life of a Christian. Some of my readers might ask, But to whom should we pray? To whom do we direct our requests, our needs, our problems, and hardships? Who listens to us and who will answer us? The answers to these questions are very important for each person to know. Each citizen of this planet must know to whom they should pray and who listens and responds to their prayers. And we can find the answer to all of they above on the pages of the Holy Word.

When Jesus' followers asked how they should pray, Jesus replied:

In this manner, therefore, pray: Our Father in heaven, Hallowed be Your name. Your kingdom come. Your will be done On earth as it is in heaven. Give us this day our daily bread. And forgive us our debts, As we forgive our debtors. And do not lead us into temptation, But deliver us from the evil one. For Yours is the kingdom and the power and the glory forever. Amen.

—MATTHEW 6:9–13

Jesus taught His disciples that they should turn to God the Father in simple ways. He told us how to pray, to whom we must pray, and who listens and answers. Let's read His words:

And in that day you will ask Me nothing. Most assuredly, I say to you, whatever you ask the Father in My name He will give you. Until now you have asked nothing in My name. Ask, and you will receive, that your joy may be full.

—JOHN 16:23–24

And whatever you ask in My name, that I will do, that the Father may be glorified in the Son. If you ask anything in My name, I will do it.

—JOHN 14:13–14

"If you abide in Me, and My words abide in you, you will ask what you desire, and it shall be done for you."

—JOHN 15:7

And whatever we ask we receive from Him, because we keep His commandments and do those things that are pleasing in His sight.

—1 JOHN 3:22

Now this is the confidence that we have in Him, that if we ask anything according to His will, He hears us. And if we know that He hears us, whatever we ask, we know that we have the petitions that we have asked of Him.

—1 John 5:14–15

We do not have to recite certain phrases with God; we can speak with simple words that come from our heart and soul. We must tell God about our circumstances, our hardships, our problems, and we must ask for His wisdom to resolve these issues victoriously. There are many examples of how we can communicate with God. For instance, when a man loses his job, he may turn to God with the following words:

Father God, Creator of heaven and Earth,

I come to you in the name of Jesus Christ, Your only begotten Son. I want to first thank You for Your love toward me, for remembering me—Your creation. I thank You for Your gift of salvation and that You touched my heart and mind, that You opened my heart to Your truth, and that You cleansed me and allowed me to have fellowship with You. I thank You that I can show You my entire soul and that I can present You with all my situations. Right now I want to tell You of my position. I lost my job, and I do not have any other means of supporting myself or my family. Please send me work; direct my steps to where I will be needed, where I can earn a living with which I can support my family. Help me, dear Lord. I ask this in the name of Jesus. I bless You and thank You for listening to my prayer. And I thank You in advance for sending an answer to my request.

In Jesus' name, amen.

When someone is sick in your family, it is important to present God with the problem. For example, say a mother got sick and is in bad circumstances, unable to help her husband or children. The entire family may pray to God with the following words:

Dear God, Creator of heaven and Earth,

We come to You in the name of Jesus to tell You that our mother is very sick. The doctors have done what they could; they have done what was in their human power to do, but her health has not improved. We come to You, dear Jesus, because we know and believe that You are the Healer of all healers. And we ask You to heal her. We love our mother, and we want her to be with us. We are still young and we need her help, her discipline. Our mother also loves us, and she wants to be with us. She wants to raise us and teach us. She does not want to leave us as orphans.

No one else can replace our mother. No one can sit us on her lap and hug us as heartily as our mother can. No one else can place their hand on our shoulder and say so lovingly, "You are my son," or "You are my only daughter," and "I truly love you." No one can do this as sweetly and lovingly as our mother does.

Dear Jesus, You were on this earth. You healed so many people from many diseases. Please heal our mother also. Jesus Christ, You came to this earth. You were crucified. They killed You and placed You in the grave, but You arose. You ascended into heaven. You sit at the right hand of God, and You intercede for us. You have great power and ability to help those who come to You and ask Your help. Dear Jesus, we, as a family, come to You and ask You to stretch Your wounded hands toward our mother

and touch her to rid her of her sickness. Give the parts of her body that are sick new life. Return her life because You are life, and You can give life to those who find that their life is leaving them. Our great Father God, we bring our mother in front of Your holy throne, and ask in the name of Jesus of Nazareth that You heal her. We truly thank You for hearing our prayer!
In Jesus' name, amen.

The Word of God teaches us to turn to God in the time of sorrow, sickness and problems and to ask for His help.

Call upon Me in the day of trouble; I will deliver you, and you shall glorify Me.
—PSALM 50:15

Call to Me, and I will answer you, and show you great and mighty things, which you do not know.
—JEREMIAH 33:3

Yet you do not have because you do not ask.
—JAMES 4:2

The Word of God teaches us to turn to our Creator, present our needs and problems to Him, and ask for His help. One of my dear readers wants to know if there is some proof in God's Constitution that God will answer his or her prayer.

Let's read the personal testimony of King David:

For You, Lord, are good, and ready to forgive, And abundant in mercy to all those who call upon You. Give ear, O LORD, to my prayer; And attend to the voice of my supplications.

In the day of my trouble I will call upon You, For You will answer me.

—Psalm 86:5–7

I called on the Lord in distress; The Lord answered me and set me in a broad place. The Lord is on my side; I will not fear. What can man do to me?

—Psalm 118:5–6

In my distress I called upon the Lord, And cried out to my God; He heard my voice from His temple, And my cry came before Him, even to His ears.

—Psalm 18:6

Let's read the story of Jonah, who did not listen to the voice of God and found himself in a risky situation because of it. He nonetheless turned to God in his circumstance.

Then Jonah prayed to the Lord his God from the fish's belly. And he said: "I cried out to the Lord because of my affliction, And He answered me. "Out of the belly of Sheol I cried, And You heard my voice. For You cast me into the deep, Into the heart of the seas, And the floods surrounded me; All Your billows and Your waves passed over me.... Those who regard worthless idols Forsake their own Mercy.

—Jonah 2:1–3, 8

Dear reader, if God heard king David and Jonah, then He will hear you too. You only must turn to Him, tell him your situation, and ask for His help. God wants to have fellowship with His creation. He loves when His creation turns to Him, and He rebukes those who do not turn to Him.

It is important for each person to know that faith without works, without fellowship with the Creator, without prayer, without the fulfillment of His commands, and without daily reading of the Bible is dead.

32

THIS IS THE GOSPEL.
THIS IS THE GOOD NEWS!

O N THE FIRST FEW PAGES OF GOD'S CONSTITUTION, WE read of how God made the first man, Adam, our great-grandfather, in His likeness. God used one of Adam's ribs to make Eve, a wife and helper for Adam. He commanded them to multiply and fill the earth with life. God the Father gave them great power to rule over the animal kingdom, and He commanded them to take care of the earth. In other words, God the Father made man the manager of the rest of creation. The Creator made a garden for the first couple, and in the garden grew trees which were pleasing to the eye and which produced fruit that was pleasing to the tongue and stomach. The tree of life and the tree of knowledge were also in the garden. The garden was also the source of four rivers. God the Father gave the first couple great wealth, as the garden had gold, rich and useful stone, and other resources. (See Genesis 2:11–12.) The young couple was surrounded with wealth and fortune. Their Creator was with them, and they had fellowship with Him. And

God gave the couple one command, which He wanted them to obey. The command was as follows:

> Of every tree of the garden you may freely eat; but of the tree
> of the knowledge of good and evil you shall not eat, for in the
> day that you eat of it you shall surely die."
> —GENESIS 2:16–17

And what happened? Did the first people fulfill this command? Did they treasure the Word of God the Father? No! Adam disobeyed, as did his wife. Eve listened to the voice of the serpent and ate from the tree of knowledge. She also gave some fruit to Adam, and he also ate. The first man broke the will of his Creator. The first people were disobedient to God, even after all the good that God gave them. When they disobeyed Him, they lost fellowship with their Creator. The consequence of their careless step was terrible. They lost authority, and they lost the privilege of ruling the Garden of Eden. They realized they were naked when they ate from the tree of knowledge, and when God came to seek fellowship with them, they hid. Their guilty consciences began bothering them, and they began fearing God. The result of this one disobedient act was that they, and subsequently, we, lost eternal life with God in the Garden of Eden.

Sin entered all life after the first man sinned. Sin became part of me and you, dear reader. I was born a sinner and you too, dear reader, are a sinner. The entire human race lost fellowship with their Creator, and sin currently reigns. The sin has become a chasm between people and God the Father. But our great and powerful God, who loves His creation dearly, does not want the chasm, the barrier, to be between us and Him. God seeks fellowship with His creation; He still wants to be united to us, the work of His hands. He wants to be in contact with each soul. For this reason, He created a way to unite us with Himself; He found a way to cleanse us from our sin—and this way requires blood.

> And according to the law almost all things are purified with blood, and without shedding of blood there is no remission.
> —HEBREWS 9:22

In the Old Testament, it is recorded that God told Moses to build the ark of the covenant, where one-year-old male animals without blemish could be brought as sacrifices. They were killed and their blood was sprinkled on the altar, scrolls, and people. (See Hebrews 9:21.) God cleansed His people, the nation of Israel, in this manner. God forgave His creation of their sinful actions when He washed them with blood. And when He washed them, He could once more have fellowship with them. He could then be united with them and actually be present among them.

The time came when God established a new method of forgiveness. This new method would once and for all shed all the blood required to cleanse us of our sins. God the Father decided to send His only begotten Son, Jesus Christ, to die for us. His Son was without blemish, and He became the one and only sacrifice that would ever be needed. When heaven and Earth were ready to receive this gift, the King of kings and the Lord of lords left heaven and His glory and came to Earth in human flesh. The Son of God was born as Son of man to the Virgin Mary. He grew, matured, and preached the kingdom of God. He called people to repentance, and He became the ultimate sacrifice on the cross. Jesus Christ did not complain about being the sacrifice for us; He was obedient to God the Father, and He accepted His fate without hesitation. He shed His holy and sinless blood for us, and He is the only sacrifice that could cover all of our sins. His blood unites us with God the Father.

This is the gospel. This is the good news!

They beat Him, ridiculed, and crucified Him. He suffered great pain for us. As He hung on the cross, and after He had received the sour wine, He said the following last words:

> "It is finished!" And bowing His head, He gave up His spirit.
> —JOHN 19:30

At this moment, it was fulfilled—salvation became possible for the entire human race.

> For God so loved the world that He gave His only begotten Son, that whoever believes in Him should not perish but have everlasting life.
> —JOHN 3:16

We receive forgiveness and salvation when we believe in Jesus Christ and have faith in His crucifixion and blood. We are united with God the Father, and we have access to His eternal kingdom when we believe. This is the good news, and it is for everyone! It is for me and for you too, dear reader.

Jesus was placed in a grave after His crucifixion, but He arose on the third day! After the resurrection, He appeared to many people, including His disciples, and He left them with the direction as to what they should do.

> All authority has been given to Me in heaven and on earth. Go therefore and make disciples of all the nations, baptizing them in the name of the Father and of the Son and of the Holy Spirit, teaching them to observe all things that I have commanded you; and lo, I am with you always, even to the end of the age.
> —MATTHEW 28:18–20

And He said to them, "Go into all the world and preach the gospel to every creature. He who believes and is baptized will be saved; but he who does not believe will be condemned. And these signs will follow those who believe: In My name they will cast out demons; they will speak with new tongues; they will take up serpents; and if they drink anything deadly, it will by no means hurt them; they will lay hands on the sick, and they will recover." So then, after the Lord had spoken to them, He was received up into heaven, and sat down at the right hand of God.

—MARK 16:15–19

Jesus Christ sits on the right hand of God in heaven. This is good news. The first chapter of Hebrews describes Jesus' role:

God, who at various times and in various ways spoke in time past to the fathers by the prophets, has in these last days spoken to us by His Son, whom He has appointed heir of all things, through whom also He made the worlds; who being the brightness of His glory and the express image of His person, and upholding all things by the word of His power, when He had by Himself purged our sins, sat down at the right hand of the Majesty on high.

—HEBREWS 1:1–3

Although Jesus is in heaven, He has not forgotten us, who are still on Earth. He has not forgotten you, dear reader.

For Christ has not entered the holy places made with hands, which are copies of the true, but into heaven itself, now to appear in the presence of God for us.

—HEBREWS 9:24

Jesus Christ went to heaven after His resurrection and now sits on the right hand of God and manages His followers. He looks after you and me, too, dear reader. Isn't this good news? Yes, of course—this is good news for the entire human race.

Let's read more from the pages of the Holy Word, which has great meaning for each of our lives. Each citizen must know these verses; we must not forget them. Every nation, generation, and race ought to know them.

> My little children, these things I write to you, so that you may not sin. And if anyone sins, we have an Advocate with the Father, Jesus Christ the righteous. And He Himself is the propitiation for our sins, and not for ours only but also for the whole world.
>
> —1 JOHN 2:1–2

> But if we walk in the light as He is in the light, we have fellowship with one another, and the blood of Jesus Christ His Son cleanses us from all sin....If we confess our sins, He is faithful and just to forgive us our sins and to cleanse us from all unrighteousness.
>
> —1 JOHN 1:7, 9

This is the gospel, the good news for all of mankind, for each person who turns to Christ and believes in Him. This is wonderful news for me and for you, dear reader. Jesus Christ is our caretaker. He is our shield in front of God the Father, and His blood has not lost its power. His blood is still able to cleanse you and me from our sin and disobedience.

What else is interesting to note is that when God forgives our sins, He never remembers them again. He doesn't recount our mistakes because He actually gets rid of them. He erases them and eliminates their record. People also forgive others, but they never fail to remember their mistakes. Even the most loving, caring, and honest person can forgive, but our human memory rarely lets us forget. Even government officials, the Department of Justice, and the police force may forgive offenders and release them from prison. But on their documents, the misdemeanors will always be recorded; they will never be erased or burned to ash. Their mistakes will be there forever, some for a hundred years. Their mistakes will live on, sometimes even after the offender's life. Their mistakes may even be read by the following generations. Let's travel through the pages of God's Constitution and see what God, who is merciful, does with our sins:

> For as the heavens are high above the earth, So great is His mercy toward those who fear Him; As far as the east is from the west, So far has He removed our transgressions from us.
> —PSALM 103:11–12

> I, even I, am He who blots out your transgressions for My own sake; And I will not remember your sins.
> —ISAIAH 43:25

> I have blotted out, like a thick cloud, your transgressions, And like a cloud, your sins. Return to Me, for I have redeemed you.
> —ISAIAH 44:22

> But if a wicked man turns from all his sins which he has committed, keeps all My statutes, and does what is lawful and right, he shall surely live; he shall not die. None of the transgressions which he has committed shall be remembered against him; because of the righteousness which he has done, he shall live. Do I have any pleasure at all that the wicked should die?" says the Lord GOD, "and not that he should turn from his ways

and live?"...Again, when a wicked man turns away from the wickedness which he committed, and does what is lawful and right, he preserves himself alive. Because he considers and turns away from all the transgressions which he committed, he shall surely live; he shall not die....Cast away from you all the transgressions which you have committed, and get yourselves a new heart and a new spirit. For why should you die, O house of Israel? For I have no pleasure in the death of one who dies," says the Lord God. "Therefore turn and live!"

—EZEKIEL 18:21–23, 27–28, 31–32

Who is a God like You, Pardoning iniquity And passing over the transgression of the remnant of His heritage? He does not retain His anger forever, Because He delights in mercy. He will again have compassion on us, And will subdue our iniquities. You will cast all our sins Into the depths of the sea.

—MICAH 7:18–19

It is worth knowing, serving, and living your life for such a merciful, loving, and forgiving God?

Now let's go to Golgotha, the place where Jesus Christ was crucified. Along with Jesus, two thieves were also crucified. The two of them were sentenced to death for their sins, and they were hung on either side of Jesus. One of them blasphemed against Jesus, but the other believed in Jesus. The one who believed admitted that Jesus Christ was a righteous, sinless man. This thief saw the Savior, Messiah, and the King in Jesus. This thief believed in salvation and received eternal life through Jesus Christ. This thief admitted his own sinful state. He admitted his sins publicly when he said:

And we indeed [have been crucified] justly, for we receive the due reward of our deeds; but this Man has done nothing wrong.

—LUKE 23:41

Hope and the desire to live in eternity were born in the heart of this thief. He didn't think for too long; he didn't lose too much time before he turned to Jesus, to the King of kings and the Giver of eternal life, with the following words, "Remember me when you get to heaven!" (Luke 23:42, author's paraphrase).

What happened next? How did Jesus respond to these words? What did He say? Jesus knew very well who this thief was. He knew what sin was in this man's life and how much pain and tears he brought to others. But the Son of God did not speak of this man's sin. He did not rebuke this man by remembering his dark past, his sinful yesterday. Jesus saw this man's heart instead. He heard him admit his sin. He heard his repentance and his faith in the kingdom of God and in eternal life. Jesus Christ had mercy on this sinner, and He blessed him by forgiving him of his sin. Jesus said to this sinner, "Assuredly, I say to you, today you will be with Me in Paradise" (Luke 23:43).

> Therefore, if anyone is in Christ, he is a new creation; old things have passed away; behold, all things have become new.
> —2 Corinthians 5:17

This is the gospel. This is the good news!

God the Father wants all of His creation, every person, to be saved and reconciled with Him. This desire is written in the Holy Scriptures:

> For this is good and acceptable in the sight of God our Savior, who desires all men to be saved and to come to the knowledge of the truth.
> —1 Timothy 2:3–4

The voice of Jesus Christ can be heard even today, throughout all continents and countries, throughout all islands, large cities, small towns, and to the farthest corners of this world. The voice of God resounds anywhere that His creation is found, anywhere there is a living soul. Everyone is called by Jesus Christ—the rich and the poor, both the educated and illiterate, white- and blue-collar workers, the popular and the forgotten, the kings and shepherds. He calls us with the following:

> Come to Me, all you who labor and are heavy laden, and I will give you rest. Take My yoke upon you and learn from Me, for I am gentle and lowly in heart, and you will find rest for your souls. For My yoke is easy and My burden is light."
>
> —Matthew 11:28–30

> Behold, I stand at the door and knock. If anyone hears My voice and opens the door, I will come in to him and dine with him, and he with Me.
>
> —Revelation 3:20

Two thousand years ago, John the Baptist was preaching in the Judean desert, and he called people to repentance with the following words:

> "Repent, for the kingdom of heaven is at hand!" For this is he who was spoken of by the prophet Isaiah, saying: "The voice of one crying in the wilderness: 'Prepare the way of the Lord; Make His paths straight.'"
>
> —Matthew 3:2–3

And today, in the twenty-first century, there are people who find themselves in a spiritual desert. They don't know why they were born, why they live, what to do, who to turn to, where they are going, or where they will go after death. But God's voice does not grow quiet today. He calls us to repentance now.

> Therefore, as the Holy Spirit says: "Today, if you will hear His voice, Do not harden your hearts as in the rebellion, In the day of trial in the wilderness."
>
> —Hebrews 3:7–8

His voice is speaking to my heart and to your heart also, dear reader. Jesus Christ is calling you to walk toward Him, to open your heart in front of Him, and to tell Him your sins, shortcomings, and offenses, be they small or large. He is waiting to forgive you, regardless of how terrible and many your sins are. He will never remember them after you repent.

> But the Holy Spirit also witnesses to us; for after He had said before, "This is the covenant that I will make with them after those days, says the LORD: I will put My laws into their hearts, and in their minds I will write them," then He adds, "Their sins and their lawless deeds I will remember no more."
>
> —Hebrews 10:15–17

These are God's promises, and they are true and effective today. The only way, the only path to salvation, is through Jesus. You will not find another way. Jesus came to say that He is the way. Another way did not exist before Him, does not exist now, and will not exist. He is the only door. He is life. No one else is life, nor can anyone else give eternal life. Salvation is only in Christ. Only He can give it to you, and it is free of charge to us—He only requires faith. This is the gospel. This is the good news for each citizen of this planet. This good news is for me and for you, too, my dear and attentive atheist.

Jesus Christ came to Earth in human flesh only once. He became a servant and was the sacrifice for our redemption. His one sacrifice destroyed the power of sin.

For by one offering He has perfected forever those who are being sanctified.

—Hebrews 10:14

For Christ also suffered once for sins, the just for the unjust, that He might bring us to God, being put to death in the flesh but made alive by the Spirit...who has gone into heaven and is at the right hand of God, angels and authorities and powers having been made subject to Him.

—1 Peter 3:18, 22

Not that He should offer Himself often, as the high priest enters the Most Holy Place every year with blood of another— He then would have had to suffer often since the foundation of the world; but now, once at the end of the ages, He has appeared to put away sin by the sacrifice of Himself. And as it is appointed for men to die once, but after this the judgment, so Christ was offered once to bear the sins of many. To those who eagerly wait for Him He will appear a second time, apart from sin, for salvation.

—Hebrews 9:25–28

Jesus will come in great glory the second time He comes to Earth. He will come for those who await His return. Daniel prophesied in the Old Testament of the Second Coming of the Son of Man.

I watched till thrones were put in place, And the Ancient of Days was seated; His garment was white as snow, And the hair of His head was like pure wool. His throne was a fiery flame, Its wheels a burning fire; A fiery stream issued And came forth from before Him. A thousand thousands ministered to Him; Ten thousand times ten thousand stood before Him. The court was seated, And the books were opened....I was watching in the night visions, And behold, One like the Son of Man, Coming with the clouds of heaven! He came to the Ancient of Days, And they brought Him near before Him. Then to Him was given dominion and glory and a kingdom, That all peoples, nations, and languages should serve Him. His dominion is an everlasting dominion, Which shall not pass away, And His kingdom the one Which shall not be destroyed.

—Daniel 7:9–10, 13–14

When the priest asked Jesus to tell him who He was, if He really was the Son of God, Jesus gave an interesting response with reference to His Second Coming:

Jesus said to him, "It is as you said. Nevertheless, I say to you, hereafter you will see the Son of Man sitting at the right hand of the Power, and coming on the clouds of heaven."

—Matthew 26:64

Not only did Jesus speak of His Second Coming and not only did the prophets prophesy of it, but the angels know and confirm that Jesus Christ will come again.

And while they looked steadfastly toward heaven as He went up, behold, two men stood by them in white apparel, who also said, "Men of Galilee, why do you stand gazing up into heaven? This same Jesus, who was taken up from you into heaven, will so come in like manner as you saw Him go into heaven."

—Acts 1:10–11

When Jesus comes for the second time, it will not be to save us, but to separate the righteous from the unrighteous:

> For the Son of Man will come in the glory of His Father with His
> angels, and then He will reward each according to his works.
> —MATTHEW 16:27

These words raise questions. When will this happen? How will
it happen? These questions were asked by Jesus' disciples; they also
wanted to know of the second coming of Christ. Jesus spoke a lot
about His Second Coming. It will benefit both myself and you, my
reader, to read from Matthew:

> Now as He sat on the Mount of Olives, the disciples came to
> Him privately, saying, "Tell us, when will these things be?
> And what will be the sign of Your coming, and of the end
> of the age?"... "For as the lightning comes from the east and
> flashes to the west, so also will the coming of the Son of Man
> be.... Then the sign of the Son of Man will appear in heaven,
> and then all the tribes of the earth will mourn, and they will
> see the Son of Man coming on the clouds of heaven with
> power and great glory. And He will send His angels with a
> great sound of a trumpet, and they will gather together His
> elect from the four winds, from one end of heaven to the other.
> Now learn this parable from the fig tree: When its branch has
> already become tender and puts forth leaves, you know that
> summer is near. So you also, when you see all these things,
> know that it is near—at the doors! Assuredly, I say to you,
> this generation will by no means pass away till all these things
> take place. Heaven and earth will pass away, but My words
> will by no means pass away. But of that day and hour no one
> knows, not even the angels of heaven, but My Father only. But
> as the days of Noah were, so also will the coming of the Son of
> Man be. For as in the days before the flood, they were eating
> and drinking, marrying and giving in marriage, until the day

that Noah entered the ark, and did not know until the flood came and took them all away, so also will the coming of the Son of Man be. Then two men will be in the field: one will be taken and the other left. Two women will be grinding at the mill: one will be taken and the other left. Watch therefore, for you do not know what hour your Lord is coming. But know this, that if the master of the house had known what hour the thief would come, he would have watched and not allowed his house to be broken into. Therefore you also be ready, for the Son of Man is coming at an hour you do not expect.

—MATTHEW 24:3, 27, 30–44

No one but the Father knows when Jesus will come again. For the Christian, the most important thing is to believe and be ready for His return.

The Word of God teaches that when Jesus comes, we will see Him, as will every eye and those who pierced Him:

Behold, He is coming with clouds, and every eye will see Him, even they who pierced Him. And all the tribes of the earth will mourn because of Him. Even so, Amen. "I am the Alpha and the Omega, the Beginning and the End," says the Lord, "who is and who was and who is to come, the Almighty."

—REVELATION 1:7–8

We read in Matthew 25 that one of plans for the Son of God is to separate the unrighteous from the righteous and to judge them:

When the Son of Man comes in His glory, and all the holy angels with Him, then He will sit on the throne of His glory. All the nations will be gathered before Him, and He will separate them one from another, as a shepherd divides his sheep from the goats. And He will set the sheep on His right hand, but the goats on the left. Then the King will say to those on His right hand, "Come, you blessed of My Father, inherit the kingdom prepared for you from the foundation of the world.... Then He will also say to those on the left hand, "Depart from Me, you cursed, into the everlasting fire prepared for the devil and his angels.... And these will go away into everlasting punishment, but the righteous into eternal life."

—Matthew 25:31–34, 41, 46

The Word of God teaches us that Jesus is the righteous Judge of both the dead and living. He will first lead the judgment over the dead and then over the living. After this, the church will meet Jesus.

For the Lord Himself will descend from heaven with a shout, with the voice of an archangel, and with the trumpet of God. And the dead in Christ will rise first. Then we who are alive and remain shall be caught up together with them in the clouds to meet the Lord in the air. And thus we shall always be with the Lord.

—1 Thessalonians 4:16–17

In the Word of God, Jesus is called the Groom and the church His bride. When He comes for the second time, He will come as the Groom to take the church, His bride whom He washed with His blood, into heaven. In parts of the Bible, the church is called the Holy City of Jerusalem. John's writing that describes the church as the bride is very interesting:

Now I saw a new heaven and a new earth, for the first heaven and the first earth had passed away. Also there was no more sea. Then I, John, saw the holy city, New Jerusalem, coming down out of heaven from God, prepared as a bride adorned for her husband.... Then one of the seven angels who had the seven bowls filled with the seven last plagues came to me and talked with me, saying, "Come, I will show you the bride, the Lamb's wife." And he carried me away in the Spirit to a great and high mountain, and showed me the great city, the holy Jerusalem, descending out of heaven from God.

—Revelation 21:1–2, 9–10

When the meeting between Jesus and His church will come, the Word of God says that this will be the marriage of the Lamb:

Let us be glad and rejoice and give Him glory, for the marriage of the Lamb has come, and His wife has made herself ready." And to her it was granted to be arrayed in fine linen, clean and bright, for the fine linen is the righteous acts of the saints. Then he said to me, "Write: 'Blessed are those who are called to the marriage supper of the Lamb!'" And he said to me, "These are the true sayings of God."

—Revelation 19:7–9

The purpose of Jesus coming to Earth the first time was to find and save the lost and to prepare the church to be a bride for her Husband. When He will come for the second time, it will be to separate the righteous from the sinners who have not accepted Jesus as their Savior and to take His righteous from this earth into His kingdom. He will come to gather His so that He can have fellowship with them in eternity. Christians and the church await the coming of the Son of man, our Savior and Groom.

And the Spirit and the bride say, "Come!" And let him who hears say, "Come!" And let him who thirsts come. Whoever desires, let him take the water of life freely.

—Revelation 22:17

Jesus, come for Your church—Your bride awaits!

Jesus Christ, as a Husband, made a promise to His believers. Being a faithful Groom, He has not concealed anything from His church. He wrote His plans on the pages of the Holy Word, and He told us to not be troubled but to believe:

> Let not your heart be troubled; you believe in God, believe also in Me. In My Father's house are many mansions; if it were not so, I would have told you. I go to prepare a place for you. And if I go and prepare a place for you, I will come again and receive you to Myself; that where I am, there you may be also.
>
> —John 14:1–3

This is the gospel. This is the good news!

This is the good news for all those who believe in Jesus Christ and commit their lives into His hands. We are living in a very special period of time, when Jesus Christ's second coming to this earth is expected soon.

> A little while, and you will not see Me; and again a little while, and you will see Me, because I go to the Father.
>
> —John 16:16

Jesus Christ left for heaven, to the Father, but He did not leave His believers as orphans.

> And I will pray the Father, and He will give you another Helper, that He may abide with you forever—the Spirit of truth, whom the world cannot receive, because it neither sees Him nor knows Him; but you know Him, for He dwells with you and will be in you. I will not leave you orphans; I will come to you....But the Helper, the Holy Spirit, whom the

Father will send in My name, He will teach you all things, and bring to your remembrance all things that I said to you. Peace I leave with you, My peace I give to you; not as the world gives do I give to you. Let not your heart be troubled, neither let it be afraid. You have heard Me say to you, "I am going away and coming back to you." If you loved Me, you would rejoice because I said, "I am going to the Father," for My Father is greater than I.

—JOHN 14:16–18, 26–28

But when the Helper comes, whom I shall send to you from the Father, the Spirit of truth who proceeds from the Father, He will testify of Me.

—JOHN 15:26

Nevertheless I tell you the truth. It is to your advantage that I go away; for if I do not go away, the Helper will not come to you; but if I depart, I will send Him to you. And when He has come, He will convict the world of sin, and of righteousness, and of judgment.... However, when He, the Spirit of truth, has come, He will guide you into all truth; for He will not speak on His own authority, but whatever He hears He will speak; and He will tell you things to come.

—JOHN 16:7–8, 13

We live in a time when the Holy Spirit is being sent to this earth. The Holy Spirit abides among believers, guides them, teaches, reminds, testifies of Jesus, convicts the world of its sin, and reminds us about righteousness and judgment. This is the Bible; this is the good news!

33

MY PERSONAL TESTIMONY

IN THE PREVIOUS CHAPTER, WE LEARNED AND TALKED ABOUT the thief on the cross who turned to God right before his death. I, like the thief, turned to our great and mighty God and asked Him to show me the path that leads to truth and salvation. I asked God's assistance in many difficult times of my life, especially in times of sorrow and despair. I think that my dear and respected reader might like to know when, where, and how I turned to God, and I will share with you all I can.

I was born in Eastern Poland, in the part that is now Belarus. I was born to simple Christian parents. My father read the Holy Word and my mother, whom I loved and treasured more than my own life, went to the church of her parents and grandparents. She claimed that her faith was the greatest, most popular, and the oldest because she saw her grandparents, as well as her great-grandparents, practice it.

I went to a school where atheism reigned, and throughout each school day I heard that there was no God and that God never had existed and never would exist. We learned that the people who believed in God were second-class citizens who were somehow neglected and allowed to populate the bottom ranks of society. But when I came home from school, I heard my father say that all I had learned in school did not please God. My father would tell me what God liked to see from His children and what He says in the Bible. On Sundays, my mother took me to church with her. I, as a little girl, stood at the crossroads without knowing who to listen to or what to believe for myself.

In school I studied hard and received high marks. I took part in school activities. But my father, all the while, would shake his finger at me and with a raised voice tell me to remember "once and for all" that my place "is not in there!" I heard my father's voice and I saw his finger directed straight at me whenever I took part in the school activities. I felt then as though I was trapped in the middle of a briar patch. Many times in bed, before I fell asleep, I cried bitter tears and asked God why He let me be born to such a terrible father. I asked God what terrible thing I did to deserve this, why He had cursed me so, and why couldn't I have been born to the neighbors. The other fathers in our neighborhood did not tell their kids not to take part in school activities such as dances and other social events.

I loved my mother dearly and I went with her to her church. I fulfilled every requirement of this church—to the last detail. I fell to my knees in front of pictures of dead saints. I told them the sorrows of my soul. I asked them for salvation and I praised them. I kissed them and awaited their help. And when my mother and I would return home, I heard my father, who said, "You go to a church where there is idol worship. The priests in those churches do not fulfill God's will and commands. They have thrown out all that is godly and have replaced it with icons, pictures, and other idols. They bow to the work of man's hands. They do all that the living God, the Creator of heaven and Earth, has forbidden—idol worship! God is not in that church. His truth is also not there." And he read the following verses from the Bible:

> You shall not make for yourself a carved image—any likeness of anything that is in heaven above, or that is in the earth beneath, or that is in the water under the earth; you shall not bow down to them nor serve them. For I, the LORD your God, am a jealous God, visiting the iniquity of the fathers upon the children to the third and fourth generations of those who hate Me, but showing mercy to thousands, to those who love Me and keep My commandments.
>
> —EXODUS 20:4–6

> Do you not know that the unrighteous will not inherit the kingdom of God? Do not be deceived. Neither fornicators, nor idolaters, nor adulterers, nor homosexuals, nor sodomites, nor thieves, nor covetous, nor drunkards, nor revilers, nor extortioners will inherit the kingdom of God.
>
> —1 CORINTHIANS 6:9–10

> But the cowardly, unbelieving, abominable, murderers, sexually immoral, sorcerers, idolaters, and all liars shall have their part in the lake which burns with fire and brimstone, which is the second death.
>
> —REVELATION 21:8

When I heard him saying this, my heart grew angry. It grew roots of hate toward my father and the Bible. And just for the sake of it, I would go to that church with my mother, as I had always done. I bowed to the icons, no matter how many there were, and I even did this twice as often as was required. But help never came; not one of the icons was there for me when I needed someone. The hurt in my soul and the hate began to grow and tear at my young heart. No one from my family knew what was going on in my life, what I was experiencing in my most innermost being. I had no one to communicate with. There was no one I could open my soul to or tell my problems and worries to. There was no one to direct me. My parents told me different things, and they pointed me in opposite directions, something which began to wound my life. I stood at the crossroads alone without knowing who to listen to, what to believe, who I could believe, or what to do next. Darkness and emptiness surrounded me.

At one point, when the hurt in my soul tore my heart and I had no escape and lacked completeness in my life, I decided to speak with God Himself. No one else apparently could offer help, and I was hopeless and lost. I decided that my conversation with God would be pleasant. I wouldn't argue, rebuke, or ask too many questions. I wouldn't cry to Him, either. I simply wanted to tell Him my problems and hardships. I wanted to show Him the hurt of my soul and heart.

And as a child in middle school, I spoke with God on a beautiful, summer day, just as I had decided I would. When I was alone in a field by my house, I sat down by my tree and looked out on a beautiful field lit up in sunlight under a clear, blue sky—it was a magnificent picture of nature. I began speaking with God in simple, childlike words: "God, if it is true that You reign and that You created heaven and Earth and all that is found on it, all of mankind, including me; if I really am Your creation, then You must listen to what I have to say to You." I continued to pour out all the hurt of my soul to God. I didn't just speak with Him—I screamed! I told Him that I didn't know who to believe, who to listen to, and most importantly, what to do. I promised that I would listen to Him and serve Him—Him and only Him—if it were true that He lives and reigns.

I promised to do this, even if I were kicked out of school or, worse, if I was burned to death for my faith. I had heard that believers were jailed and killed, sometimes by fire. I didn't know if this was true or if they were just stories meant to scare people like myself into obedience, but I wasn't even afraid of death. I believed that death was just the transition from life on Earth to eternity, and with my young mind I decided that my soul could not be burned to ashes as my body could because my soul will be with God in heaven. I asked God, "Tell me who is right, who I should listen to, and what I should do." I told God everything that day. I promised to serve Him faithfully all the days of my life, and I awaited His direction.

Time passed quickly, as always; the days turned into weeks. In school I still heard that there was no God and at home that God was displeased with me. The same rituals continued in church—I worshiped the work of man's hands, and I bowed to idols. The pain and sorrow continued in my heart.

Not much time had passed when everything changed. Something unexpected happened. My father continued reading the Holy Word, and he shared the Word not only at home, but also with other people. But just this once, as he opened the Bible and began to read, I listened. I listened under the pretense that I wasn't really listening—my head was buried in my schoolbook. Though he read in Polish, a language I could not speak or read, nor understand the alphabet, I could still understand it. I understood what he read, which happened to be Matthew 10:16–39:

> Behold, I send you out as sheep in the midst of wolves. There-
> fore be wise as serpents and harmless as doves. But beware of
> men, for they will deliver you up to councils and scourge you
> in their synagogues. You will be brought before governors and
> kings for My sake, as a testimony to them and to the Gentiles.
> But when they deliver you up, do not worry about how or what

you should speak. For it will be given to you in that hour what you should speak; for it is not you who speak, but the Spirit of your Father who speaks in you. "Now brother will deliver up brother to death, and a father his child; and children will rise up against parents and cause them to be put to death. And you will be hated by all for My name's sake. But he who endures to the end will be saved. When they persecute you in this city, flee to another. For assuredly, I say to you, you will not have gone through the cities of Israel before the Son of Man comes. A disciple is not above his teacher, nor a servant above his master. It is enough for a disciple that he be like his teacher, and a servant like his master. If they have called the master of the house Beelzebub, how much more will they call those of his household! Therefore do not fear them. For there is nothing covered that will not be revealed, and hidden that will not be known. Whatever I tell you in the dark, speak in the light; and what you hear in the ear, preach on the house-tops. And do not fear those who kill the body but cannot kill the soul. But rather fear Him who is able to destroy both soul and body in hell. Are not two sparrows sold for a copper coin? And not one of them falls to the ground apart from your Father's will. But the very hairs of your head are all numbered. Do not fear therefore; you are of more value than many sparrows. Therefore whoever confesses Me before men, him I will also confess before My Father who is in heaven. But whoever denies Me before men, him I will also deny before My Father who is in heaven. Do not think that I came to bring peace on earth. I did not come to bring peace but a sword. For I have come to "set a man against his father, a daughter against her mother, and a daughter-in-law against her mother-in-law"; and "a man's enemies will be those of his own household." He who loves father or mother more than Me is not worthy of

Me. And he who loves son or daughter more than Me is not worthy of Me. And he who does not take his cross and follow after Me is not worthy of Me. He who finds his life will lose it, and he who loses his life for My sake will find it.

When I heard that children would turn against their parents, it felt as if I was hit by lightning. In that moment, my soul told me that the Book my father read from was holy and that I was that child described in it. In that moment, I felt like the sinner that I was. When I raised my head and looked at my father, I saw him in a light I never had before. To my amazement, he was handsome; his eyes looked holy. I decided then and there that I wanted to be like him. I decided to read the Holy Word and tell others of God's truth.

The pain and emptiness in my soul were replaced with peace, something I had never experienced before that moment. I felt love toward my father—something I could not remember feeling for a long time. From that moment, my father became not only my earthly father, but also my spiritual one. I realized that he was a man of God.

Doctors and psychologists cannot change a man's heart and make him turn completely from his old habits. They cannot change hate into love, pain into joy, darkness into light, or hopelessness and emptiness into a spiritually fulfilling life. Only God and the Holy Spirit can do that.

I did not stop loving my mother. I did think of her differently, though. In my heart I knew that she was pretty, nice, and gentle. She was the best mother in many ways, but she did not read the Holy Word. She didn't know God's truth. At her request, I still went to church with her, but spiritually I was dead to her church. I didn't take part in the religious ceremonies as I had earlier. I didn't bow to the pictures and idols. I saw the worship of these man-made objects as idolatry. They were merely things, and ungodly at that.

I began to notice that some icons were broken, with missing limbs that needed to be fixed. They were just there, collecting dust throughout the years. I observed them and could not believe that not long before then I had asked them for their help. I bowed to them after all, though the icons were dead! I was embarrassed and guilty and ashamed for choosing them over the living God.

During one service, there was a ceremony wherein the priests of the church carried pictures and icons around the church. People fell to their knees when the priests passed them. When they got to me, I stood there like a post. My friends, who had bowed, pulled the hem of my dress and asked me why I was not bowing to these holy things, but all I could think of were the words I had read from God's Constitution:

> You shall not make for yourself a carved image—any likeness of anything that is in heaven above, or that is in the earth beneath, or that is in the water under the earth; you shall not bow down to them nor serve them. For I, the LORD your God, am a jealous God, visiting the iniquity of the fathers upon the children to the third and fourth generations of those who hate Me, but showing mercy to thousands, to those who love Me and keep My commandments.
>
> —EXODUS 20:4–6

> Do you not know that the unrighteous will not inherit the kingdom of God? Do not be deceived. Neither fornicators, nor idolaters, nor adulterers, nor homosexuals, nor sodomites, nor thieves, nor covetous, nor drunkards, nor revilers, nor extortioners will inherit the kingdom of God.
>
> —1 CORINTHIANS 6:9–10

I stood there without moving, as though my feet were cemented to the ground. I was grateful for God's Word; it was my victory and

I thank God for it to this very day. If my memory doesn't err, this was the last time I visited the church of my mother. I looked at that building and my soul knew that God's commands were nowhere to be found in it; there was no room for them, or me, in that church.

I often listened to my father reading the Holy Word with great attention and interest. All the words in that Holy Bible, every will of God, touched me deeply. I believed and believe still that this Book is holy. It is God's Book. But even after listening to its words, I wasn't sure if God had forgiven me for my sins. I felt I was a great sinner. But other than that, I had few problems in school at that time. Some students called me old-fashioned, which did not bother me all that much. The negative comments rolled off of me in middle school. But in high school, many trials came my way.

The headmasters of the school committee required every student to become members of a special, but ungodly, organization. All students did this without protest, but I went to the school committee and told them that I could not join their organization.

My protest did not sit well with the headmasters, and they sent me home to fetch my mother. My mother became my shield and took all the blame upon herself. So the committee allowed me to return to school. When the students remained after school for the meetings, the headmasters would make it a point to say, "Who is not with us is against us and is our enemy; the enemies must leave us." And I, a tall, young girl, would stand from my seat at the back of the class and walk to the door. The class would laugh, clap, and scream, "Victory!" as I left. Their remarks echoed what my father read from God's Word: Christians will be persecuted.

So I went through trials. But these trials seemed insignificant to me because I awaited longer, harder trials. The Passover approached, and I realized that the celebration of the resurrection of Jesus Christ would be on two days, both Sunday and Monday. I knew that this was an important event—the resurrection of Jesus—and that there was class on Monday. Without too much thinking, I decided to observe the Passover and not attend school on Monday. My decision had a great impact on the headmasters, who decided to get back at me. On Tuesday when I entered the school building, I saw many students in the hall. They were rowdy and their voices were raised as they looked and talked about what was posted on the wall. I continued walking, and I saw that they were talking about the school newspaper, which happened to be taped on the wall. When I looked closer at it, I saw that the cover page was of a large cross with a girl on her knees and arms raised next to it. The caption read, "Janina Bobrel didn't attend school yesterday because she didn't have time. She was praying to her God." When I saw the picture and read my name, I experienced an unearthly joy, which had no doubt eluded me before. A thought raced through my mind, "They are persecuting me for God's Word, for His truth. This means that I am saved!"

The joy of knowing this cannot be explained with human words. This was the day when I was born again. I felt I was forgiven for my sins; I felt saved and near to my Creator. The students yelled, criticized me, and pointed at me. Others said that the school did not act right toward me, that they were too hard on me. But during that day, I was so happy, I was ready to kiss everyone and tell them what happened to me—that I was saved! Every moment reminded me that I was saved by Christ Himself. Physically, I was in school, I sat at my desk in the back of the classroom; but spiritually, I was in heaven. I had heavenly happiness.

After class as I walked home, I saw a new world. The trees, the houses, everything seemed prettier, lighter, and softly whispered to me, "You are saved." I will never forget that day. I felt that my name was written in the Book of Life. I was born again from heaven into a new life with Christ.

God's Constitution writes about rebirth. Let's read it together:

> There was a man of the Pharisees named Nicodemus, a ruler of the Jews. This man came to Jesus by night and said to Him, "Rabbi, we know that You are a teacher come from God; for no one can do these signs that You do unless God is with him." Jesus answered and said to him, "Most assuredly, I say to you, unless one is born again, he cannot see the kingdom of God." Nicodemus said to Him, "How can a man be born when he is old? Can he enter a second time into his mother's womb and be born?" Jesus answered, "Most assuredly, I say to you, unless one is born of water and the Spirit, he cannot enter the kingdom of God. That which is born of the flesh is flesh, and that which is born of the Spirit is spirit. Do not marvel that I said to you, 'You must be born again.'"
> —JOHN 3:1–7

These words became truth in my life. I lived them personally. They brought me joy and faith in salvation, which has not left me up to this day. I am saved. I have eternal life with Christ. The old has passed away and the new has arrived.

> Therefore, if anyone is in Christ, he is a new creation; old things have passed away; behold, all things have become new.
> —2 CORINTHIANS 5:17

This is my life, even today.

The next day, Wednesday, came. It was a calm day and the halls of the school were quiet. The school paper was not posted on the walls anymore.

My beloved mother eventually came to believe in Jesus Christ. She accepted Him as her personal Savior and committed her life to Him through water baptism. Praise the Lord.

I completed high school with big problems and with God's great blessings in my spiritual life. After graduation, I went to Minsk, the capital of Belarus. I began working and studied some more to have the tools to begin some sort of profession. I discovered a church that believed in the Holy Word and in God. The people of the church did God's will and praised Him.

I attended services often and listened as they preached the Word of God, which continued to touch my heart and soul. I believed that the Author of the Bible was not man, but the Holy Spirit and that the words in the Bible were really God's. I believed that the gospel was powerful and was the good news. The words of Jesus became fact in my life, my reality, and I believed them with all my heart and soul. I decided to take the next step, water baptism. I began to fulfill the words of God, "Go into all the world and preach the gospel to every creature. He who believes and is baptized will be saved; but he does not believe will be condemned" (Mark 16:15). I heard the gospel and I believed each word, and in a river near the city of Minsk, I was baptized with water in front of people and heaven. I proclaimed that Jesus Christ is the Son of the living God, that He came to this Earth to find and save the lost—me—that He was crucified and shed His holy blood, and was in the grave for three days but arose on the third. I proclaimed that He arose into heaven and now sits at the right hand of God and intercedes for me. I promised to serve Him faithfully and to praise Him as long as I live on this Earth.

These promises I keep even today; they are alive and true. They give me strength to be victorious during all my hardships. They give me strength for all my trials and every obstacle that I must overcome, and I go through life with victory and a smile. My life is not decorated with roses, but it is indeed blessed by God.

I earned an accounting degree in school and then moved to Western Poland. I felt very lucky. It seemed that the whole world belonged to me. So with my diploma in hand, I had my life ahead of me in Poland. But many obstacles met me when I got to Poland. Poland is a pretty country, and the people there are excellent—but they speak Polish. I understood Polish, but I could not speak it. Because I grew up in Eastern Poland, which had been occupied by Russia since World War II, I wasn't in the position to communicate with this nation. I had attended Russian school, spoke the Russian language, and knew only the Russian government. Former Polish president Wladyslaw Gomulka once said that though the Russians had taken the land, he would demand that they return the Polish people. So my family moved to Western Poland.

It wasn't easy for me to adapt to this new country, and wherever I turned, all I saw was obstacle after obstacle. At one point I was told of a place that might need my help. I went there and presented them with my referral. A man asked me to write a petition and an autobiography so he could get a sense of my capability. I asked him what language the assignment should be written in. This man's eyebrows rose and, without smiling, he said, "In the Polish language." I was completely open with him and said, "Sir, I cannot do that because I don't even know the Polish alphabet." The man rose from his chair, his face turned red as he wrinkled his forehead and said, "Ma'am, we only accept people for the accounting position who can read and write Polish." When I heard this, my stomach turned.

Since there was no point in speaking to the man further, I left the building. I could not walk very far, and so I sat there on the steps. It was fall; the day was cold and dark. The coldness of the steps quickly brought me back to reality. I walked to the streetcar very meekly. In my head I heard, "Why did you come here? Who asked you to come? You can't even write, read, speak, or understand the Polish language completely. You don't even know the alphabet! You must look underdeveloped to these people. What have you done?"

Hopelessness surrounded me, as did darkness and despair. I turned to God and said, "Dear God, tell me what I should do. How am I to begin my life in this country?" And immediately, it was as though everything was illuminated. A solution hit me like thunder: "Learn the alphabet! It is only thirty-two letters. Learn to write and read. It is not that hard. You have learned so much already in your life, and there is just a bit more." When I heard this, my heart filled with joy.

Everything else seemingly was the same—the day was still cold and gloomy. I was surrounded with the same circumstances, but there was hope in my heart. This solution was from God Himself, who said:

> Call to Me, and I will answer you, and show you great and mighty things, which you do not know.
> —Jeremiah 33:3

With time, I learned to read and write in Polish. I found a job, and after being an accountant for a firm for a couple of years, I was promoted to manager.

I took an active part in my church, and I taught Sunday school for ten years. This was a treasured and blessed time in my life. I had the opportunity to pour God's truth, will, and laws into the hearts of little children. I taught them to believe in God and to believe God, to have faith and hope in Him through all of life's circumstances, to read and love His Constitution—the Word of God—to have fellowship with Him, and to listen to His voice.

During these years, God was unfolding a plan to answer a childhood prayer of mine. When I was young and still in school, my favorite subject was geography. I liked to study about other countries, and from my birth have been a lover of nature; I see life in every plant, tree, and flower. Late one winter evening while my family was sleeping, I stayed up reading my geography book. It was below freezing outside, and the snow was piled nearly seven feet tall. Our small house had only one room. The roof was made of straw, the floor was made of clay, and our only light was one kerosene lamp. As I was reading, I reached a chapter about North America and began to read about the state of California. I learned that during the winter in California, there is no snow, and flowers are in bloom year-round. In my small heart, such a strong desire was born to go there that I began to ache inside. Living behind the iron curtain and knowing the rules of the government, my childish mind thought that the only way to go abroad would be to become a bird and fly away. Though at the time I still wasn't sure whether or not I believed in God or, if He did exist, whether or not I liked Him, my dream compelled me to pray, "Lord God, I want to become a bird and fly to California, if only for one single day. I want to fly all over the state, see the beautiful nature, and return home. If you do this, in my whole life I will never desire anything more." In spite of my disbelief in Him at the time of that prayer, God loved me and heard my voice. I imagine Him watching me, smiling, and saying, "You do not have to become a bird. I created you a woman, and I have a much better way for you to go to California."

As the years passed, I forgot about California and my childhood prayer. God, however, did not forget. Far away, a handsome man named Paul who lived in California decided to get married, and he would only agree to take a wife from Poland. He called a pastor in Warsaw and asked him to find a beautiful, kind lady to be his wife. Though this request wasn't easy for the pastor to fulfill, he agreed to try. After searching and thinking about many beautiful Polish girls, the pastor decided to recommend me and gave the man my address. Paul sent me a letter, and I responded. After a few months, he sent me an invitation to visit California for forty-five days, along with a round-trip ticket from Warsaw to San Francisco and back. With military discipline, he wrote, "Remember, I invite you only for forty-five days to visit California." As I read that line, I said to myself, "Almighty God is a good God; He is an awesome God." My prayer had been to go to California for one day, and suddenly I was preparing to spend forty-five days there! God had given me so much more than I asked for.

After so many years, my childish dream came alive. I was so excited! I accepted Paul's invitation, and the day of my departure arrived quickly. When it came time to leave our home, I kneeled before my parents for prayer. My father was on my left side and my mother was on my right, each laying one hand on my shoulder and stretching the other out to heaven. They prayed, "Lord God, our daughter is leaving our home. She is going to a far-away country, on a different continent. Please be with her, guide her, protect her, and give her power and strength to remain faithful to You in all circumstances of her life. Lord God, we give her into your hands. Bless her and keep her. Amen." With their blessings, I took my suitcase and began my trip. In Warsaw, I met the pastor Paul had contacted about finding a wife, and he prayed over me, blessed me, and blessed my journey and future.

Well equipped with God's blessings, my feet soon stepped onto new soil—California, U.S.A. The first time Paul and I saw each other was at the San Francisco airport. Paul looked at me and said, "You will not see Poland anytime soon." Of course, we started to quarrel and exchange our points of view on the subject loudly. Fortunately, security guards were not called. We resolved our conflict, and after four days of being in California, Paul and I got married. Perhaps some of my dear readers will want to know, did we argue in our life together? Of course we did, sometimes pretty loudly, but our neighbors never complained. Our journey together lasted for thirty-three years, two months, and twenty-one days. During our marriage, I visited Poland only once. My husband's prophesy got fulfilled, as did my dream. Our journey was not easy, but it was blessed by a living and mighty God.

Arriving in a new nation brought its own problems for me. California is a beautiful state—just as my old geography book said, there is no snow in San Francisco in the winter, and the flowers are in bloom throughout the year—but life for a newly arrived immigrant is not easy. I had to start from scratch. I had to learn to read, write, understand, and speak English. This was not easy for me, but I knew what moving to a new country entailed. I was ready for the challenge, and I knew my good and mighty God was watching me in California also. Other problems that I was not prepared for arose, but the prayers and blessings of my parents reached to the heavens—to the throne of God. He gave me patience and wisdom, power and strength to go through very hard circumstances without murmurs, grumbles, and complaints. I did not let my problems concern me, and I did not pay very much attention to them. I marched with God's help heroically and victoriously through all situations. Four years went by, and eventually I understood English well enough to look for work. I found a position as an accountant at a firm, and I also took up work among the women in my church. I thank God to this day for the opportunities He gave me to share His truth with women.

Highways in the U.S. are impressive, but unfortunately about fifty thousand people die on these roads in any given year. People pass to eternity in their cars and no longer live among us. Many times death stared me straight in the face on a California road, though it never touched my car or me. Many times while driving I turned to God and said, "Dear God, You do not yet want to take me to heaven. You still have plans for me here on Earth. I still have work to do here for You."

California is well-known around the world for many reasons. Not only do magnolias bloom in December and the acacia and Chinese cherry trees in February, but there is snow in the mountains year round. It is also infamous for the fact that it is an earthquake zone.

You must be ready for eternity, both day and night. There are constant quakes there. Sometimes they are small, and other times they are large. Courses in earthquake preparedness are given at schools and sometimes workplaces. People are taught how to act during an earthquake, what to do and how to help the injured.

I have lived through an earthquake, a large one at that. It was October 17, 1989, shortly after five in the afternoon. I was home from work and had just finished doing the dishes from our meal. My husband was on the phone with a new immigrant, and I was turning on my tape recorder to tape an English lesson that was about to air. The house was full of noise and life. And at that moment, the entire house shook. We had been taught to leave the house if possible during an earthquake, and Paul and I tried to do just that. As I was walking through the corridor, I was pushed to one side, and then to the other. I felt as though I was walking on wood that was floating on water. I admit I was scared when I got outside and saw that my potted plants had fallen over. This was frightening. The ground under my feet was shaking and I couldn't stand. My husband also had come outside.

The earthquake lasted for sixteen seconds and measured 7.1 on the Richter scale. The electricity in our house was out; the phones did not work. Paul turned on a small radio that he had and we listened to the latest broadcast, which was at that moment announcing that there was massive damage in San Francisco—a bridge was damaged and people were killed.

I for some reason felt I needed to sleep. I told Paul I was going to bed, but he said, "You will die tonight in the house." My response was that I wasn't afraid of death—I was saved and ready to leave this earth at any time for the kingdom of God. I hadn't finished preaching yet when Paul said that he also would go to bed with me. We went inside, raised our hands, and said, "God, our lives are in Your hands." We went to bed, pulled the covers over ourselves, and with our backs to each other, peacefully fell asleep.

There wasn't any electricity in the morning, and I left for work without listening to the radio. As I drove, the roads were unusually empty. When I got work, I found the parking lot empty also. Though no one was there, I went into the building anyway and made my way to our company. When I opened the door to my section, I stopped in my tracks when I saw what happened. There were documents on the floor. The flowers that decorated the building were spread on the floor, too. When I entered my room, it was in the same disarray. I tried the lights and the phone, but neither worked. The owner also showed up, and we began to clean the place. It was just the two of us—no one else came to work that day.

Geologists predict that there will be another quake, maybe in thirty years, and it will detach part of California from the mainland. But people, not God, foretell this. This may or may not happen. Though there are constant smaller tremors of different proportions here, they probably affect people differently each time. Sometimes a person may wake at night upon feeling one and not be able to fall back asleep. At other times, one may feel the walls and their bed tremble, but not think anything of it. They might roll over and think, "It's only a quake," and with their trust in God and His Word and promises, they fall back to sleep.

> Therefore we will not fear, Even though the earth be removed, And though the mountains be carried into the midst of the sea; Though its waters roar and be troubled, Though the

mountains shake with its swelling. Selah. There is a river whose streams shall make glad the city of God, The holy place of the tabernacle of the Most High....Come, behold the works of the LORD, Who has made desolations in the earth.

—PSALM 46:2–4, 8

O LORD, You have searched me and known me. You know my sitting down and my rising up; You understand my thought afar off. You comprehend my path and my lying down, And are acquainted with all my ways. For there is not a word on my tongue, But behold, O LORD, You know it altogether. You have hedged me behind and before, And laid Your hand upon me. Such knowledge is too wonderful for me; It is high, I cannot attain it. Where can I go from Your Spirit? Or where can I flee from Your presence? If I ascend into heaven, You are there; If I make my bed in hell, behold, You are there. If I take the wings of the morning, And dwell in the uttermost parts of the sea, Even there Your hand shall lead me, And Your right hand shall hold me. If I say, "Surely the darkness shall fall on me," Even the night shall be light about me; Indeed, the darkness shall not hide from You, But the night shines as the day; The darkness and the light are both alike to You. For You formed my inward parts; You covered me in my mother's womb. I will praise You, for I am fearfully and wonderfully made; Marvelous are Your works, And that my soul knows very well. My frame was not hidden from You, When I was made in secret, And skillfully wrought in the lowest parts of the earth. Your eyes saw my substance, being yet unformed. And in Your book they all were written, The days fashioned for me, When as yet there were none of them.

—PSALM 139:1–16

In times of danger, in minutes of hardships, we can turn to God, His Word, and His promises. When we read His Word we can sleep peacefully all through the night. Knowing the almighty God and living with His Word is truly great.

Sickness is prevalent throughout the earth. It touches everyone, be they rich or poor, educated or simple; it affects everyone at one point or another. Sickness touched me also. It touched my heart. I once visited a doctor in San Francisco who told me that at least one of my arteries was blocked. He didn't know yet if only one was blocked, or if there were more, but in a calm voice he continued to explain what could be done. If only one or two were blocked, he could simply clean them. But if there were more, then he would have to perform open-heart surgery.

On average, three out of every five hundred surgeries end in death. These people go to eternity on the operating table. The doctor reminded me that I could be one of these also. With that said, he gave me the consent form for further tests. I smiled at him, took the papers, and said, "I have received many promotions in my life. I've been promoted everywhere I have worked. Maybe this consent form is the means to my greatest promotion: from Earth to heaven."

I signed the papers and gave them back to him. But my promotion did not happen, for I had only one blocked artery. With faith I can say that my promotion will happen eventually, for the Word of God says those who have been born will die.

The one who has been born will die! And then what? Then eternity! Only two places make up what we know as eternity. In one, there is eternal peace and fellowship with God, our Creator. In the other, there is constant darkness and separation from God's presence. Those who believe in God accept Jesus as their personal Savior and fulfill His teachings in their life. They will be in the first place. But those who have not accepted the gift of salvation, those who have not had fellowship with Him here on Earth, will not have fellowship with Him in eternity. This is a fact because it is written in the Bible. Those who believe will be saved, and those who do not will be judged.

> Most assuredly, I say to you, he who hears My word and believes in Him who sent Me has everlasting life, and shall not come into judgment, but has passed from death into life.
> —JOHN 5:24

> And this is the will of Him who sent Me, that everyone who sees the Son and believes in Him may have everlasting life; and I will raise him up at the last day.
> —JOHN 6:40

> Jesus said to her, "I am the resurrection and the life. He who believes in Me, though he may die, he shall live. And whoever lives and believes in Me shall never die. Do you believe this?"
> —JOHN 11:25–26

> Let not your heart be troubled; you believe in God, believe also in Me. In My Father's house are many mansions; if it were not so, I would have told you. I go to prepare a place for you. And if I go and prepare a place for you, I will come again and receive you to Myself; that where I am, there you may be also.
> —JOHN 14:1–3

I believe in these words with all of my heart and soul. I believe that Jesus Christ is the Son of the living God, that He left heaven and came to Earth to save sinners. I believe that only He is the only Savior. There is no other savior, and there will never be another.

Jesus Christ is the only path through which we can have salvation. There is no other path. Salvation is only in Christ, as it is written in Acts:

> Nor is there salvation in any other, for there is no other name under heaven given among men by which we must be saved.
> —Acts 4:12

Salvation is only through the name of Jesus because there is no other name under heaven with which a man can be saved. Jesus Christ is the only Truth; there is no other. Only He can give life; only He is life. You cannot find eternal life in another. I came to Him and told Him my sins and mistakes. I asked for His forgiveness, and He gave it to me.

Today, I try to witness to people, to the world, to heaven, and all the hosts of heaven, and to you, too, my dear and respected reader, that Jesus Christ is my personal Savior, my Redeemer, Leader, and my God and King. And I am His—I am His servant, His new creation. I must say that there is no better advantage on this Earth than knowing God's truth. There is no better option than believing God and having fellowship with Him.

I have worked with the wealthy, with America's millionaires here in California. I managed their finances, and I must say, being wealthy is not a bad thing; having money is not a sin. Having material wealth is good, but riches do not give fellowship with God and they do not lead into the kingdom of God. Money cannot buy eternal life. I knew people who were very wealthy and had everything a person could ever desire, but who never thought they needed to be saved.

Life on Earth is very short, and you cannot take your riches with you into eternity. All your wealth will remain here. A man is born naked, and he leaves naked. He does not take his material wealth with him. There are many wealthy people who lack fellowship with God. Because of this, they are spiritually poor. And there are poor people who, though they lack material wealth, have accepted God's plan of salvation, His gift of life, and they are spiritually wealthy. I am that person.

I am rich in Jesus Christ. I am blessed because I know Him, and I have never regretted giving Him my life. Though I walk in the narrow path, I do not miss anything that is found on the wide path. God has lead me over mountains and through valleys, through success and failure, through hardships, defeat, victory, and joy. He has never left my side. He is always with me. I have experienced His help during my entire life, something for which I'm forever thankful. Jesus Christ, by the Holy Spirit, was with me here on this earth, and I will be with Him in my future. I know He will be there to meet me at the gates of heaven when it is my time to leave this planet.

Is not this world arranged wonderfully by God the Father? Yes, it is! Glory and praise to Him forever!

34

THE CALL TO REPENTANCE

I HOPE THAT MY DEAR AND RESPECTED READER HAS BECOME aware that each man is a sinner in need of salvation. Salvation comes only from believing in Jesus Christ. Our past is irrelevant when we believe. God the Father forgives us when we turn to Jesus Christ, admit our sins and lawlessness, and heartily ask for His forgiveness and mercy. The blood of Jesus washes us and makes us a new creation that is saved and reconciled to God.

This book did not find you by chance—it is no accident that this book is in your hands. This is God's great love for you. You were created by God in His likeness; you are God's creation and your Creator remembers you. He wants to have fellowship with you. He awaits your return until He can assign you your work here on Earth. He longs to hear your voice.

Turn your attention now to yourself and see how lovely you are. Another person like you will never exist. Your smile cannot be found on anyone, nor will it ever be duplicated. Eyes like yours cannot be found anywhere else. Your Creator did not forget to give you your unique fingerprints. You are an unrepeatable, original person. You are the work of God's hands. He has even counted the hairs on your head. You are important and treasured in the eyes of the almighty God.

God the Father wants to have fellowship with you. He wants to bless you here on Earth. He would like you to be saved and have eternal life in His kingdom with Him. All that you must do is turn to Him in a simple way, with simple words, as a child turns to their parents.

Maybe in your life you have never spoken with God. Today, in this moment, you have the opportunity to take this step. Do not put this off until tomorrow, because tomorrow is not yours. Tomorrow could be too late. Take this step today. Simply turn to Him with the following words:

> *Dear Jesus,*
>
> *I believe that You are the Son of the living God. I believe that You left heaven, Your throne and glory, to come to Earth to save all sinners. I believe that You are the one and only Savior, the only way. I come to You and admit that I am a sinner. I admit to You all of my sins and lawlessness, and I ask Your forgiveness. Wash me with Your holy, clean blood, which cleanses from all sin. I want to be clean.*

Now open your heart in front of Jesus and tell Him everything. Admit all your wrongdoings. You remember them well. You know what you have done wrong. Maybe not a single person from your immediate family knows of your deeds. But you know and remember them. Your conscience, which God imparted to humanity during the creation of the first man, speaks to you and reminds you. Admit it all. Do not hide anything. God the Father will hear your admissions and will forgive you. He will not tell anyone else. He will not share them with any of your loved ones. He will not report your sins to the police department. Instead, He will toss your wrong deeds into the sea of forgiveness and will never again remember them or remind you of them. Make a covenant with Him by repeating the following:

Dear Jesus,

Thank You for forgiving my sins, for salvation, and for eternal life. I give myself into Your hands, and I desire to be a child of God, Your very own. I promise to serve You faithfully all the days of my life. Lead me in Your path and be my Guidance in my life. I desire to hear Your voice, to fulfill Your will, and to have fellowship with You here on Earth and in eternity. Give me physical and spiritual strength daily. Teach me to do Your will.

Amen.

And as is written in the Bible, Jesus' response is the following:

The one who comes to Me I will by no means cast out.

—John 6:37

Our great and almighty God, Creator of heaven and Earth, established a single plan, a single way through which we, a sinful people, can be reconciled with Him. The way is through the sacrifice of His only begotten Son. The person who wants to be saved and reconciled with God the Father must adjust him- or herself to this plan. We must believe in God's Son. We must trust in Him and accept His teaching for our life. In other words, we must make Jesus Christ the Lord of our existence. God the Creator has prepared so many wonderful things for His creation. He prepared everything to ensure that we will have the opportunity to be saved and have fellowship with Him. He requires so little in exchange—only obedience and the willful acceptance of His gifts to us. Now thank your Creator for His forgiveness, salvation, and the opportunity to know Him more.